LARRY DE

REENTRY REALITIES

A SURVIVAL GUIDE FOR REINTEGRATION

Hanusz Publishing LLC
Toledo, Ohio

www.hanusz.com

Reentry Realities: A Survival Guide for Reintegration
by Larry Dean Thompson

Softcover ISBN 978-1-938283-22-2
Hardcover ISBN 979-8-88831-864-5

For bulk purchases of *Reentry Realities* and other works by Larry Thompson,
please visit www.larrythompson.net or email info@larrythompson.net.

Praise for *Reentry Realities* from Inmates

Reentry Realities is a must-read book. I think every prisoner who's soon to be released should read the book. The book has so much great information and powerful messages, I think it's vital to every prisoner's reentry back to society. I urge everyone to read the book. It will challenge you. And if you read it with an open mind and heart I promise it will make you view freedom in a totally different way. *Reentry Realities* is the truth. – KEVIN

—∾—

Reentry Realities has given genuine substance, shape and form to words I've heard all my life, such as accountability, maturity, and moral values. It clearly demonstrates the power that can be unleashed in someone's life through the practice of principles like real courage, commitment, and consistency. This book clearly demonstrates the life transforming power of truth, self-examination, personal responsibility, and many more principles.

I have always been suspicious and uncertain about religion. I was amazed at how this book takes the principles of the Bible and turned them into powerful tools for everyday life as well as successful reentry. There's no question, we were created to live a life of design, not random chaos. This book has literally brought new hope into my life and completely changed my focus. – LENNY

—∾—

This book has brought me insight, tears, and new dialog with my family. What surprised me was most books seem to have some interesting chapters and some not so interesting. Every single page of *Reentry Realities* is loaded with golden nuggets of insight and revelations that really speaks to the heart.

Reentry Realities reflects the truth in a unique way that has helped me to see crime as a symptom of deeper issues such as maturity issues, relational issues, and compulsive/addictive issues.

When these are severe enough it reflects a level of an arrested maturity that prevents success in an adult society. I have never read a book like this that speaks in simple language so directly to what I have suffered in my life. Adult male life is truly meant to reflect principle centered maturity as this book portrays. The powerful tools in this book are solid principles to secure any man's reintegration into society.

It has been an honor to read this life changing book. – JAMES

—∾—

It is said the best way to overcome something is to understand what it is and where it comes from. This book does exactly that. It gives you the information to put a name on what it is that we go through in respects to dealing with our everyday problems that might cause us to re-offend. I am an avid reader and this by far has to be the top 3 books that I've ever read and applied to my life. I highly recommend reading *Reentry Realities*. It is a very powerful book, if applied. – FIDENCIO

—∞—

If insanity is defined as doing the same thing over and over again while expecting a different result, then my previous three attempts at reentering society were just that – Insane.

Finally, someone has developed a program to address all the issues I so vividly remember from my past attempts. *Reentry Realities* should be mandatory for every inmate at every level of incarceration. – GARY

—∞—

Before I read this book I didn't understand my condition or have a clue of the solution. *Reentry Realities* is not only informative but challenges you to a call of action. This book has given me new hope and a solid reason to believe I can succeed at reentry. The principles in this book are at the heart of what it takes to succeed at reentry. It has helped me to see that my crime was a symptom of a self-centered lifestyle. More importantly, it has helped me to see that the key to my success in reentry is a life of principle- centered maturity. Mr. Thompson's insights are from actual experience, and from a lifetime of suffering. He speaks directly to the heart, hopes and fears of everyone who is incarcerated. I believe every inmate needs to read this book before they leave prison. Thanks for taking the time to write this book, Mr. Thompson. – AL

—∞—

I am deeply grateful for the opportunity to read this book. It reveals clear and convincing evidence of not only the human condition, but the cause and cure for crime and incarceration. It challenged me in every way: mentally, emotionally, and spiritually. *Reentry Realities* provides answers to questions that are at the core of how I came to prison and what it will require to remain free once I am released.

This book needs to be in every single prison and in schools across America. I can see now that the faster we catch these developing symptoms, the less likely anti-social behavior and crime will manifest.

Today my goal is to be a model of principle-centered maturity and practice these principles in all my affairs. – FELIPE

Endorsements

This book, *Reentry Realities* written by inmate Larry Dean Thompson, paints a very clear picture of the issues facing offenders upon their return to the community. He speaks from his own experiences having endured years of incarceration followed by multiple failed attempts to successfully reintegrate into the community. In his own words he is encouraging, honest, and straightforward, as well as challenging to the reader.

As a Reentry Community Advocate this book indeed speaks to not only the offender but to those of us who work with this population and their families. Larry has seen the error of his past actions and is now focused on assisting those inmates who are also still behind prison walls awaiting another attempt at reentry.

This book is an excellent tool/survival guide for those seeking to change their lifestyle and successfully reintegrate into society. Larry has done a commendable job with the assistance of his support system in getting this book completed. We challenge those readers to take advantage of this roadmap and to navigate the journey wisely.

LENORA BARRY
FORMER REENTRY COORDINATOR/REENTRY COALITION OF NORTHWEST OHIO

—❈—

It has been said, 'The man with the experience is never at the mercy of a man with only an argument.' As an inmate, Larry Thompson has the goods on reentry. His book, *Reentry Realities*, has been birthed out of his own personal struggles and experiences with prison life and reentry.

These experiences, coupled with a hard core grasp on reality, have qualified Larry to write a book that will impact many lives. It will equip inmates with the necessary tools to make a successful transition from prison life to home life. I also believe this book has the potential to change the disastrous rate of recidivism inmates now face. I highly recommend *Reentry Realities* to every inmate. If you're just beginning your sentence or coming to its end, this book is for you. It can make the prison experience both redemptive and your last.

JOSEPH HOEFLINGER
RESTORED HOPE PRISON MINISTRY

Table of Contents

Table of Contents

Foreword

I have known Larry since 2013 when I was introduced to him by a friend who was working with Larry on a book dealing with reentry. At the time, I was very active in federal court reentry programs. Our friend asked me to take a look at the book for suggestions. This is when I learned Larry was serving a sentence for aggravated robbery and other crimes. Sadly, as is far too common, his crimes were driven by alcohol and drug abuse.

Larry was a model prisoner while incarcerated. He used his time to further his education. But Larry is not only book smart, he is people smart. He dedicated himself to helping other inmates reenter society upon release. He has been a profound inspiration to those who have taken his program, which has helped others successfully avoid the self-perpetuating cycle of recidivism. This book outlines that program and now serves as a guide for multiple state institutions.

I was particularly drawn to Larry's situation because I had come to learn that it was important for those leaving incarceration to prepare for their return to the community *before* being released. In other words, the chances of success are much higher if the person can hit the ground running. Larry's efforts while incarcerated, aside from this book, are remarkable. The graduation ceremonies are a source of pride for the inmates, families, and all others involved.

Perhaps Larry's initiative is all the more remarkable because he is telling the story from the inside – with his firsthand knowledge of what it's like on the cell block. And with his release this year, he now has the opportunity to continue spreading his message from the outside.

This book reflects Larry's heart and mind, along with his passion for restoring the fallen to a life of purpose and meaning in their communities. Those familiar with Larry's story know that it is one worth retelling.

Judge Jack Zouhary
United States District Court
for the Northern District of Ohio

Introduction

This book is written for incarcerated men and women, although anyone may benefit from its principle centered concepts. Many books have been written about us, a few books have been written to us, and even fewer books have been written by us. I am one of you. This book represents my journey from brokenness to healing and from bondage to freedom. We wrestle our crowns of victory from the inner giants we conquer. Now a precious message of light has come from the dark shadows of captivity.

I do not have the experience or the background to address the issues that affect women and reentry. I trust God will call out a woman who will meet this need in due time. However, I believe women can benefit from reading this book in order to better understand the challenges incarcerated men will face upon release. I believe all who are involved with released ex-convicts can gain insight here.

This is a map and a survival guide for genuine reintegration into society. It offers hope and insight to those men who are searching for a path that leads to freedom – those who are tired of suffering under the weight of their own poor choices and misguided directions. This book holds no clinical status. It is inspired by four prison numbers and twenty-eight years of experience in suffering from repeated incarcerations. Sorrow and suffering are common scars found on the face of insight.

If I represent anything, my hope is that it would be a man who refused to give up – who refused to accept failure as his legacy. The Master Model of Manhood (Jesus) proved to the world that the ministry of thorns is far greater than the ministry of thrones. He also proved that every book worthy of reading has been written in the author's own blood. The fingerprints of tribulation and grief mark every great accomplishment. This book is not my accomplishment; the ability to claim with integrity that I have genuine freedom is.

HOW THIS JOURNEY BEGAN

This five-year project came about as a result of a visit from a pastor and friend, Joe Hoeflinger. When Joe asked me if I would be interested in sharing my experience with others in writing, I was shocked and extremely intimidated by such an idea. In the natural, it made no sense for a four-time loser to write a book about how to be successful in reentry. I struggled deeply with Joe's proposal.

Joe told me to look at this writing like a research project. The idea was that I had made several expeditions back and forth between the two different worlds of prison and society. I was merely to reflect and write my first-hand experience in each of them. From this perspective it made a little more sense to me, even though I was still filled with uncertainty at that point.

Finding the time to work on a project like this was also an issue for me. I was in my first year of a four-year Bible college and that required several hours of work each day. The immense responsibility of a quality writing that was accurate and truthful did not escape me.

I struggled with the idea for some time, even after I had started it, because I was only looking at things from the natural. I was a weak and broken man from a human perspective. I had no idea at the time that God was trying to answer my prayer for change and create something that would cause me to have a deepening encounter with Him. I was about to enter a crisis of belief – I would accept the challenge handed to me or recoil from it.

If God has called us to His highest and best for our lives, each of us will have a crisis of belief. This is when all our abilities and resources have failed, and when we face either complete ruin or something better than we could have ever dreamed. God was far more interested in me having an intimate encounter with Him than He was me getting the job done. The book was merely the medium to create the encounter – a God-sized assignment that only He could do. I realized I could not do it on my own. If He didn't help me it would fail. There was no way to see it come to pass unless God provided it.

The crisis of belief was that the God who led me to the task of this book would provide the revelation and the resources to bring it to pass. When it comes to a God-sized assignment, if you can handle it alone, it probably is not of God. At some point on this journey, I came to understand the real assignment was my experience with Him. It changed my focus and changed my life. I went from focusing on the end result of the book to the end result of my encounter with God on this journey. Now it can be your journey too.

A CALL TO RELATIONSHIP, NOT RELIGION

This is not a book about religion but rather a book addressing manhood through relationship. It contains no Bible stories, sells no religious tradition of man, and uses no theological language. This is a book that addresses the nature of the problem, which is the problem of the human nature. It sheds light on the heart of the problem, which is the problem of the human heart.

Reentry Realities is a reentry book that takes a hardcore look at the realities of reintegration back into society. It provides solutions through a relationship with God and the guidance of His wisdom in the context of how we manage our lives by design upon release from incarceration. It takes a look at how we deal with authority and supervision, how we define freedom, choose relationships, navigate job hunting, respond to support, reenter or create a family, become an asset to our community, and many more areas of reentry and reintegration.

God is in the business of turning males into men of moral integrity, strength, character, and value to the community they enter. Your open response to the wisdom of His principles and disciplines casts the deciding vote. His wisdom offers us full reconciliation and restoration to life in all of its fullness. Through the master model of manhood (His Son), God longs to show you that freedom and liberty are gifts that can only be preserved through the boundaries of manhood.

The scriptures themselves have profound power and authority that is greater than any human words. It still remains the best-selling book of all time. Fifty Bibles are sold every minute, seventy-two thousand a day, and twenty-six million a year. For this reason I have frequently quoted Bible passages throughout the text so readers can easily examine the powerful principles of scripture supporting my conclusions.

When I was a child, I talked like a child, I thought like a child,
I reasoned like a child; now that I have become a man,
I am done with childish ways and have put them aside
1 CORINTHIANS 13:11

THE PRINCIPLES THAT GOVERN ALL LIFE

The Bible stands alone among the books of the world in that it is a revelation from God to man. It claims man as its subject and cries out for his obedience. The Bible is a revelation of the reason for man, the nature of man, and the destiny of man. It is a revelation of the laws of operation that govern man and reveals the path to the highest levels of success in every field of life.

In accordance with His purpose, who works out everything
in agreement with the counsel and design of His [own] will
EPHESIANS 1:11

We go to school and they introduce us to the laws of physics. We still don't understand much about them as average people, and we pay little attention to them as we go about our daily lives. All that we are likely to remember about them is that the laws of physics govern all matter and motion, from the unseen sub-atomic particles all the way up to the motion of the stars and planets.

A deep understanding of the principles of physics has led to mastering the air – flying around the world and even to the moon and back. When we operate within the boundaries of the principles of physics we can accomplish great things. If we miscalculate those principles we crash and burn. We cannot change those principles to suit us or break those principles without breaking ourselves, and we accept that.

15

The principles of physics are not "like" the principles of God; they are the principles of God. The laws of physics are simply the principles of His "counsel and design" that govern matter and its motion. The principles of His "counsel and design" that govern all operations of human life are just like the principles of physics – except much easier to understand and apply. When we operate within them, our lives soar and we accomplish great things. When we try to break them, we break ourselves against them, and we crash and burn. What's important to understand is they were not given to us to limit us. They were given to us to protect us and remove the limits of success in our lives.

I have given you the choice between life and death,
between blessing and curses…Oh, that you would choose life
DEUTERONOMY 30:19

A BROKEN HUMANITY

This is also a story about man's long history of breaking himself against the principles that govern all operations of human life. God warned man that breaking these principles would result in spiritual death, and the fall from the design of his manhood (Genesis 2:17). Man's rebellion means that he no longer had a Creator and offspring relationship with his God. He had fallen to only a Creator and creation relationship.

As the centuries passed, man fell further and further from the design of authentic manhood. No one even remembered what it was supposed to look like anymore. There were no longer any models left that even remotely resembled it. Man began to create his own definitions for manhood. Every man claimed his own brand of manhood.

Man regressed more and more from maturity to immaturity, and more like an animal than a man made in the image of his Creator. The earth became corrupt and filled with violence (Genesis 6:11). It was every man for himself and his own selfish desires. Man has become so selfish, self-centered, and self-obsessed that he has never experienced a period of peace without war longer than twenty-five years since the recording of history began.

CRIME IS A SYMPTOM

The fall from manhood exists as a major crisis in our world today, and it is reflected in the vast number of adult males who are incarcerated and their high rates of recidivism. The fall of man was not something that happened; it is still happening. The loss of the inner image of manhood is still causing us to regress. The quadrupling of America's prison population and the number of returning offenders dwarfs anything previously seen in American history. Well over half a million Americans will leave prison and return to society each year, an estimated sixteen hundred per day. A staggering two-thirds of the more than six hundred thousand prisoners who are released each year will return to crime and prison where the cycle begins all over again. The question you face now is, will you be one of them?

The crisis in our rising prison population is a crisis of an arrested psycho-social development and the maturity issues, relational issues, and the compulsive/addictive issues that result from it. This devastating issue of an arrested development seems to have the power to shackle our responses and narrow and limit the range of individual choice.

These issues have a major impact on society. The arrested development is the source of all wars within ourselves and is reflected in our battles with others. The potential for anti-social behavior and crime are embodied in our lack of wholeness and the missing parts of our developmental maturity. The crime is but a symptom.

SET UP TO BE RULED BY EMOTIONS

The arrested development means to be emotion driven. We are pleasure driven instead of principle driven. To be principle driven makes no sense to the person with an arrested development that is governed by the self-obsession for restoration. If at some point it does make sense to us, we don't own enough of ourselves to initiate the inner controls necessary for a life or principle-centered maturity.

When emotion and desire are unbridled by the inner controls of maturity, they are unquenchable, and we live out our lives in a desperate attempt to satisfy the never satisfied disease of more. It is a psychic imbalance; a sickness of the soul initiated at the fall of man. Without this psychic balance, no real and genuine connection with another human being is possible. Our relational world as adults is severely limited and handicapped and sometimes severely twisted and distorted. Since the pleasure driven life is a form of self-referential immaturity, it is a type of self-obsession that is ever manifesting itself through the alternating obsessions of predator and parasite.

Adulthood in society demands that we have the inner controls of maturity that provide self-control, such as discipline, morals, and boundaries. When these inner controls are not in place or are not functioning, society initiates outer controls that serve as a secondary safety mechanism to protect others. Outer controls such as incarceration are rarely, if ever, effective at causing a person to live through a process of inner controls. As a consequence of the arrested development, the inner controls are just not in place to be activated.

RETURNING TO SOCIETY SEVERELY HANDICAPPED

We return to society expecting to skip over some of the vital stages of rebuilding our lives and vital stages of growth. Our goal is to save ourselves from the pain of problem solving, while still expecting to reap the desired rewards of maturity in adulthood. What often ends up happening after release is we live our lives with the desperation and panic of someone trying to steer themselves out of a bad crash. The prolonged desperation causes us to over-steer at some point (make poor choices), making the crash inevitable. The result once again is conflict with society that leads to incarceration.

Interdependence and cooperation within society are critical to its freedoms. A society of freedom cannot be fostered in an atmosphere of recklessness, lawlessness, and the instability of adult males with an arrested maturity. We are men who have been unwilling and unable to live life on life's terms instead of our own.

The arrested maturity is an inner psychic wound and self-rupture of the soul that violates our will, our rights, and our needs. We are driven to compensate for this chronic imbalance with various forms of self-inflicted replacement therapy. We try to fill the emptiness with all sorts of things: sex, money, possessions, social status, alcohol and drugs, relationships, achievement, excitement, work, and even exercise.

The chronic craving for wholeness is never filled – a perpetual self-obsession to connect with some fix for our restoration. We are adult males who have never fully negotiated all the stages of adult consciousness and have not acquired all the skills necessary for a mature adult life in society. We have been frozen in various forms of dependency, warring, and striving for proof of independence in a world that functions through interdependence. The crisis is far worse than we realize. It's about millions of adult males who look like men, but are in reality without the consciousness of adulthood.

THE CORRECTIVE EXPERIENCE

Man has a desperate desire and need for restoration to his original design. The desire is reflected in all of the ways he seeks to fill his emptiness and fix himself. The need is reflected in the countless ways he continues to break himself against the principles that were designed to govern his operations. God honored man's desperate desire and need, and refused to give up on His creation. Man had represented His literal offspring and was simply too valuable to be left to his own destruction.

One last Adam came to humanity and provided the path for the corrective experience of restoration to the original design of manhood (1 Corinthians 15:45). He restored man's ability to walk in the spiritual life that represented his inner image of manhood – the image and likeness of his Creator. The last Adam is our Master Model of Manhood, the Son of God. He walked out the principles that govern human life with unwavering perfection.

Reintegration into society is a call to manhood and maturity in adulthood. It can be seen as nothing less. Reentry Realities addresses the corrective experience using spiritual principles and disciplines and relationships to address the arrested development within each man. Psycho- social development, like spiritual development, can continue throughout our lifetime. The goal is to reignite these processes, becoming an atmosphere of change, and then the soil for future functionality.

Reentry Realities takes a look at principles that are in harmony with the natural laws of growth and development according to God's intended design. Reentry Realities uses the corrective experience to move us progressively on a maturity continuum, from childlike self- obsessions to the natural place of social beings called interdependence. The work begins with our private successes – steps toward character growth. We grow mentally and emotionally from this work and, as a result, we grow relationally. Our personal successes translate into our public successes. As we become genuinely independent, we develop a foundation for interpersonal relationships. We have our character development from which we can work on our more public successes of consistent cooperation and teamwork within our communities.

With the overwhelming challenges one faces today upon reentry, along with the statistical majority of ex-offenders re-offending, it has become imperative that we approach reentry holistically. We have an inner life and an outer life. They are not separate; the former determines the latter. Investing in programs that provide the tools to pro-socially adapt to life in the community prepares one to have the specific skills to manage his outer life. Investing in our inner life provides the inner controls of self-control that lead to discipline, morals, and pro-social boundaries. Together they create a complimentary approach which leads to success in the social reality of an adult world.

My efforts in this book have been geared toward being encouraging, yet with brutal honesty, straightforward, and challenging. I believe you can respect that. I really have been there, and my prayer is that you and I will never return to prison. My hope is that you will be able to relate, and that you will not see yourself as different from the rest of us who hope to remain free. In light of the two-thirds who return to prison, hopefully you will not be indifferent.

I am sure this book has its oversights and shortcomings in the subjects discussed.

Followers of spiritual truths are always traitors to some degree. I have been aware of the Holy Spirit's guidance in response to the hundreds of hours of prayer for this book; His giving me strength, courage, and an unwavering desire to complete this work. The Holy Spirit, along with my own experience, has shown me the necessity of such a book.

This journey is about changing our inner man – the hidden man of the heart
1 PETER 3:4

The hidden man of the heart is the real person inside each of us. The hidden man of the heart rules the outer man of the senses. If we can face the changes that need to be made in the inner man of the heart, the temptations, struggles, and disappointments of reentry will produce growth instead of self-destruction.

I know prison is a real and present problem. The question is, how can we navigate it in such a way that it actually becomes a fulfilling and life-changing experience, one that helps us to understand who we are, our strengths, and our own value? If we can learn to view our journey in this way, it becomes the heroic journey.

There are no real barriers to this thing. You can change or you can choose to stay the same. You can enjoy this thing called life by making the most of it, living life on life's terms, or you can let who and what you might have been pass you by. It's all your choice, but while you are still sitting on the sidelines of life, think well – choose well. You will never get back the time and opportunity you give up. I am confident you will find yourself in these pages. If you do, you can reach those not reached and tell the untold, as I am. Go ahead and turn the page and begin with my story.

POST-RELEASE UPDATE
This is the second edition of *Reentry Realities*. The first printing had such an impact on its readers, we decided to repackage it and give it a suitable launching. I spent the last eight years teaching this course with its accompanying workbook in multiple prisons. This book as a course led to new insights that created the seed for a second edition, which is now in a completed manuscript and ready for publication.

The game we practice while incarcerated is the game we will play upon release. I have been released from prison since the first printing, and have been able to put these principles into practice in my own release. I planted and cultivated, and now I am reaping the harvest with great success in every area of my life in reentry. This law of the harvest shows no partiality. This success awaits you as well.

Larry Dean Thompson
Toledo, Ohio
October 2022

CHAPTER ONE

My Story of the Oppression of Self-Obsession
—∞—

A PRINCIPLE LIKE GRAVITY

*If you always think what you have always thought, you will always feel what you
have always felt. If you always feel what you have always felt, you will always do
what you have always done. If you always do what you have always done, you will
always get what you have always got. If you always get what you have always got,
you will return to thinking what you have always thought.*

— UNKNOWN —

My hope is you will be able to relate to some of my own experiences.
If we purposely determine to focus on what is common between
us rather than our differences, we may find we are more alike than
either one of us realized. We may be different ages and come from different
generations. We may have different skin colors and may have been raised in
different cities with different people. We may have completely different circumstances that brought us to prison. Regardless of these things, I believe what
goes on inside each of us is far more common than any external differences.
If we peel back all these surface layers of identifying ourselves and look at the
dynamics of our inner lives, it might be hard to tell us apart.

Maybe, like me, you lived your whole life with an inner thirst nothing
ever seemed to be able to fully satisfy. There was always this big search for
something I knew was out there. I was never able to catch up to it or make
the connection between where I looked and the cost of searching there. The
good times of the search always seemed to be short-lived and the bad times
from searching in the wrong places never seemed to have an end. In spite of
the costs, I remember the search was relentless and had to be satisfied. I didn't
know it then, but the word of God speaks about this unquenchable thirst:

*Wait and listen, everyone who is thirsty! Come to the waters…Yes, come, buy [priceless,
spiritual] wine and milk without money and without price [simply for the self-surrender
that accepts the blessing]. Why do you spend your money for that which is not bread, and
your earnings for that which does not satisfy? Harken diligently to me, and eat what is
good, and let your soul delight itself in fatness [the profuseness of spiritual joy]*

ISAIAH 55:1,2

AN UNQUENCHABLE THIRST

Can you imagine walking through your whole life and never being allowed to drink a glass of water to satisfy your thirst? This is what my life felt like with my unquenchable desires. I tried everything imaginable, and my thirst remained. I tried it more often, more of it at one time, different mixtures of it, and nothing worked to relieve the obsession. The thought should have crossed my mind, "If no desire I search out can quench this inner thirst, maybe it wasn't supposed to."

All who drink of this water will be thirsty again. But whoever takes a drink of the water that I will give him shall never, no never, be thirsty any more. But the water that I will give him shall become like a spring of water welling up (flowing, bubbling) [continually] within him unto (into, for) eternal life
JOHN 4:13-14

I had no idea at the time that this was more spiritual than physical. Yet its effects were just as real on every aspect of my physical nature. The question I should have asked myself was, "Is life no more than a constant desire or thirst that can never be satisfied?" From my own experience of the chase, I could have easily said yes. Yet I saw a different law at work in the natural world. To satisfy my hunger for food, life provided bountiful resources to supply my needs. If I was physically thirsty, life provided an abundance of resources there. It was clear that life provided for every single need for every single creature. Why is it, then, that while life supplied every single need, did I go through life with such an obsession – an inner longing, emptiness, and thirst – that often bordered on the insane?

THE COST OF PURSUIT

Insanity has been defined as doing the same things over and over and expecting different results. Clearly that definition of insanity accurately described my life. There I was, 45 years old with my 4th prison number and the same scenario once again repeating itself in my life. The prison door slamming in my face. A tomb with a light in it. A jungle of concrete and steel where the only things breakable are the men in the tombs. The truth is, I was already broken. I was here because I was not all there. A place made for broken men – and once again society was a little safer.

I am forgotten like a dead man, and out of mind; like a broken vessel am I
PSALM 31:12

All I could think about was what the judge had said to me: "You have a college degree. You have been trained as a counselor. Mr. Thompson, you have been through more programs, and have taught more programs, than anyone who has ever stood before me in this courtroom. You still haven't applied what you've learned to your own life, and you are a menace to society. What you need is some time to do some serious soul searching. I am sentencing you to ten years for aggravated robbery, five years for abduction, and one year for a criminal tool. You are hereby warded to the Ohio Department of Rehabilitation and Corrections for the duration of sixteen years."

In the blink of an eye and the swing of the judge's gavel, three years of hard work to rebuild my life after my last incarceration was gone. In those three years, I went from a ten-speed bicycle in a halfway house to a newly remodeled home. I had two trucks and my own construction business. Every personal item I owned I lost with my arrest. I also lost my place in my community, my friends, my dog, and even my hopes and dreams were gone as if they never existed. All I left in the wake was more victims.

How could this happen all over again? What went wrong? What was wrong with me? I was sure the answer was not more knowledge. Like the judge said, I had enough of that. I had spent years in Alcoholics Anonymous. I could quote the steps and the principle of the program forward and backward. Yet I never held more than a year of sobriety unless I was locked up. In previous incarcerations, I completed and worked as a program aid in just about every program the state had to offer. What more could I be taught?

> Surely I am too stupid and brutish to be called a man, and I have not
> the understanding of a man [for all my secular learning is as nothing]
> PROVERBS 30:2

INTENTION ALONE IS INSUFFICIENT

In one respect, I was just like you in my attitude toward the release from prison that you will face. Each time I was released from prison, I was done with the things that put me there. I was sure of it while I was incarcerated. I knew what I had to do to stay out of prison, and I wanted to do it. I knew the mistakes I had made and vowed not to repeat them.

This time, however, I was becoming aware that while I had plenty of pro-social tools and information, I really didn't have a changed heart. No changed heart means no permanently changed mind – only a fool who was only fooling himself. Each time I was released back into the liberty of options, voices equaled choices, (I-Self-Me) and the thirst for more raged on even with the new tools and information.

I am confident no one reading this ever valued their freedom more than I did each time I was incarcerated and released. I applied myself in those programs both in and out of prison. I went because I genuinely wanted to learn, not to receive pats on the back, fancy certificates or degrees. I went the extra mile in reentry, always remaining employed and living independently.

I believe I became a better and more functional human being as a result of each incarceration and release. Stumbling and falling doesn't necessarily mean you haven't made progress. It just means there is more progress to be made. You're never really a failure until you stop trying to succeed.

MATURITY RESISTANT AND DANGEROUS

I wasn't resistant to learning. I was resistant to growing up. I simply lacked the courage. I understand that today. The difference between gaining knowledge and growing up is a difference that is profound. Our problem of incarceration can never be solved but only outgrown. It means bridging the longest eighteen inches in the human anatomy, which is from the head to the heart. The inner man – the hidden man of the heart – was still a self-obsessed child. Today, I believe I was one of the most dangerous people in my community because of that. I had adult head knowledge and childlike self-centeredness. Such a person has no problem learning right from wrong. It's just that his self-obsession is so pronounced that it overrides all thought and conviction of it.

Trust not in oppression, and become not vain in robbery:
if riches increase, set not your heart upon them
PSALM 62:10

IT'S ALL ABOUT LARRY

A good example of just how far my self-centeredness had progressed was clear when I stood in front of the judge during my last sentencing. I was guilty of crimes against society. I violated the basic human rights of people in my community. I brought danger and terror into my community and violated their trust and acceptance. My actions violated the freedoms every American soldier ever died to protect and every public servant sought to maintain.

Civil authorities are not a terror to [people of] good conduct, but to [those of] bad behavior. Would you have no dread of him who is in authority? Then do what is right and you will receive his approval and commendation. For he is God's servant for your good. But if you do wrong [you should dread him and] be afraid… He is God's servant to execute His wrath (punishment, vengeance) on the wrongdoer
ROMANS 13:3-4

None of this was significant to me at my sentencing, of course; it was still all about me. Once again, I was able to take this experience and make it all about Larry. I was full of self pity, indignation, fear, and anger over my consequences. Now all of the sudden what was fair, right, and merciful somehow became extremely important to me at my sentencing. I was now an expert at deciding and executing justice – above the learned and elected civil authorities – especially when it came to me.

In the light of the behaviors that put me there in front of them, it sounds incredibly insane. It was no less than rebellion against the consequences I would be required to pay and was the sum total of my immature, self-obsessed thinking. As I look back now, it amazes me how self obsession can progress to such an extreme from childhood to adulthood. What amazes me even more is that I had absolutely no ability to see it. Like some undiagnosed allergy, all I could see was the symptoms.

THIRST OR ITCH - IT'S ALL THE SAME

Self obsession is sort of like poison ivy of the mind. The person infected with this childlike immaturity becomes covered with a rash of selfish self-centeredness which incites an intense and all-consuming itch. As the person gives into its constant demands to be scratched, it spreads to all areas of life, becoming all the worse and harder to resist scratching. If the infected person does not scratch it, he can think of nothing else and feels as though he might go insane. Yet if he scratches the itch until he bleeds, hurts, and is exhausted, a few minutes later it would itch all the more. As long as he scratches the itch of his self-centeredness, it never goes away. Like real poison ivy, it's always asking to be scratched; always promising relief. To scratch it is to cause pain and once again intensify the itch.

LIKE CHASING THE WIND

Some would suggest the Bible is thousands of years old and cannot be relevant to us today. The truth is, there is nothing new under the sun when it comes to the itch of human desire. King Solomon was the wisest man who ever lived according to the Bible. When God asked him what he desired, King Solomon asked for an understanding mind (1 Kings 3:5-14). God was pleased with his request. God not only made him wise but also gave him riches, power, and an era of peace in his kingdom. Solomon had everything a person could ever want. He had all the pleasures and all that was thought to give life meaning and happiness. The success and riches of his kingdom certainly supplied opportunities for these experiences far beyond our creative desires. Let's take a look at what King Solomon had to say about it. His final view of it may surprise you:

Anything I wanted I would take. I denied myself no pleasure. I even found great pleasures in hard work, a reward for all my labors. But as I looked at everything I worked so hard to accomplish, it was all so meaningless – like chasing the wind. So I came to hate life because everything done under the sun is so troubling. Everything is so meaningless – like chasing the wind (Ecclesiastes 2:10, 11, 17). What happened? Why did wanting everything and then having it leave him so sour? He pursued them as an ultimate end to personal satisfaction is why. He realized chasing the thirst and scratching the itch of personal satisfaction alone is empty and as temporary as your next pursuit and accomplishment. Like "chasing the wind," human desire and satisfaction are always moving and changing directions. It could never be caught; never held on to.

King Solomon's pursuit and attainment didn't free him. Like us, it imprisoned him in the chase. Everything he tried, tasted, or tested had been meaningless, useless, pointless, and most of all, empty. King Solomon's hope in writing such wisdom was the same as mine: to spare future generations like ours the bitterness of learning the hard way – by personal experience.

For many of us, this is not the first time we have heard these warnings. Yet because we remain plugged into the illusions of our own self obsessions, we believe the lie that we are unique and different, and somehow if we manage it right, we can satisfy our obsessions. We believe if we can't there is no fulfillment left for us. Nothing could be further from the truth. The twisted distortions of extreme self obsession is no lifestyle at all but rather a death style. It is the cause of all our wars within and our battles without. It is the cause of incarceration, broken relationships, lost dreams, and broken men.

What leads to strife (discord and feuds) and how do conflicts (quarrels and fightings) originate among you? Do they not arise from your sensual desires that are ever warring in your bodily members? You are jealous and covet [what others have] and your desires go unfulfilled; [so] you become murders. [To hate is to murder as far as your hearts are concerned.] You burn with envy and anger and are not able to obtain [the gratification, the contentment, and the happiness that you seek], so you fight and war

JAMES 4:1, 2

LARRY THE PARASITE AND PREDATOR

People who suffer from the oppression of self-obsession are like a virus invading the lives of other people. We seek to remain fully fed and charged in a life that serves our purposes. We are driven to be pleased and satisfied, and the lives of others and the world revolve around us.

When the feeding and charge are not at full capacity, we suffer fear and pain from the emptiness the self-obsession can never fulfill. To live a life plugged into the thirst and itch of selfish self-centeredness means to live a life operating on the alternating obsessions of parasite and predator.

The most potent weapon in the hands of the oppressor is an oppressed mind. When I was sober I was a parasite that devoured anyone foolish enough to get close to me. When I consumed alcohol and drugs my level of oppression became extremely elevated, and I preyed on those in my community as a predator. Every thing and every person were used for the express purpose of advancing my own interests and avoiding the pain of emptiness. This is how everyone behind the razor wire gets there. If you refuse to take these things seriously, you may ruin your chances of ever having a life of real value and lasting freedom.

My self-obsession would never allow me to see things that way. It demanded a strong commitment to avoiding truth and reality, which like emptiness, only produced a discomfort I was not willing to tolerate. I was always telling the courts and the people in my life how sorry I was. From the standpoint of who I am today, the words "I'm sorry" seem more like an insult than a remedy. Being sorry, even genuinely remorseful, doesn't take back the things done, heal the harmed, or fix the people that were hurt by them. In light of my repeated acts of parasite and predatory behavior, it meant very little at all.

MY WORLDVIEW

Very early in life I began to view the world as chaotic, dangerous, and frightening. Life appeared as a ruthless place of survival of the fittest. I didn't know it then, but that view dramatically affected the way I responded to the world. Instead of growing up and maturing as a result of facing life's problems head on and solving them, I used avoidance and escape to respond to the world.

I had always been willing to believe life had some deeper meaning. I just didn't have any idea of how to get past all the chaos and ruthlessness to tap into it. Today, however, I realize the world is actually a nurturing place in most ways, even in the many forms of emotional pain that are an inherent standard of it. This change in my perceptions would have never been possible without discovering a source of genuine courage to challenge and confront my old worldview. From the standpoint of an evidence-based model, I am able to see the world as a place governed by principles designed to reward me for my positive efforts and exact a price for my destructive actions (Galatians 6:7). Like gravity, these principles are always operating and governing our lives to our advantage or our destruction.

Before I had this revelation, the oppression of self-obsession left me imprisoned in my eight by ten mentally. In my old experience-based model, it made sense to me to live from one fleeting desire to the next; grabbing whatever pleasure whenever and wherever I could. I was not about to pass up any quick fix or shortcut to personal gratification in the present, since the future seemed so unstable and uncertain anyway. The longer I lived by this worldview the more my actions created situations to reinforce it, and the more time I spent in eight by ten prison cells.

A PRINCIPLE LIKE GRAVITY

For as he thinks in his heart, so is he
PROVERBS 23:7

If you always think what you have always thought, you will always feel what you have always felt. If you always feel what you have always felt, you will always do what you have always done. If you always do that you have done, you will always get what you have always got. If you always get what you have always got, you will return to thinking what you have always thought." I created the world I believed in and then I believed in, the world I created. For by whatever anyone is made inferior or worse or is overcome, to that [person or thing] he is enslaved
2 PETER 2:19

THE UNNATURAL NATURE OF SELF OBSESSION

My self-obsession was a set of thinking patterns and habits that had become a lifestyle of unnatural attempts to fulfill my most natural basic human needs. What I really needed I believed I could not get, so I couldn't get enough of what I didn't need in response. I needed what everyone needs – security, belonging, acceptance, and love. Unfortunately, the ones who often need these things the most are the ones who deserve them the least. I worked hard to fill myself with the things around me, a temporary fix, until I resolved the needs within me. I looked outside of myself for a supporting cast of characters; something that would fill the emptiness and offer pleasure and satisfaction. I began to associate the high and the euphoria of chasing the thirst and scratching the itch with fulfillment of my needs. The more I sought to fulfill the emptiness, the more my unnatural efforts intensified it.

Therefore remove [the lusts that end in] sorrow and vexation from your heart and mind and put away evil from your body, for youth and the dawn of life are vanity [transitory, idle, empty, and devoid of truth]
ECCLESIASTES 11:10

THE IMPRINT OF IDENTITY AND VALUE

In the blueprint of life and according to God's intended design, family was the place of my source relationships. Family is our place of many beginnings, where the foundation for our lives is constructed. My family was to be the source where, for the first time in my life, I would learn about who I am and my own personal value. These relationships were designed to be the source of my first experience of what it felt like to have my needs met; to know what it felt like to belong, to be accepted, and loved. Family was to be the source of an environment that allowed me to resolve my natural occurring conflicts, such as trust, intimacy, attachment, and other conflicts. For well over a decade the parents are the most important part of a child's world.

My beliefs about myself came from my parents, not the world or my own immature non- logical mind. As a child, I could only know myself from the reflections I received from my source relationships. Since those reflections are mirrored by remarkably imperfect human beings, they are naturally inaccurate, incomplete, and often unavailable. For this reason, the most responsible thing parents can do for their child is to reflect the image God reflects in His Word of that child's value.

The imprint of identity and value and its lifelong impact are made possible by the magical part of a child's thinking. It allows them to view their parents as godlike: all knowing, and all powerful. There is absolutely no greater privilege and responsibility in the life of any parent. This magical thinking provides a survival value for the child. No harm can come to him and all his needs will be met as long as he has his parents. The child's greatest terror and harm is a parent who is unavailable and not meeting the child's needs. Likewise, the magical thinking of a child offers a self-preservation value. Since parents are seen as all knowing and all powerful, children are eager to learn from them the meaning of the world around them. There is no greater inspiration to seek God as the loving Father He is, or to scorn Him and reject Him in adulthood.

And did not God make [you and your wife] one [flesh]? And why [did God make you two] one? Because He sought godly offspring [from your union]
MALACHI 2:15

The magical idealization of my parents had as much potential for harm as for good. As a child, my parents were unavailable and that influenced my core beliefs about myself. Since my father was absent and my mother was present but often unavailable, I had no alternative than to internalize it as a reflection of my own value and worth. It wasn't possible for me at that age to rationalize the inadequacies and imperfections of my parents. Their absence could only mean I was worthless: worth - less than their time, attention, and direction. The more I felt worthless, the more uncertain I was about who I was and my personal value. I felt unworthy of having my needs met.

BASIC HUMAN NEEDS AND CONFLICT RESOLUTION

The imprint of identity and value becomes preparation of the soil of a child's soul, making it fertile so that God can fill it with His seed of life (1 Peter 1:22-23). The needs and conflict resolution of a child are the building blocks, of wholeness and completion. The child can enter life and experience what it means to be fully human. Like any child, I needed both my parents throughout my childhood. When a child is alienated and alone like I was, he is in a constant state of unresolved conflict and unmet needs. I felt a gnawing sense of emptiness, as though something of profound importance was missing.

In such a condition, the design and order of nature is reversed. The lower drives and pleasure centers dominate reasoning and logic in an aborted attempt to resolve conflicts and meet needs. Beyond this, there is no inner life, no basic sense of value; only an inner barrenness with no other alternative than to seek people, places, and things outside of self to feel whole, complete, lovable, and worthwhile. It is a kind of soul murder that results in a kind of death in life.

A CASE OF SUBSTANDARD MATURITY

Physically I became an adult. My inner development was set up to be governed by emotion and self-centered thinking, much like a child or a teenager. The part of the brain that governs reasoning and judgment is called the prefrontal cortex. In the normal cycle of development, it increases in its awareness of the inner dialogue of thought, emotion, and desire. Maturity results as reasoning and judgment gain dominion over emotion and desire. When our development is arrested, this dominion is never fully negotiated. The way we were designed to operate and function is literally turned upside down. When this happens, emotion and desire rule and reasoning and judgment are dominated by them.

Under these conditions I was set up for problems with relationships and society. It was a wound I felt on the inside; one that separated me from both myself and others. It is the psychic imbalance that fuels the self-obsession. Forged in the matrix of my source relationships, it conditioned the way I would approach every other relationship in my life.

This accurately describes my level of functioning throughout my entire adult life. It was a level of substandard maturity that barred me from functioning in the normal operations of an adult life. I had poor impulse control. I was unwilling and unable to delay personal gratification. The fulfillment of my "want to" ruled my life – not pro-social reasoning and judgment. I wanted what I wanted when I wanted it. Like the short sighted view of a child (in an adult's body), there was nothing else to consider beyond the "want to," and it often spiraled into many forms of darkness.

THE SPIRAL INTO DARKNESS

The fantasy and hope of fulfillment of the thirst and itch overshadows any past experience of the emptiness and sorrow it always creates. The more a person is controlled by self-obsession, the less they are able to see it. Slowly and progressively it destroys the person's ability to comprehend it. When a person insists on chasing the thirst and scratching the itch of self-obsession, there comes an unforeseen time when they give up personal power to have any control over it.

The way of the wicked is like deep darkness; they do not know over what they stumble
PROVERBS 4:19

Self-obsession is a beast that grows in proportion to how much you feed it. As the person pursues his self-obsession he finds everything he chases will eventually lose the power to satisfy him. It gains power over him while everything it feeds on loses its power to satisfy. Each time he gives into his extreme self-centeredness it tightens its grip on him and is strengthened. The more he listens to the voice of (I-Self-Me), the more it demands. The longer he lives a self-obsessed life, the less he is likely to ever change.

As a person crosses this unseen barrier, he begins to view everything differently. He will plunge from one depth of darkness to the next until his life is out of control. He can no longer be counted on to make sound decisions and his life begins to quickly unravel. His mind no longer thinks sanely. His self-centered thinking has become twisted. He finds himself thinking and then acting out things that are insane because of his narrowed view of self-obsession.

But if your eye is unsound your whole body will be full of darkness. If then the very light in you [your conscious] is darkened, how dense is that darkness
MATTHEW 6:23

Deeper and deeper he sinks into darkness. In time, darkness will consume his heart, and it will become calloused. The more he slips into self obsession the thicker the callous becomes. He is unmoved by fear of consequences. His only aim is satisfaction. The next fix of life is on his terms: sex, relationships, money, social power, and chemical highs. Each of us have our own history and list where we have "acted out" our self obsessions as parasite and predator at the expense of others – even at the expense of our own lives and freedom.

To all my enemies I have become a reproach, but especially to my neighbors, and a dread to my acquaintances, who flee from me on the street
PSALM 31: 11

Unfortunately, there will be many who never turn away from this path. Once self obsession is the master of a person's life darkness prevails. Where darkness prevails it signifies a lack of light and illumination in the person's thinking. I was not able to see this progression in my life until freedom was more important to me than the pain the light of truth might create.

Truth and communication are the first things to go, and the first things that need to be reestablished if one is to be loosed from its bondage of slavery.

THE CRISIS OF OUR DAY

My crime was a symptom of the nature of my self-obsession. I was having an allergic reaction to life as a result of chasing the thirst and scratching the itch, and I kept breaking out in a rash of jails and prison institutions. The more psychologically deprived a person is, the more self obsessed they become. The thirst and itch of self obsession that results from an arrested development is the tragedy which releases the rage that dominates the crisis in our prisons today. The rage is either directed by means of projections toward others or is directed toward ourselves. The arrested maturity which fuels the self obsession is acted out in the alternating obsessions of parasite and predator; crime, and violence.

This knowledge does not in any way provide an excuse for our behaviors or offer an avenue for blame. There is no viable excuse for anti-social behavior and crime. There is no one for a full grown adult to blame. Excuses are for children and cowards and are designed to avoid personal responsibility. It is just the opposite. Such knowledge points to a solution that demands responsible action on our part.

Even a child is known by his acts, whether [or not] what he does is pure and right
PROVERBS 20:11

TRIMMING VERSUS UPROOTING

Friend, you can complete all the programs, get your certificates and gain a lot of tools.

You should do these things. They most certainly have their value. Upon release you can get a job, find suitable housing, buy a car and obtain all the essentials, but you can't fix yourself. You can trim a lot of dead things in your life, but you can't remove their roots. You can't even see them. After you accomplish all these honorable challenges, you will still live with a desire projected into everything you do to fill the emptiness and satisfy the thirst.

Who can say, I have made my heart clean
PROVERBS 20:9

Although you go through all the motions of cleaning up the outside, the real wars that must be won are in the hidden recesses of the heart and character. Self obsession has a "want to" problem. Don't be fooled into thinking you can stop the "want to" any time you want to; you can't. There is something inside you that's stronger than you are. Until I was willing to recognize this in my own life I could not change. Stopping the act and still having the "want to" springing up in your life is not freedom. A long as you are separated from God and plugged into the child like obsession of (I-Self-Me) the "want to" will still be at work in your heart. A temporary retreat in prison does not mean that it is dead, but that it is very much alive and waiting.

If our own histories have shown us anything, it should be that our hearts are exceedingly deceitful and untrustworthy (Jeremiah 17:9). Without the light of the law of the Spirit of life residing in our hearts, our inventory will be exceedingly poor. We will minimize some area of self-centeredness and hold on to it. We will believe others are gone when they are not and miss some completely. This is one of the ways the Spirit of God assists us in our lives. He will reveal any self-centeredness that needs to be removed. His conviction will remain on you until you can no longer live with that area of self-centeredness.

Who can discern his lapses in error? Clear me from hidden [and unconscious] faults
PSALM 19:12

THE GREAT I-SELF-ME
Could there be a more horrible picture of slavery than self obsession? It's impossible to satisfy its demands. The one who worships the idol of (I-Self-Me) finds he will destroy himself long before he will ever meet its demands. Self obsession is design gone wrong – playing God in our own lives. We have worshiped in self-centered thought and served in selfish, self-seeking action. No god has ever demanded more and offered less in return, nor had a more faithful follower. This is serious business – as serious as it gets. We will never get back the days of our lives we have forfeited to our false idols.

Their sorrows shall be multiplied who choose another god
PSALM 16:4

It took me eighteen years in prison and four prison numbers to be willing to surrender to the right God and become the man I am today. I thank the one true God daily that I survived and lived to tell about it. There are so many who have not survived it. Four prison numbers is still not the worst thing that could happen to me; neither is dying, although it would be worse than prison. I realize today that the worst thing that can happen to me is being alive and never really living. This understanding led me to no longer regret the past nor wish to shut to the door on it. I know my experience can benefit others, so that's my focus today.

Even when I am old and grey-headed, O God, forsake me not,
[but keep me alive] until I have declared Your mighty strength to [this] generation,
and your might and power to all that are come
PSALM 71:18

33

THE RIGHT REFLECTION

All our lives we have been receiving the wrong reflections. Until I received the right reflection I never knew who I really was. My genuine reflection came when I began to view myself through the lens of God's perspective. It changed everything. Today, I have come to know through personal experience that there is a special place God created in me that allows Him to satisfy the thirst and the itch in a way only He can.

Programs will provide you with valuable tools for reentry, but they can't show you who you are and the value connected to it. They are incapable of meeting basic human needs and resolving lifelong inner conflicts; only right relationships can do that. When you have these things and the program tools, life will work best for you.

Create in me a clean heart, O God, and renew a right,
preserving, and steadfast spirit within me
PSALM 51:10

HOW TRANSFORMATION WORKS

The liberty of the law of the Spirit of life residing in the heart, combined with the maturity-centered principles of His Word, renews the heart and mind of man. It alone curses the allergy of self-obsession. It's like having radical surgery. You get a new life as a result of a new heart and a new mind. Each experience of applying the principles of the Great Physician is like spiritual radiation treatment. It kills a few more of those fast-growing cancerous cells of self obsession, and making us immune to their power to dominate our lives.

He sends forth His word and heals them
PSALM 107:20

The principle-empowered spirit acts as a mediator between the mind, emotions, and will, enabling us to move from self-centered immaturity to principle-centered maturity. We can reach a point where there is more satisfaction in the application of the principle than satisfying our selfish desires. It's called maturity. It doesn't mean we are redeemed from having desires. We're just redeemed from our desires having us.

What amazed me about the word of God is that He doesn't promise the ability to manage self obsession. He promises complete freedom from its slavery. Any lingering "want to" is brought into extinction and vice is traded for virtue. The voice of our old conditioning (I-Self- Me) are reconditioned with the voice of the Spirit and His principles. It transforms us and dramatically expands our world with the voice that speaks a new language of (We-Us-Ours).

SLAVE OR SERVANT – YOU WILL CHOOSE

You will choose a master, there's no question about that. It will determine the type of slave or servant you become. The same is true when we enter the family of the living God and become a son. The issue of identity is forever resolved, needs are met, and conflicts are resolved through community and relationship. Everything changes because you have. Prison is no longer a setback but rather a set up for what God has in store for your life. Something I've learned on this journey is that all purpose is given birth in a problem. Said another way, once you find your purpose in God, your problems shrink in proportion to the degree you walk in that purpose. With God it's never too late to become what you were designed to be.

DEVELOPING THE RIGHT PERSPECTIVE

I'm not talking about becoming religious. That can just as easily become another form of bondage. God's desire for our life in Him is simply relationship – the very thing He created us for. He wants you to experience the wholeness and healing He has for you. Once you do, you will not be able to do anything else but love Him back with the very love He has shed abroad in your renewed heart. We are transformed from parasite and predator to partner with God and our community. Right relationships always have their boundaries, responsibilities, and common goals. God is no different. When you meet these mutually shared expectations, the result is your life becomes more than it ever would have otherwise.

O Lord my God, I cried to you and you have healed me
PSALM 30:2

There is no greater path to lost opportunity than contempt for prior investigation. Call out to God in prayer; ask Him to show you He is real. He will not disappoint you. I promise you, the only regret you are likely to have is the one you will share with me. I only regret waiting so long to take this seriously. That is why I am writing this book, so you don't have to wait as long. You can start right now. Take a few moments to consider what parts of my story you can relate to your own life.

- What methods did you use to try to satisfy the thirst and scratch the itch of self-obsession? What lingering "want to" do you have that may sabotage your freedom?
- What type of losses have you experienced in your pursuit of chasing the thirst and scratching the itch of self-obsession?
- What's different about you today? Do you still have the same worldview you came into prison with?

One of the questions I had in the beginning of my search for truth was, is there evidence for God outside of the Bible and personal testimonies? What I discovered about God was above and beyond overwhelming evidence to show himself in his creation. Let's look at some of that evidence together in the next chapter.

CHAPTER TWO

The Human Design Model (Part One)

—◆—

One cannot be exposed to the law and order of the universe without concluding that there must be design and purpose behind it all…the better we understand the intricacies of the universe and all it harbors, the more reason we have found to marvel at the inherent design upon which it is based…

To be forced to believe one conclusion – that everything in the universe happened by chance, would violate the very objectivity of science itself…what random process could produce the brain of a man or the systems of the human eye?

They (evolutionists) challenge science to prove the existence of god, but must we really light a candle to see the sun? They say they cannot visualize a designer.

Well, can a physicist visualize an electron? What strange rationale makes some physicists accept the inconceivable electron as real while refusing to accept the reality of a designer on the grounds they cannot conceive him?

— WERNER VON BRAUN —

Director of NASA and father of the American space program

Everywhere we look we see design. This is especially true in our post-modern world of technology. Today we have cellphones, laptops, smart watches and electric bicycles with more onboard power than the Apollo spaceship that landed on the moon in 1969. This is sure to make reentering society after incarceration an interesting and exciting adventure.

Precision designs like these always require intelligent designers that have a plan and a purpose for their design. We call them precision designs, because they contain a vast amount of interactive components that are built to an exactly calculated specification to allow the design to function. When this is accomplished, the hope is that it will have the potential to fulfill the designers predestined purpose.

The problem with the designs of man is that they are never perfection. Once a design hits the market and is put to the test, consumers find the imperfections. Even if the design appears to work well, someone will always come along and build it a little better. The competition will perfect a design that already exists or build a completely new and better model.

The Apollo spaceship is a good example. The world was excited about a design with such quality to get mankind to the moon and back. It was still far from perfection. The spaceship was a disposable design and could not be reused. In 1982, the world was introduced to the reusable space shuttle and new excitement emerged.

However, the more advanced a design becomes, the greater the need for technical precision. By January 26, 1986, man's inherent inability to design perfection was made painfully clear to the world when the space shuttle Challenger exploded seventy-three seconds after takeoff, killing all of its passengers. On and on the cycle goes of advancing designs and discovering flaws. Nothing man designs will ever reach ultimate perfection.

Webster's Dictionary defines design in part as pattern; intention. For example, let's say you are driving down a highway observing some majestic mountain range and its rocky cliffs. To your mind the scattered rock formations would be random, without pattern and intention, so you would conclude it was without design. However, if you were driving down the highway in South Dakota next to Mount Rushmore, your conclusions would be totally different. The busts of four presidents are carved into the side of the mountain. Immediately, you would recognize there is a pattern here. There was a reason behind its creation. There was an intention for this design and there must, therefore, be a designer. You may even recognize the faces of George Washington, Thomas Jefferson, Teddy Roosevelt, and Abraham Lincoln. Your mind may begin to wonder who the designer was and what the designer's purpose and intention might have been.

THE CASE FOR SUPER INTELLIGENT DESIGN

We seldom see, and often take for granted, the designs that man did not create – the heavens, the earth, and even ourselves. In some ways, this should surprise us if not shock us. Why? Nothing mankind ever created or ever will create is as complex and precision designed as the things he did not create. We seldom wonder about the perfection of this design that cannot be perfected. Often it is because we understand little about the Designer and the design of creation. The end result is we live our lives taking creation's unwavering consistency and perfection for granted.

The late Carl Sagan, a brilliant scientist and best-selling author, made a similar statement concerning this lack of understanding: "We go about our daily lives understanding almost nothing of the world. We give little thought to the machinery that generates the sunlight that makes life possible, the gravity that glues us to an earth that would otherwise send us off spinning into space, or the atoms of which we are made and on whose stability we fundamentally depend." (Stephen Hawking, *A Brief History of Time: From the Big Bang to Black Holes*, 1988, introduction by Carl Sagan, p. ix).

Professor Sagan addressed this issue by dedicating his life to introducing scientific thought to a non-scientific public. Here is another of his conclusions: "Except for children, (who don't know enough to not ask the important questions), few of us spend much time wondering why nature is the way it is; where the cosmos came from, or whether it was always here." (ibid).

The majority are likely to feel we lack the skills to investigate the mysteries of the universe, our planet, and ourselves. We may even feel there is no need or that it would be a waste of time. Neither of these assumptions is correct. We may even be wondering what such knowledge and discussion has to do with reentry into society. I believe these questions will be answered by the end of this chapter and certainly by the end of this book. The ability to ask the right questions and understand the answers lies in the way we are wired and is part of our makeup. A general understanding is not only possible for the average layman; it has the potential to lead us to life's most important questions and their answers.

Is all that exists a matter of super intelligent design? Why are we here? Is there a purpose for our lives? If the answer we discover is "yes," then it is critical to ask a few other very important questions. If there is a purpose for our lives, is that purpose linked with the existence of God? If there is a design, how can we best live out this design in our day to day lives upon reentry?

These are fundamental question, indeed. We need to ask and seek answers to these questions. The way we view their answers profoundly affect the way we conduct our lives once we are released from prison.

Have you squarely faced these questions?

It may very well be that we are missing a vital perspective in the way we write the pages of rebuilding our lives after incarceration. We can find answers to these questions. Evidence of a super intelligent design is available. Let's look at some of the evidence, asking and answering questions basic to our search for freedom, meaning, and purpose in reentry.

The heavens declare the glory of God;
and the firmament shows and proclaims His handiwork
PSALM 19:1

A UNIVERSE OF SUPER INTELLIGENT DESIGN

A growing number of scientists in astronomy, physics, chemistry, botany, biology, and other major disciplines have recently declared the universe anthropic. This simply means that it bears clear and convincing evidence that it was designed by a super intelligence. At first, this declaration was not widely welcomed by the majority of the scientific community. However, this assertion began to change after an astonishing number of complex scientific variables were discovered that fit into a very narrow range of tolerance and balance that governs our solar system and allows life to exist on our planet. Paul Davies,

39

Professor of mathematical physics at Australia's University of Adelaide, sum-marizes the growing findings of scientists from many fields: "A long list of additional 'lucky accidents' and 'coincidences' has been compiled . . . Taken together, they provide impressive evidence that life as we know it depends very sensitively on the form of the laws of physics, and on some seemingly fortu-itous accidents in the actual values that nature has chosen for various particle masses, force strengths, and so on.

Suffice it to say that, if we could play God, and select values for these quantities at whim by twiddling a set of knobs, we would find that almost all knob settings would render the universe uninhabitable. In some cases, it seems as if the different knobs have to be fine-tuned to enormous precision if the universe is to be such that life would flourish (Davies, *The Mind of God: The Scientific Basis for a Rational World*, 1992, pp. 199-200).

What Professor Davies is implying here is overwhelming evidence of in-tricate design in the universe as a powerful indicator of an intelligent designer. Sir Isaac Newton said that, "This beautiful system of sun, planets, and comets could only proceed from the counsel and dominion of an intelligent and pow-erful being...." The wisdom and steady hand of an almighty God, not the Big Bang theory, place things strategically and with precision. Let's take a look at some of this precision design.

- The earth is an intelligently calculated 93 million miles from the sun. As-tronomer Hugh Ross points out this intelligent calculation: "In the case of planet earth, a change in the distance from the sun as small as 2 percent would rid the planet of all life." *The Creator and the Cosmos*, 1993, p. 135).
- The earth travels through space at 66,000 miles per hour as it orbits the sun. This speed perfectly offsets the sun's gravitational pull and keeps the earth's orbit at the proper distance from the sun. This orbit is so precise that if it were one inch less per 18 miles it would burn; one inch further the earth would freeze.
- There is nowhere else in our galaxy that planet earth could have been positioned and still sustain life. Our planet is carefully placed between two violent asteroid belts where there is a small amount of asteroids that quickly burn up in earth's atmosphere. If we were positioned in any oth-er location, the dust particles that flow through the asteroid belts would block out the light from the stars.
- The moon plays a critical role for life on earth as well. Its size and distance are exact to light our nights and create the precise tidal movement for our oceans. If the moon were closer, it would create tidal waves every tide. If it were further, tides would be too weak, oceans would become stagnant, plant life in our oceans would die, and the earth would be without most of its oxygen.

The Lord, who gives the sun for a light by day,
and the fixed order of the moon and the stars for a light by night
JEREMIAH 31:35

John Polkinghorne, a theoretical physicist and president of Queens College at Cambridge University states: "The intellectual beauty of the order discovered by science is consistent with the physical worlds having behind it the mind of a divine creator...The finely tuned balance built into the laws determining the very fabric of the universe is consistent with its fruitful history being the expression of divine purpose (*Serious Talk: Science and Religion in Dialogue*, 1995, p. viii).

Since man first gazed into the splendor of the night sky, he has been moved in wonder and awe. What are those tiny specks of light sparkling in the darkness of space? How did they get there? What lies beyond them in the unimaginable reaches of the universe? The grandeur and magnificence of the shimmering heavens raise questions not just about the universe but our part in it. Could it be that arousing these questions was the intention of a super intelligent designer?

You alone Lord, you alone; you have made the heaven of heavens, with all their host, the
earth, and all that is on it, the seas and all that is in them; and you preserve them all,
and the hosts of heaven worship you
NEHEMIAH 9:6

Some of the most clear and convincing evidence of God's existence is in the magnificent universe structured on and sustained by innumerable laws of physics. These laws are so finely tuned in harmony with a multitude of other laws; it's like balancing a needle on a razor's edge. This requires a law giver – a creator who expresses Himself through wholeness, relationship, balance, and order in all that He manifests.

A PLANET OF SUPER INTELLIGENT DESIGN

Unlike any other planet yet discovered, Earth is a shimmering blue ball, finely tuned for life to exist and thrive. Inside its atmosphere there exists a vast amount of diversity sustained through remarkable and intricate common relationships. Some scientists have concluded that Earth may be the only planet in the universe that harbors life. The conditions necessary for life are so exacting that the possibility of life on other planets is infinitely remote. Let's take a look.

• Without the earth revolving every twenty-four hours like a precision designed watch, one-half of our planet would be frozen in darkness. The other half of our planet would be a barren desert from continual exposure to the sun.

41

- As Earth moves through space in its precision orbit around the sun and turns in its finely tuned twenty-four hour rotation period, it remains tilted at a 23.5 degree angle. This precision tilt allows for the seasonal variations that produce an abundance of crops that feed our planet's population. Without this tilt, it could not feed its inhabitants.
- Earth's atmosphere is yet another way our planet is finely tuned for life. No other planet discovered in our universe has anything remotely like it. If this atmosphere were just a few degrees thinner, it could not retain the ozone layer that blocks out cancer-causing radiation emanating from the sun. In addition, a much thinner atmosphere would not be capable of retaining warm enough temperatures for life to exist.
- The atmosphere of earth contains a mixture of gases in not just close but perfect proportions for life to exist as we know it. Oxygen makes up 21% of our air. This perfect balance allows for breathing to be effortless; if it were much thinner we would be stopping every few feet to catch our breath. Everyday survival would become difficult if not impossible.
- Nitrogen and carbon dioxide make up most of the rest of our atmosphere. Rain brings nitrogen to the soil where it acts as fertilizer for plants. Likewise, plants require carbon dioxide which they take in while giving off oxygen. Could it be just another precision accident that plants take in carbon dioxide and release oxygen, while humans take in oxygen and release carbon dioxide?

Dr. Paul Davies had this to say about the possibility of design: "The temptation to believe that the universe is the product of some sort of design, a manifestation of subtle aesthetic and mathematical judgment, is overwhelming. The belief that there is something behind it all is one that I personally share with, I suspect, a majority of physicists." (*New Science Magazine*, June 1983, p. 638)

Our universe works like a giant finely tuned watch. Our planet and its precision laws that govern it are just some of the mechanisms within the watch. On Earth we can chart the position of the stars and planets for any given day, month, or year – forward or backward – with incredible accuracy. Calendars are useful because of the universe's precision laws that govern their interacting relationships.

How could there ever be a precision watch without a precision universe to measure it by? Furthermore, could a Rolex be the result of random chance? If that question seems ridiculous, so does a random-chance precision universe. Like the design of man, the function that results is from a vast number of finely tuned and intelligently designed interactive components – designed by an intelligent designer – who never experiences breakdowns or malfunctions.

By the word of the Lord were the heavens made,
and all their host by the breath of his mouth
PSALM 33:6

A HUMAN KIND OF SUPER INTELLIGENT DESIGN

Do we as human beings display the same super intelligent design as the universe and our planet? I think you will soon discover the answer is a resounding yes! Lewis Thomas addresses this: "What is the earth most like? It is most like a single cell." (*The Lives of a Cell*, 1974, p. 93) Science has made remarkable progress in the understanding of not only outer space but inner space. Research into cells has revealed an astonishing complexity and unmistakable evidence of design.

These discoveries reveal that the simplest living cell is so intricate and complex in its design that even the possibility of it coming into existence through a series of fortunate accidents and lucky coincidences is unthinkable. The English Astronomer Sir Fred Hoyle, professor of Astronomy at Cambridge University, had this to say about the possibility of accidents and coincidences: "The chance that higher life forms might have emerged in this way is comparable with the chance that a tornado sweeping through a junkyard might assemble a Boeing 747 from the materials therein." (Hoyle, "On Evolution, Nature", vol. 294, November 1982, p. 105)

The tornado scenario is just not going to happen. Likewise, neither would such a well designed, finely tuned, and information-packed living cell. Let's take a look at just a few of these unthinkable coincidences.

- Zoology Professor, Richard Dawkins, notes that the cell nucleus "contains a digitally coded data base, larger than all thirty volumes of the Encyclopedia put together. And this figure is for each cell. The number of cells in the body of a human is about ten trillion." (*The Blind Watch Maker*, pp. 17-18, 1986)
- Your DNA database will not only determine whether you will be a human being, but all the vast amount of personalized data that defines you personally. It will custom design your skin, eye, hair color, much of your personality – all the way down to the sound of your laughter.
- Each of us begins as a tiny ball about the size of the period at the end of this sentence. The cell is a miniature super factory using DNA language-coded instructions to divide your colossal 100 trillion cells into two hundred different varieties. They will have specialized jobs, such as brain cells, eye cells, and everything that makes us who and what we are.

Advancements in the realm of information technology have allowed us to put greater and greater amounts of information into increasingly smaller computer chips, circuit boards, and micro processors. This micro-information technology has radically changed and improved the way we design computers, cars, phones, televisions, and just about everything else. Today's designs are smarter and have more functional abilities than ever before as a result of these advancements. The designs of humankind, however, pale in comparison and are child's play when compared to the amount of information in a single human cell.

For you did form my inward parts; You did knit me together in my mother's womb. I will confess and praise You for You are fearful and wonderful and for the awful wonder of my birth! Wonderful are your works, and that my inner self knows right well

PSALM 139:13-14

THE SUPER INTELLIGENT DESIGN OF THE HUMAN EYE

Consider the case of the human eye, constructed from the information coded in your DNA, and ask yourself if such an astounding system of interactive components could be anything less than design perfection? You are reading this page with a set of specialized camera-type eyes that contain a vast amount of precision components that work together as an organized system, allowing you to "see" the image before you. What we are about to see is the stunning and bewildering complexity of the machinery in the human eye is a testimony to a super intelligent designer. Let's take a look.

- Astonishingly, the eye describes what it sees to the brain through the communication medium of chemical and electrical signals. In other words, your brain interprets that you are looking at a sunset and that the sunset is a beautiful one, not by pictures, but rather chemical and electrical signals sent from the eye to the brain.

- The human eye contains a vastly complex wiring system. The optic nerve at the back of the eye has a staggering one-million nerve endings which connect to another one-million nerve endings in the brain. Even for a master electrician, requesting that he run a million lines in a home would be enough to put him in a strait jacket and out of a job.

- This amazing system of interactive components that make up the design of the human eye allows us to interpret size, shape, distance, color, and speed in a moment's time. What makes it even more amazing is that scientists have discovered that the image we receive in our eye is upside down; the cell design in the eye reverses the image before sending it to the brain for interpretation.

Yet we are often impressed when we open the hood of the latest sports car or learn of the latest satellite computer technology.

THE SUPER INTELLIGENT DESIGN OF THE HUMAN BRAIN

The information in your DNA that begins about the size of a period contains the genetic information to build the human brain. The brain is the most complex organ in the human body. This human command center is controlling heart, lungs, and blood pressure, all while you read the newspaper, eat your breakfast, and notice the big story on the news. Scientists have still yet to discover how it can function on multiple levels of consciousness such as this.

In the past, the brain has often been referred to as a supercomputer. It can handle vast amounts of data operating at 100 mph. Like a computer, it can process, analyze, store, and retrieve information. However, scientists have recently considered this supercomputer analogy as falling short of describing the brain's amazing abilities. Let's take a look and see why.

- The brain has a unique quality to it called plasticity that puts this organ in a realm completely of its own. This plasticity refers to a quality like a moldable plastic. In fact, the brain's constant activity means it is continually changing and making new connections. The communication between these information cells never stops, even while you sleep. By the time you get done reading this chapter, your brain will have changed by making new circuits.

- Thanks to advancements in computer imaging, research has been able to tap into the brain and learn what parts control hearing, sight, speech, reasoning, emotions, and so on. Scientists were awe struck when they also discovered that when a specific part of the brain is injured, it will rewire itself so another part of the brain can pick up on the lost function. This would be like building a car with enough intelligence that when the windshield wipers quit working, the power doors would take over the function. This type of technology just does not exist.

- Another super intelligent design of the brain is its cauliflower-type folds. If all these folds were taken out the brain would be several times too big to fit into your skull. Scientists say it's like taking a large piece of paper and crumpling it up to create vast amounts of folds so to fit into such a small area. Yet instead of crumpling it up, each and every fold is precisely made.

There are qualities of the brain we may never fully understand. For example, scientists know the brain operates through a process of electrical and chemical signals, yet they have no idea how this creates consciousness. For that matter, scientists are not completely sure how to define consciousness. They know at a very basic level it means awareness. The human brain is the only organ that has such acute awareness as to analyze itself as we are doing here.

Scientists are still baffled about how the brain manifests creativity. Where does it come from? What makes it work? Researchers are eager to understand how we can remember a childhood experience in our lives, recall the emotional energy connected to it, or even how we can recall it from the brain. The experience, such as reading this book, becomes a biological reality stored in the vast and complex human brain.

WHY DESIGN AND REENTRY

From the vastness of the universe to the space between our ears, we cannot begin to scratch the surface of the huge amount of evidence that overwhelmingly points to design in the world we live in and in our own lives. I believe any thoughtful observation of the evidence will lead you to conclude you were created by a super intelligence the Bible calls God. Clearly our world and our lives unanimously qualify as design far above the four heads of presidents carved in stone. We are likewise still far more advanced and precision designed than the latest cell phone, lap top computer, or sports car.

Dr. Michael J. Behe, a renowned biochemist appointed to the National Institute of Health at Bethesda, Maryland, has come to terms with the unavoidable evidence of design. Can you? "The resulting realization that life was designed by intelligence is a shock to us in the twenty- first century who have gotten used to thinking of life as a result of simple natural laws, but other generations have had their shocks and there is no reason to suppose that we should escape them." (*Darwin's Black Box*, 1996, p. 253)

What should shock us as men behind the razor wire is just how poorly we missed seeing it. We have paid a heavy price for this. Our lives have exploded like the space shuttle Challenger shortly after takeoff. However, the flaw was not in our design, but rather our inability to see our design.

Reflect on yourself for a moment.

- Would you be willing to investigate how you were designed to function and apply yourself to it if it meant living successfully in every area of your life?
- Next, is it important to you to be able to manage your life once you are released? What would it mean to you for your life to make sense once you are released from prison?
- Is it possible that your greatest handicap is your inability to see your potential in a life lived by design – according to how you were created to live?

With this in mind, let's look at the second part of the Human Design Model.

CHAPTER THREE

The Human Design Model (Part Two)

—∼∼—

THE DESIGN OF LIFE
(INTEGRATED LIFE)

If there is a design,
how is that design best lived out in our day to day lives?
I am convinced
how we answer this question
will have a profound impact
on how we govern our lives upon release.

— THE AUTHOR —

Part one revealed convincing evidence that a supernatural God created our extremely complicated universe. In His infinite wisdom, God created all things with specific design and working perfection. Throughout part one we were able to see everything He designed contains four essential principles which allow everything to work and support life. For this reason we will call them life support factors.

Wholeness: All essential parts are present that signify the design.

Relationship: There is an inter-active connection between the parts.

Balance: All the parts are present in necessary qualities and quantities.

Order: The parts are arranged in specific ways for operating potential.

I am convinced human design is no different. Every human being is a precision design of God. Our lives work for us as a result of inter-active components, witnessed in the design of the universe, our planet, and our genetic make-up. Part two will begin to outline our super-intelligent design. The goal of this chapter is to answer the question asked in part one: If there is a design, how is that design best lived out in our day to day lives? I am convinced how we answer this question will have a profound impact on how we govern our lives in reentry.

MODELS CREATE UNDERSTANDING

Design involves something put together a certain way (pattern), and functioning a certain way (intention).

Design: Pattern	Goal: Intention
1. Spiritual Maturity	1. Becoming
2. Mental Maturity	2. Becoming
3. Emotional Maturity	3. Becoming
4. Physical Health	4. Becoming = Wholeness in design of manhood
5. Family Unity	5. Relating = Modeling
6. Social Unity	6. Achieving = Service

The way a design is put together is geared toward how it is intended to function. For example, a sports car is put together a certain way for speed and performance. If it did not function according to those design standards, you would say it is not fulfilling its potential and purpose. We need to begin to view our design as human beings in the same way. We need to ask ourselves an all-important question: How am I designed to function?

To study human design we need to understand the various parts and the connections between the parts. To help us accomplish these goals we will first take a look at how the life support factors play a critical role in allowing our lives to work for us. This requires a model of operation which best describes our design. The six areas in diagram #2 represent human powers we will call potentials. If they are rightly relational to each other, balanced, and ordered, they create a system of functioning that guides us to operate through a process of principle centered maturity. It becomes the defining factor of what we BE-COME, how well we RELATE, and what we ACHIEVE.

Each area has a different role in our lives. Each role must be refined for effective living. They operate as a system within the whole system. The end result is harmony within the whole that provides a foundation for effective life management. Like any complex design, breaking it down into components and roles in these areas make it easier to relate to and understand how a break-down in one area affects the relationship to the whole. Diagram 2:

THE SIX COMPONENTS OF OUR DESIGN EXPRESSING
THE FOUR LIFE SUPPORT FACTORS

1. Wholeness   3. Balance
2. Relationship   4. Order

Wholeness means all the components are refined and working for us. Wholeness – maturity – manhood are terms representing the same ideal. They cannot be separated. We cannot have one without the other. What we now have are the potentials to enter wholeness in the six areas of our design. All essential components are present which signify our design of (manhood) and allow us to operate in (maturity). Such a concept provides new perspective to the ideal of maturity in manhood through wholeness. It reflects all the self-governing powers necessary to live competent adult lives.

Traditionally, we have not addressed wholeness in manhood according to human design. We only address problems which are symptoms of our lack of wholeness. If we only have problems, we can get sympathy and compassion from counselors and therapists. Man always looks for new definitions and better methods – putting band-aids on major wounds. We continue to live out our lack of wholeness while still trying to escape reality and escape adult responsibility.

It is true we are only young once, yet we may live immature our whole lives. The maturity of manhood cannot be the product of aging. If it were we would all achieve it 100% of the time. While we may feel we are the one who made it to maturity, we can all agree many have not. Our crimes, our life problems, and the tragedies we have created in the lives of others cause people to question our ability to function in adult society. The paradox of immaturity is that we don't know how immature we are now until we become more mature than we are now.

If we are remotely honest with ourselves, we could look at our crimes and ask this question, "What would maturity in manhood have done?" For some of us an honest answer might be, "I really don't know." Whatever the case, in the light of our consequences we can be sure a much higher ideal exists than what we lived out. No doubt, what the maturity of manhood represents has many characteristics. We can begin by admitting it involves the ability as adults to negotiate the reality of an adult world without costing us years of our lives locked up in prison and away from society for its safety.

MATURITY AND DECISION MAKING

It is likely our idea of maturity in manhood is narrowed by our self-serving opinions and lack of objectivity, and that it is partially or totally incorrect.

They have nothing to do with outward attributes. Maturity and manhood are measured by internal qualities of character. One becomes a man of maturity through consistently making decisions based on enduring principles that build one upon the other. This strengthens and forges one's character to maturity through a framework of higher values. Such a framework guides us to make right choices and sound decisions in reentry that become increasingly complex and ultimately affirm and strengthen those principles and values.

The framework of values we use in our day-to-day decisions (the little decisions) will determine how we handle major decisions in our lives. Little decisions, one built upon another, make the man. When life's many moments of challenge and crisis of circumstances come there is strength of character already strong enough to make the best possible decisions, even in the midst of life's greatest pressures.

Men of maturity are still prone to mistakes, wrong attitudes, lapses in judgment, and even failure. They are men who still experience fear and self-doubt in the face of tremendous crisis and challenge. What sets maturity apart from immaturity is this: The decisions to stand firm for right principles in the face of overwhelming pressure to bow to intense emotions based on impulse or bend with the immoral majority. The only way to succeed in manhood, maturity, and reentry is just that – doing the right thing despite the pressures.

And may the God of peace…make you pure and wholly consecrated to God; and may your spirit and soul and body be preserved sound and complete
1 THESSALONIANS 5:23

PARTLY A WHOLE AND WHOLLY A PART

Relationship means human design functions in such a way that each component has a direct relationship to every other component. Each area has the potential to enhance the other areas to our direct benefit or inhibit them to our direct disadvantage. Each component retains its own function while inter-acting and determining our ability to function as a whole. For example, our spiritual life has a direct impact on our family life and so on. The process of inter-active relationship between our components can be replicated by starting at any one area. Each area impacts every other area.

The degree of impact – positive or negative – relationally can be subtle or extreme. For example, if we neglect our physical health completely the affect on the other five areas would be more obvious. If we short ourselves on sleep, or we are not eating properly, we may not be so quick to relate the changes in the other five areas to mismanagement of our physical well-being.

If we do not see the interactive relationship between our potential powers, more often than not we will attribute the problems that result to outside factors such as people and circumstances. One thing is certain, subtle or dramatic, all components affect each other relationally. Life management is never motionless. We are either consciously moving toward life at its best, or we are unconsciously moving toward a breakdown in our ability to function in reentry.

STRONG AS OUR WEAKEST LINK

Balance means when one part of the system is out of balance, it creates imbalance throughout the other parts and, our life begins to become imbalanced. The idea of living balanced lives has long been a phrase for life at its best. People are seldom sure what it is they are supposed to be balancing. The human design model clarifies what this balance is. When the idea of balanced living comes to mind, we usually think of family, work, and possibly some other area of importance. This limited view represents a life out of balance. What balance means is no single component of our design can compensate for or replace another. Each potential power needs to be producing and empowering our lives.

For example, if family and work represent our idea of a balanced life and we neglect our spiritual values, what guidance center of principles are we to use to best govern our family and navigate our employment? What about our physical well-being? Shouldn't we consider our personal health enough to want to be around to support our family in a challenging world or have the energy to be involved in their lives? Where does our social life come into play? If we neglect the social component of our life, how does this affect the self we present to our family and the world around us? How can we choose to introduce our family to solid social support networks if we are not involved with them? Or, for that matter, how do we expect to successfully reenter society?

Another example of a life out of balance is the intellectual type whose textbooks and knowledge have become his imbalanced and incomplete human experience. Then there is the fitness guru whose life is swallowed up in the size of his biceps. There are those shackled to forms of religiosity who ignore health and sometimes family all in the name of service to their religion. There is also the socialite. He is the man who is everything to everybody and nothing to himself. All of these examples represent narrowed lives and a shallow human existence. The worst case scenario is when the imbalance is severe enough to cost us our freedom or our lives.

In diagram two, we see this model represents more than just a circle with six areas. All areas are equally balanced with no area intruding or eliminating the quality of the other. True to life, if one area in the diagram increases, one or all the others must decrease. This decrease would represent some degree of neglect in that area and a life that is suffering from imbalance. Think about this for a moment. What would your model look like if it accurately represented your life? Would all the areas be present? Which areas would be large, and which ones would be small? What your circle looks like represents your life management. Can you make any connection to how this led to your incarceration?

BALANCE REQUIRES PRIORITIZING

The lines in the model dividing the six components are not fixed or rigid. What this represents in the model is also true to life. There are times in our lives, days, weeks, or even months, when one area dictates priority and a significant more amount of time and attention.

For example, a family crisis would require greater focus on family than any other area for an undetermined amount of time. Life may call us to a period of extended education or work.

You may need increased focus on recovery upon release or personal spiritual growth. There are a multitude of reasons why life may call upon you to prioritize one specific area for a period. Not prioritizing when life calls us to do so is just as irresponsible as living a life that is destructively out of balance.

Whatever circumstances you may encounter upon release, no component of your super intelligent design should ever be totally neglected. After the period of prioritizing passes we consciously choose to move back toward a fuller degree of balance. When major events transpire such a reentry, we often prioritize certain areas of our lives. Once the event passes there is a tendency to never move back toward balance. The other tendency is to prioritize the wrong areas upon release – not fully understanding our design needs. What will you prioritize upon release?

WARNING SIGNS OF IMBALANCE

The first warning sign of imbalance is our emotions. Our emotions are inner gauges designed to let us know where we are at in getting our needs met. When we are living our life out of balance warning signs begin to appear in the form of stress, depression, anger, and other emotions in an unconscious effort of your life to regain balance. If warning signs are not acknowledged, we run the risk of moving from a life out of balance to a life out of control. When we acknowledge these warning signs for what they are, (a call to move back toward wholeness and balance), we can put forth conscious effort to make necessary adjustments and regain balance. The necessity of balance is particularly important for the individual reentering society after a period of incarceration. A balanced lifestyle is developed on the inside and transplanted and expanded upon release.

Be well balanced (temperate, sober of mind) be vigilant and cautious at all times
I PETER 5: 8

PRINCIPLES PROVIDE ORDER

Order allows the design to function. If you change the order you alter the design and our lives no longer function according to its potential. Like the other three principles, this principle applies to all design and even more to intricate precision designs like ourselves. The idea of order in design can be seen in a wristwatch. If the parts are not ordered it could not function. It is order that allows a Rolex watch to execute precision functioning and operate with extreme predictable accuracy. We are no different.

The design of the human eye alone is far more complex than a man-made Rolex watch. How much more the complete, magnificent human being who forms an orderly whole greater than the sum of his parts? Without order there can be no detection of life by design. Where no order exists only random chaos is found. Disorder and random chaos result in our lives when the most basic components of our human design are not ordered.

Life by design is only effective when it operates through effective life management. For life management to be effective it must operate within specific principles best suited for our welfare and success. Our design is mature manhood, and a principle centered character is the defining factor. This pattern and intention can only be fulfilled through a life based on specific principles and disciplines that govern our design.

Life by design involves more than connecting relationships between the various parts called integrated life. If we depart from this ordered life process we get premature fruits (immature) in each area of our lives which are neither ripe nor flavored and which soon decay.

Without a principle centered foundation that leads us to orderly life management in all six areas, we are fractured and fragmented and therefore incomplete in our developmental process.

This is why any experience of genuine fulfillment is elusive for so many. Fulfillment can only come through wholeness. No one ever finds fulfillment in any single component. Maturity in our manhood requires an inner life dependent on spiritual principles and disciplines. It can create our BECOMING a man outwardly that expresses a character of mature manhood. This type of independent manhood can extend his principle centered character to his outer image by RELATING to family and ACHIEVING through service in his community. This is called interdependence.

This process is illustrated in diagram three. Take the time to study it and relate it to your strengths and shortcomings in your life management. The rest of this chapter will discuss the impact of the presence or absence of a principle centered life (See Diagram 3, next page).

Diagram 3:

Outer image reflecting inner image of manhood	**Social Component #6** Employment Community Service Fellowship Friendship Association	**Areas 5-6** Extending foundation of principle centered self to others
Interdependence	**Family Component #5** Function as model Beliefs-Rules Meet needs	**Relating/Achieving**
Outer image of manhood Independence	**Physical Component #4** Sleep Exercise Nutrition Recreation Hygiene Relaxation	**Areas 1-4** Foundation of principle centered self
	Emotional Component #3 Inner gauges for Needs-Boundaries-Healing Will – Energy of action	Basis for determining beliefs, rules, needs **Becoming**
	Mental Component #2 Perception Imagination Reasoning Intuition Judgment Conscience	
Inner image of manhood Dependence	**Spiritual Foundation #1** Principle based guidance center Wisdom-Virtue-Discipline Character-Maturity-Manhood	Developmental source: Empowerment carried into other 5 areas

Integrated/Development life management

THE DESIGNER'S PRINCIPLES

The principles the designer handed down to us for our design are in the form of a life doctrine – for instruction and correction in right living (2 Timothy 3:16-17). It is given to not only guide, govern, and guard us, but unite us in a remarkable orchestration of interdependence that marks the flow of all life. It has the power to defeat the inner wars we carry into the battlefield of the world and promises "greener pastures" of inner peace (Psalm 23:2). To the degree we experience inner peace: interdependence between human beings is possible. This doctrine of life principles is the "still waters" that provides us with an accurate reflection of ourselves (Psalm 23:2). It is the "strong tower" that protects us against being bound in strongholds of moral error (Psalm 61:3). It becomes a "lamp and light" in the deep darkness of uncertainty life often presents to us (Psalm 119:105).

BREAKING MINDSETS

The principle centered life contains power to mold and mature our character to the point that it creates the corrective experience and restores our soul (Psalm 23:3). It restores our soul by taking old mindsets captive as a result of submitting our thoughts to the authority of higher values. If we "order our steps" by the principles that govern our design, we are guaranteed error will not have dominion over us and continue to govern our lives. Error can only be purged by principles of truth (Proverbs 18:17). The masterful genius of principles is that they are created to cover every possible situation and circumstance without addressing every detail.

In all your ways know, recognize, and acknowledge Him,
and He will direct and make straight and plain your paths
PROVERBS 3:6

Moral error is a mindset. The old mind set keeps us bound (Proverbs 5:22-23). It operates like a form of programming. Without principles written on our hearts (Proverbs 4:21), we are drawn back and doomed to repeating the same past failures. The power of this pull to repeat the past is much stronger than most of us might be willing to admit. The prisons are full of people with multiple prison numbers who repeated the same past mistakes. I am guilty of this myself.

Each release was a different place, different people, but same mistakes. The underlying problem for all of us is the same. It is our unwillingness to submit to the authority of higher principles and values.

OUR DIRECTION INDICATOR

Principles and values, or the lack thereof, are powerful indicators of the direction and outcome of an individual life. It determines all our choices and has tremendous impact on our world view. When we have no foundation of higher principles and values we are left with what is self-serving and narrowed to our own impulses and desires. The focus is always on ourselves. It is a self-reliant life with no foundation for absolute right and wrong.

Most of us cannot relate our lives to the life of Jeffery Dahmer. His life is a good example of how far out of control our lives can get when we refuse to submit our lives to the authority of higher principles and values. We must always remember that he didn't begin where he ended; he only ended where he ended. It was a progressive and powerfully seductive process. Here is a glimpse into the mind of Dahmer: "If a person doesn't think there is a God to be accountable to, then, then what's-what's the point of-of trying to modify your behavior to keep it within the acceptable range. That's how I thought, anyway.

I always believed the theory of evolution as truth that we all came from slime. When you died, you know, that was it, there is nothing else." (Jeffery Dahmer (serial killer) in an interview with Stone Phillips, Dateline, NBC, November 29, 1994)

DESIGNER WARNING LABELS

There are whole generations being raised to believe there is no God (Psalm 14:1). It's no wonder we have the crime, violence, and bloodshed we see in our world today. We have set ourselves on the throne of our lives, to decide our own rules and our own truths. The real battle for each of us is not rampant crime in our society, the epidemic of addiction, or the search for self-satisfaction. The real battle for humanity is its self-serving lack of humility for ultimate authority. Many of us wanted life according to our own will; our own definitions and God gave us what we wanted (Romans 1:24, 28).

For ever since the creation of the world His invisible nature and attributes, that is, His eternal power and divinity, have been made intelligible and clearly discernible in and through the things that have been made (His handiworks). So [men] are without excuse [altogether without any defense or justification]. Because when they knew and recognized Him as God, they did not honor and glorify Him as God or give Him thanks. But instead they became futile and godless in their thinking [with vain imaginings, foolish reasoning, and stupid speculations] and their senseless minds were darkened
ROMANS 1:20-21

UNHEEDED WARNINGS EVERYWHERE

A news story aired as I was formulating this chapter. It told a very sad and ugly story. A middle-aged man was going through a divorce. He went to his in-laws on Christmas Eve dressed up as Santa Claus. When an eight-year-old girl opened the door she was the first one shot. Before it was over, he killed nine people and torched the house. When flames began to melt his Santa suit to his body he took his own life. That was not the end of it. When authorities searched his car it exploded. It was rigged with a bomb. The news is full of stories such as this, and so are the prisons. When the fragile and uncertain things people build the foundations of their lives on crumble so do they. This was not God's design but man's choice, and God honored it.

BILL'S STORY

The following story is a good example of the struggle to put principles into practice upon release. Recently I was mentoring a friend I will call Bill. He posed a challenging question, at least for him – he was the one who would have to live up to its answer. He said he was getting out of prison soon and wanted to know what I thought about returning to live at his girlfriend's house. I knew the decision he was about to make would have a profound impact on his future.

Whether he based this decision on preference or principle would determine the kind of impact.

I knew Bill's future freedom hung in the balance. I believed I owed him total honesty and led my response with my own human imperfections. I shared with him how, up until this time, I would not have been able to make the right decisions in my own life. I would have taken the path of preference which always involves the way of least resistance formulated through shortcuts and quick fixes.

Bill's alternative to staying at his girlfriend's house was a six-month reentry and discipleship program. He admitted this not only looked like more hoops to jump through to freedom but also more delay in rebuilding his life. I was well aware of Bill's addiction issues, poor decision-making skills, poor life skills, and his unhealthy mental and emotional dependence on his girlfriend.

In a very deep way I understood these issues, because I had suffered under them myself.

Bill reasoned he was already right with God (as if that was all there was to it). He believed he needed to get a job right away to help his girl. She was barely treading water on mortgage payments and other bills. Bill believed he was sincere and from there he could still find a mentor and fellowship to keep him growing.

HONESTY IS SELF-PRESERVATION

I listened to all Bill had to say. He wanted to get his thoughts out of the way, and then he would listen to my view. My message to Bill was: "This is not your first prison number. You have failed at this before. I think it is important to keep that in mind. I can only answer your question with other questions, and you will have to create your own answer."

I continued: "Is the rest of your life as a free man worth a six-month investment of your time? Forget what time you were incarcerated. Hopefully that was growth producing. That was paying your debt to society. I am talking about once you are released from that debt. Is your freedom important enough to make the right sacrifices in your life by willing choice? Do you think you owe it to yourself to go to any length necessary this time? Are you willing to invest in securing your freedom or is the pull of short cuts and quick fixes still too powerful for you to turn down?"

FAMILIAR VOICES SPEAK THE LOUDEST

I expressed to Bill my belief that he had a general understanding of the principles to living right and free. I asked him if he could speak to me about principles that addressed his most serious issues. He could not answer. My next question was, how did he hope to protect himself against repeating the same poor choices when moments or challenge or temptation arose?

VOICES ALWAYS EQUAL CHOICES

The words written deepest upon our hearts will speak first and loudest. If it is still (I- Self- Me) we are likely to repeat the same past mistakes. If it is principles and values we have written upon our hearts, they will guide our decisions. Principles and their voices are the "weapons of warfare" (Ephesians 6:17) in renewing our minds (Romans 12:2). If we can't recall them they can't speak to us in the midst of our time of need. When "the law of the spirit of life" is written upon our hearts, we are no longer like children (immature) tossed to and fro and carried away by the cunning and craftiness of the things that only destroy us (Ephesians 4:14).

FEELING DOMINATED IMMATURITY

Bill agreed with my logic. He said he would write a letter to the program requesting acceptance. He felt genuinely good about it, because he knew it was the right investment. His choice was no longer based on easiest or hardest, but something beyond that – correct principles. Bill and I ended our conversation – both of us pleased with the outcome. About two weeks later Bill informed me he did write the letter, and his girlfriend was impressed with his willingness to do whatever it took to build a life based on principles. However, Bill's last comment set me back. He stated there was a 30-day program he could take as well as the six month program. He said, "If I feel I will be all right once I get there."

Every way of man is right in his own eyes
PROVERBS 21:2

This is the powerful pull of old mindsets and repeating of past mistakes as if they never happened. I felt Bill and I were back to square one. I said, "What do you mean if you 'feel like you will be all right?'" You're going to be experiencing the euphoric high of post release and just about everything is likely to feel right. Do not base your decisions on your feelings, Bill, that's what put us into these positions in the first place. Base your decisions on right principles regardless of what you feel or desire and things will work out."

I haven't heard from Bill yet. I hope and pray he makes the right choices. If he does they won't be based on feelings and desires anymore. Regardless of the investment required they will be based on principles. Such hard choices translate into maturity and lasting freedom.

WHAT RULES YOUR MIND? WHAT VOICES HAVE DETERMINED YOUR CHOICES AND GOVERNED YOUR LIFE?

How shall a young man cleanse his way? By taking heed and keeping watch [on himself] according to your word [conforming his life to it]
PSALM 119:9

DESIGN OR DEFAULT DETERMINES DESTINY

Phillip Brooks notes: "Someday in the years to come, you will be wrestling with the great temptation, or trembling under the great sorrow of your life. But the real struggle is here, now… Now is being decided whether, in the day of your supreme sorrow or temptation, you shall miserably fail or gloriously conquer. Character cannot be made except by a steady long continued process."

The words of Mr. Brooks speaks volumes to the incarcerated who will one day face the challenge of release from prison. Each of us already has some form of character made by a steady, long-continued process. The factor which determines if we miserably fail or gloriously conquer is, was that character the result of living by default or under the authority of design?

The character we develop living by default (failure to live by design, neglect of organized management) is a dangerous liaison between the inward chronic pain of arrested maturity and outward performance of adult responsibilities. Effective life management by design allows us to thrive in the realm of adult responsibilities through the execution of correct principles. It works best in all circumstances, because it provides a foundation of unchanging truths to navigate the ever-changing realities life brings us. For those who hope to change and never return to prison it offers us special hope. Life by design offers to us the corrective experience which leads to wholeness (maturity) and opens the door to relationship while fostering balance and providing order in our lives.

[For skillful and godly wisdom is the principle thing.]… Get understanding (discernment, comprehension, and interpretation)
PROVERBS 4:7

WHERE DO WE GO FROM HERE?

We cannot avoid the struggle ahead of us. We do have a choice between struggles. We can choose to remain in never-ending chaos and disorder of a life by default. We can choose the "growth pains" of a principle centered life by design. The game you practice is the game you will play.

The hardest place you can be right now is not prison, but rather thinking you know everything and believing nothing. There is no greater barrier to change and freedom. A life by design is a search for the truth. If you choose this struggle, it will be the only possible proof that you have not been conquered.

Take a few moments to reflect on how your life represented the Human Design Model.

- What areas of your life need improvement?
- How might have your life mismanagement led to your incarceration?

With the answers to these questions in mind, let's look at the third part of The Human Design Model.

CHAPTER FOUR

The Human Design Model (Part Three)
—⟫⟪—

LIFE MANAGEMENT BY DESIGN
(DEVELOPMENTAL LIFE)

No man is more totally enslaved
than one who falsely assumes he is free.
He will soon discover unprincipled free will
is not freedom at all,
but rather bondage to his own unbridled desires.

— THE AUTHOR —

I n part two we examined our unique design. We briefly outlined our six potential powers and took a more in-depth look at the four life support factors. We were able to conclude our design is competent manhood, and the life support factors foster maturity to fulfill our design. This means the principles of wholeness, relationship, balance, and order in our life management provide assistance in completing our natural growth and development. They promote the emergence of personal and social qualities adequate to and necessary for adult life. The result is the ability to function and respond to life in ways that promote our freedom and liberties.

The requirement is our dependence on the right principles and values. The outcome is a platform of independence to extend ourselves into the highest level of mature interaction called interdependence. This process is considered the corrective experience. It moves us away from the isolation and destructive pattern of self-obsession, (the defining trait of our arrested maturity) and toward a more meaningful connection to the world around us. The freedom from self-obsession offers us the liberty to develop skills for becoming inner directed and other connected. These skills are discussed in the next chapter.

LIFE REQUIRES CONSCIOUS EFFORT
Our first inclination may be to view these design concepts as complex and confusing, but this is not the case. We are so far removed from our design that these concepts have become foreign to us. Chaos and disorder are far more confusing than concepts such as wholeness, relationship, balance, and order.

If a lifestyle of chaos and disorder can become a familiar pattern of habit, so can the pattern and intention of a design for living. This results in far less negative consequences and far greater stability. It's not so much that life by design is complex; it just requires conscious effort. It requires that we value our future enough to become familiar with our design and put forth the effort to grow and change.

THE RESPONSIBILITY OF FREE WILL

A primary component to our chaos and disorder is also part of the cure. God wanted to create a creature who would willingly choose to follow His principles and values. These principles would mold and shape the inner man and be expressed in the outer man. Any other design would not constitute the authority and dominion of authentic manhood in the purest sense.

For this special type of design to be possible God created man after His own image and likeness (Genesis 1:26-28), and the awesome power of free will came into play. The ability to choose was the highest honor God could bestow upon our lives. To crown us with this honor would set us above any other creature He ever created – setting the stage for man to have dominion and authority on earth as God had in heaven.

1. **Image:**   Resemblance: Representative figure   -Dominion/Authority
2. **Likeness:**   Similitude; Model; Pattern; Shape   -Principle centered maturity

We should ask ourselves, if there really is a God, why wouldn't He intend for His creation to live successful lives of design? Are we willing to believe a super intelligent designer could create this magnificent universe, our beautiful and diverse planet, and even ourselves without a perfect plan of operation? Chaos and disorder are what we chose to bring into it. We may not have the power to change the world, but being made in His image and likeness empowers us to return to His design.

The power of free will has left us with a responsibility in this process. Even if He designs us in His image so we resemble Him, we are responsible to walk in His likeness through modeling the principles He has set down for our success. We find it hard to comprehend such ideas in our disordered state – living in the world of disorder with nothing in sight to compare it to.

The process of passing on principles is modeling. We all need personal models of authentic manhood in our lives. One of the hardest barriers to overcome is not the science or the evidence of God. It is the way man presents Him to the world. It may not be that we refuse to accept Him and His design for our lives, but rather the way human beings portray and model Him to a world that is hurting and searching for answers. There are times we certainly fall short of expressing His love, compassion, and understanding. This is why we look to the Creator and not the created to glimpse His stainless perfection. A Master Model of these principles does exist. He is revealed in this chapter.

The first step away from disorder, and toward an effective life by design, is to acknowledge the responsibility bound to the privilege of free will. If we are not going to remain stuck in a repeating cycle of self-destruction, we must accept responsibility for how the power of choice created the world we know. We must see how the power of choice can turn any paradise into a living hell and any hell on earth into paradise.

MANTRAS AND VERBAL SYMPTOMS

The constant mantras of I-Self-Me are verbal symptoms of our arrested maturity and our crimes. They are deeply embedded roots in our character, grown out of the seeds of self- obsession. We have cultivated these mantras of I-Self-Me in the matrix of our arrested development. They have penetrated the deepest regions in our hearts and grownup to wrap themselves around our conscious.

Once cultivated they seem to take on a life of their own and viciously resist being uprooted. It might mean we cease to exist, at least as we have come to know existence.

Uprooting these mantras of our self-obsession is impossible, nor can we cut them off at the surface level with behavioral modification or positive thinking. The unseen roots of our arrested maturity will remain.

THE CONCEPT OF TRANSFORMATION

Genuine transformation is changing from one state into another. We must experience a process which transforms us from a state of self-obsessed immaturity into a state of principle centered maturity. It is the only chance we have; the only thing that will work for us. Nothing else can reach the well-hidden and deeply embedded roots of our unresolved developmental conflicts that have given life to our self-obsession. We will look at these conflicts in the next chapter.

The concept of transformation is often seen as unrealistic. We prefer terms like growth, change, and recovery. I might have agreed a few years ago, but from my experience, transformation is not only possible but necessary. It is more about addressing the right issue.

Growth, change, and recovery are merely vehicles in this process. Transformation is the corrective experience, the design, that puts manhood back into the male. This chapter is a journey into the role of each area of our design and the impact each represents in manhood.

THE SPIRITUAL COMPONENT

OUR SEARCH FOR IDENTITY

Manhood has an inner image as well as an outer image. It is more about what we are on the inside than what we are on the outside. The moment we grasp this truth we can tap into the potential of all we might become. Manhood and its potential are measured by the inner image of the human spirit. It has nothing to do with physical size, age, or external prestige. It has everything to do with the spirit's empowering influence in the other areas of our design. If only we could grasp the inheritance hidden in the mystery of our design – how drastically our lives would change.

The greatest miracle would be for God to create us in His image; God did that. The greatest tragedy would be for us to destroy that image; man did that. We did that trying to create our own image. We were not made to create an image but reflect the image of our creator; Jesus revealed how to do that. Creating our own image left us as runaways from our creator and our inheritance. We have chosen to live as spiritual orphans, designers of our own destinies, lords of our own futures, and rulers of our own worlds. We left our position as law enforcers over the law of the Spirit of life to be slaves under the law of moral error and death (Romans 8:2). As runaways we hid in the darkness and the darkness consumed us. (Isaiah 60:2).

And God looked upon the world and saw how degenerate, debased, and vicious it was,
for humanity had corrupted their way upon the earth and lost their true direction
GENESIS 6:12

We desperately need to rediscover how God originally designed man to be and reclaim our inheritance. The word of God explains a unique and special reason why His life is the missing element of our design of manhood. He has given us a human spirit with the unique capacity to be united with His Spirit. The life and nature of God in man is the fulfillment of man in His image. It provides the power of an endless life and enables God through our consent to guide our lives into the fullness of manhood in this life.

It is essential we do not confuse the human spirit with the human soul, although they are inseparable from each other. When united with the life of God they form an unseen entity capable of an endless life after the death of the physical body. The human soul is described in the next component.

Humans can reproduce only human life, but the Holy Spirit gives birth to spiritual life.
Just as you can hear the wind but can't tell where it comes from or where it is going, so
you can't explain how the people are born of the Spirit
JOHN 3:6,8

THE FOUNDATION OF OUR DESIGN

Created in the image and likeness of God, the spiritual life is the foundation of our design we are to build the superstructure of our lives upon. Without this foundation the other five areas crumble down upon our head over and over again. It is not the storms of life that knock us down, but the foundation we build our lives on that cannot withstand them.

> *For everyone who comes to me and listens to My words (in order to heed their teaching) and does them, I will show you what he is like: he is like a man building a house, who dug and went down deep and laid a foundation upon rock. And when the flood arose, the torrent broke against the house and could not shake or move it, because it had been securely built or founded on a rock. But he who merely hears and does not practice doing My words is like a man who built a house on the ground without a foundation, against which the torrent burst, and immediately it collapsed and fell, and the breaking and the ruin of that house was great*
>
> LUKE 6:47-49

To enter the law of the spirit of life (Romans 8:2) is to enter everything that transforms the male into manhood. Without this principle centered image of God in this male, there is no manhood according to God's design and the chaos and disorder of pleasure and desire reigns. The human spirit without the life of God residing in it is like a ship on the sea of life without a sail, tossed about by every storm it encounters. They are storms that are the self made results of the lust of the flesh, lust of the eyes, and the pride of life (1 John 2:16). He is a male who becomes easy prey to all the detours, traps, and trouble of the destructive influences which the dark side of life portrays as light.

The life and nature of God in man is the profound wisdom of an all-knowing God expressed in His ultimate design – man. It alone saves man from the hopelessness of victory over the inner wars that constantly rage within. Without this divine provision of indwelling God power, the call to a life of manhood always ends in the bitter frustration of failure time and time again. The male without the inner image of manhood only represents the sorry spectacle of self- obsession and immaturity. It is a life constantly frustrated by the failure of his own inadequacy, alternating between man-child and animal. He will spend his days trying to survive the storms around him until he calms the storms within him.

> *Then we will no longer be immature like children. We won't be tossed and blown about by every wind of new teaching. We will not be influenced when people try to trick us with lies so clever they sound like truth...*
>
> EPHESIANS 4:14-15

THE SOURCE OF LIFE - LIGHT - LOVE

The mystery of the spiritual birth is the ultimate of mysteries, based on an intimate relationship with the Creator through His Son, Jesus. He is the One all religions call the Great Prophet; the One many call the Savior of the world. Some people know Him as Lord, and some know Him as the Master Model of Manhood. He is the One the Word of God calls all of the above. Whatever we comprehend of Him now can only grow deeper if we will search the truth about Him.

As a Prophet, Jesus was led to speak God's word to man (Luke 7:16). He was Savior because He reconciled us to God through His death and paved the way for us to receive the life and nature of God through His resurrected life (John 1:4). He is Lord because God set Him above all principality, power, and might. God gave Him dominion above every name that is named (Ephesians 1:21). As Lord he set forth the principles that would guide man to walk in dominion and authority over his own life and create success in the every area of his existence (John 1:3). Finally, Jesus was the Master Model of manhood because He walked this thing called life out for us in perfect conduct according to the principles He laid down for us (John 8:29).

God sent Him to not only reveal God to man but man to man. The mystery of who Jesus really is can be settled in our hearts if we are willing to seek Him with all our hearts (Jeremiah 29:13).

1. **Prophet**: Divinely inspired speaker; One who speaks the word of God.
2. **Savior**: Person who saves or rescues; to bring salvation; to set free; to deliver spirit, body, and soul from death; to give victory; to preserve.
3. **Lord**: Supreme in authority; person of absolute power, self-existent; God.
4. **Master Model**: Person to be copied, or imitated, perfect, just right, especially in conduct, pattern; design; example; representative figure.

SPIRITUAL NOURISHMENT

Dominion and authority expressed through the morality of the law of the Spirit of life are planted in our spirit the moment we are born again. The basis of this Holy spiritual seed becoming the principal centered inner image is the right nourishment. We will not grasp this concept until we realize the word of God is far more than a collection of divinely inspired promises. It is a living force and carries within it the power to mold us into the manhood it describes and make its promises a reality in our lives.

For with God nothing is ever impossible and no word from God
shall be without power or impossible of fulfillment
LUKE 1:37

This concept can be difficult to grasp. The idea of a spiritual life seems so distant from the life we understand. The idea that God would implant His seed of life in us and His words written in a book could act as transforming nourishment can challenge our reasoning. However, we see it all the time in the natural world.

You have been regenerated (born again), not from a mortal origin (seed, sperm),
but from one that is immortal by the ever living and lasting word of God
1 PETER 1:23

I could show you an acorn seed and explain to you that within that tiny seed lies the power to produce a tree thousands of times bigger than the seed. It will produce deep roots that will travel several feet down and outward. Huge branches will extend great distances in all directions from its mighty trunk. It will produce soft green leaves and be filled with new acorns. The tiny acorn has been transformed into a mighty oak tree. The small unimpressive acorn doesn't look capable of such a feat. However, from our experience in the natural world, we know it can happen.

Jesus says the word of God works by the same principle. There is miraculous power within it. This nourishment fed to the soul and born again spirit will transform the human heart. A clear mind absolutely requires a clean heart. If we are to experience the kind of maturity Jesus described in the word we have to model His principles (imitate Him). We have to put the principles of the inner image to work through action and then speak them over our lives. The word will generate manhood in the likeness of the Master Model – Jesus (2 Corinthians 3:18).

Therefore be imitators of God (copy and follow His example)
as well-beloved children (imitate their father)
EPHESIANS 5:1

THE EMPOWERMENT TO WHOLENESS

The spiritual and the natural are not separate. It is wrong thinking to believe they are and this creates a barrier to our wholeness and healing. We try to divide them like rivals, different and unrelated. We must understand how the spiritual is brought in and walked out in the natural so wholeness and healing is complete. For example, the next chapter will look at psycho-social conflicts which have been discovered to occur in the natural for everyone. This discovery does not make the spiritual answer wrong or invalid. Likewise, the spiritual life does not make these natural conflicts invalid. We must see how the spiritual governs the natural. One influences the other.

The natural is merely a shadow of the spiritual. For example, the principles of the law of the Spirit of life God has set down for us to live by are an outward revelation of the nature and character of God as it would exist in man, if man were to have His nature. It is God's perfect standard lived out. This means Jesus is the life and the nature that the principles of the law of the Spirit of life are but a shadow of. God's gift of His life not only makes us spiritually fit and prepares us for eternity, it will make us fit for life on earth and change our earthly destiny. It will determine our condition in both worlds: redeemed or lost, success or failure and mature or immature.

That (we might arrive) at really mature manhood (the completeness of personality which is nothing less than the standard height of Christ's own perfection), the measure of the stature of the fullness of Christ and the completeness found in Him
EPHESIANS 4:13

The instant we trust Christ as Savior and Lord of our lives, we will become supernaturally empowered in the inner man, and this will begin to filter through every other area of our lives. The natural is an extension of the supernatural. Our spiritual foundation will flow like "rivers of living water" (John 7:38) into every other area of our being. We will be guided into new ways of thinking and perceiving. We trade an inherited emotional life of inner shame for a new nature and a new identity. Fear is traded for love, and love is the source of all courage.

We will trade inner storms for inner peace and sorrow for joy. There will be new health as our lifestyle changes and moves into harmony with the guiding light of God's principles. Only then will we appreciate our body for the temple of God's life it has become.

THE TRANSFORMED PARADIGM

The enabling power of the life of God in man is essential for man to face himself. The reality of what his life has come to represent is illuminated. It will take this process of male into manhood – spiritual birth to see the truth about ourselves and no longer deny or hide from it. For no man is more totally enslaved than the one who falsely assumes he is free.

He will soon discover an unprincipled free will is not freedom at all, but rather bondage to his own unbridled desires. The regenerated man sees life through a transformed paradigm; one that allows him to face life on design terms. He lives on principled terms and remains free, never again to be incarcerated.

When we choose the regenerated life we begin residing under a higher authority and see our value as God sees us. We no longer see ourselves by what others say we are. We will turn from the labels the world assigns to us and embrace the identity God gives us. Then we will be able to extend this life by design to our family and social circles. We will be all they so desperately need us to be, all they would respect in a man's man, in a God's man of authentic manhood.

(Habitually) live and behave in newness of life
ROMANS 6:4

In every circumstance we will be able to relate everything that arises to the sufficiency of our principle centered inner image of manhood. There is no situation that can arise for which the inner image is not sufficient. No matter the problem or pressure, the morality of the law of the Spirit of life makes us more than a conqueror (Romans 8:37). We need only apply these principles to every situation upon reentry in the future. When God controls the inner man, the world cannot mislead the outer man.

THE MENTAL COMPONENT

THE NAVIGATION CENTER OF LIFE

The trinity of mind, emotion, and will, are what the word of God refers to as the human soul. They are distinct powers that operate as one single unit and cannot function completely independent of each other. We must address them individually to understand them as separate powers that operate interdependently.

And the Lord God formed man of the dust of the ground, and breathed into his nostrils the breath of life; and man became a living soul
GENESIS 2:7

The human mind is the most advanced organ in the universe. It is capable of highly complex tasks through problem solving and decision making. The mind accomplishes these skills through the power of reasoning and memory. Despite its great potential, this fascinating organ has one limitation to using these skills and powers – it requires information.

THE HUMAN SUPERCOMPUTER

These skills and powers are really just processing tools. Like a computer, the mind requires data – facts from which conclusions can be processed. The mind and the computer are both data processing machines and operate on common principles. The computer was created to calculate like the mind, only quicker.

69

No computer ever made is remotely close to the complexity of the masterful design of the human mind.

With its vast abilities and common principles, the mind is widely referred to as the human supercomputer. Regardless of potential, it still functions on the most common computer principles of input and output. What you put into your mind is what it will process, store, and reproduce. What goes in is the only thing that comes out, becoming the foundation for how we govern our lives. Truth in and truth out, false in and false out, is how it works. From this information alone we should clearly see there is a link between what we believe and the consequences we suffer. Our imprisonment should challenge us to question what we believe and how we think.

The next most common principle between the human mind and the computer is that they both operate through software and hard drives. For those not computer savvy, let me explain.

Software is the feature that determines how the mind and the computer operate and handle the information received. The hard drive is the disc in the computer that stores information like memory.

THE SOFTWARE CALLED PERSONALITY

Here is where common relationships between man and machine begin to show differences. Computers often share the exact same software. Not so for humans; they have unique personalities. There are seven billion people on earth – with no two individuals sharing the same software. There is a reason for this immense variety. Every piece of information our mental computer registers must go through what is called the subjective mental filter. Here is how this filter works.

All the information we receive is filtered through what our mental computer has stored as beneficial and truthful. It is largely made up of our own ideas and opinions. This is what forms our unique mental software we call personality. This diversity in humanity makes life interesting as we share with other personalities what is best, efficient, and most rewarding.

1. **SUBJECTIVE**: opinion; existing in mind; belonging to thinker rather than object.
2. **OBJECTIVE**: real; existing outside of the mind; factual; truthful; as things exist.

This activity within our soul can be damaging as well as beneficial. It can be damaging when what is stored as beneficial and truthful is destructive and inaccurate. From regular use we are conditioned by it and treat these distortions as objective. We create images and concepts and form entire belief systems with it. These mental maps become the final product of how we view the world.

Our subjective filter can be damaging when our software has been programmed to seek only momentary pleasure or forms of instant gratification. It would be like needing successful life skills software for your mental computer but installing "101 fun and exciting things to do" software on your computer. This would be damaging, because it would give you none of the information you needed to navigate life. Your belief of "best" is inaccurate. You used no objective truth to filter it through.

THE DANGER OF MEMORY FILES

The soul has memory files like a computer, yet with the added feature of imagination which man has been unable to duplicate in machines. Memory and imagination in the soul work together through the subjective mental filter to blend the unique power of creativity. It is here principle centered morality or moral error is orchestrated.

Casting down imaginations, and every high thing that exalts itself against the knowledge of God and bringing into captivity every thought to the obedience of Christ
2 CORINTHIANS 10:5

This process begins in the form of a suggestion. Your mental software provides flash ads to review a file in your mind much like a computer does when you connect to the internet. These flash ads offer potential choices from what our mind has registered and stored as beneficial and truthful. If the desire button is pressed and not released, desire is allowed to manifest in full power. This pulls up more flash ads until signals are sent to the memory hard drive to open the complete file in your mind.

Here is where the trap of mental bondage or freedom and liberty are developed. Suggestion signals desire, then desire signals intention, and the intention triggers an act. The act itself becomes a memory recorded in the memory files of our mind with its own flash ads. At some later point you wander through your memory files and see an interesting title. The title triggers the flash ads that become the suggestion to hold down the desire button and bring up the complete file. If viewing that file signals desire, and desire signals intention, it becomes a new act of experience. Then we have another file with its own title and flash ads stored on our memory hard drive.

This process repeats itself over and over, shaping the software we call personality. It is here man rises to the heights of his most noble ideas or falls to the level of his most destructive desires. It is here man becomes a productive member of society or a criminal, locked behind the razor wire of human warehouses called prisons.

Apply your mind to instruction and correction and your ears to words of knowledge
PROVERBS 23:12

Computers are purged when they have an excess of unusable date or a virus. Files can be created and files can be erased. The same is true for people; people can unlearn thinking patterns that affect them unfavorably. We are the designers of our software, whether consciously or unconsciously. We can renew our mind with the right software program. We can use our processing skills and powers to decide what goes and what gets stored in our memory hard drive.

Be transformed (changed) by the [entire] renewal of your mind (by its new ideas and new attitude, so that you may prove [for yourselves] what is the good and acceptable and perfect will of God…
ROMANS 12:2

THE ELEMENT OF HUMAN DESIRE

The challenge for us is met in the realm of desire and emotion. Desire is the energy level of emotional input. It is desire which determines the value we place on memory files and choose to review and relive them in new experiences. This process inspires man to move from building airplanes to building spaceships; from reading books to writing one; from theft to armed robbery.

You cannot put virus infected software into your computer and expect it to operate well. All designs have standards of operation which protect their ability to function, and we are no different. Some things were never intended to be introduced into our mental software. When files programmed into our mental computer are destructive to our design of manhood, they act like a computer virus and unfavorably distort human desire.

It removes our ability to regulate desire as we were designed to regulate it. This short circuits our system, and we develop a tolerance to its ability to stimulate us. The result is that it will take greater and greater levels of intensity to satisfy us taking us further and deeper into the destructive act to create the same desired results.

After you review the same virus infected file in your mind, and have the experience once or twice, it has to be raised to a new level of intensity to stimulate the same levels of subjective pleasures. Do you see the danger in this process when it comes to our unbridled and unprincipled desires? Every time we commit such an act we have made it easier to commit another until it completely desensitizes us. There is no built-in mechanism to regulate it. The warnings shut down, and we reach a point where we can no longer tell right from wrong. We are no longer able to determine the truth from the falsehood.

WHAT ABOUT YOU?

This is the same process which led Jeffery Dahmer to go as far as he went. It is the same process that gave us something in common with him. We are society's outcasts. What about you? Is your life nothing more than sitting in prison with your mind feeding on your past memory files while basking in the bitterness of defeat? I'm asking you, the reader, right now. Are you nursing memories of things that led you to prison, perfectly content in your belief that you will not return or spend your life there? Are you resisting the thought you need to be anything other than you are?

> *You shall not do according to all we do here [in this camp] this day,*
> *every man doing whatever looks right in his own eyes*
> DEUTERONOMY 12:8

EMBRACING OUR BROKENNESS

That's why we all came to prison; every man did whatever was right in his own eyes. Maybe that's where you're at right now, still doing what you say is right for you in your own eyes. You can claim you will remain free, never coming back to prison. But that statement can only be validated by a "walk" that indicates an entirely new way of thinking. You can't change your thinking with the same mental software that created it. If you continue living in the prison of a broken man (self defeated and refusing to change), one who never realizes causes or sees the need to change, freedom will mean nothing. It will mean nothing because you remain a broken man and a broken man will not remain free.

> *As a dog returns to its vomit, so a fool returns to his folly*
> PROVERBS 26:11

I understand what it's like to leave prison a broken man and not remain free. I have experienced that sorrow, and I am seeking a genuine image of manhood in my own life. First I had to experience a revelation that the image my life represented wasn't it. We want our freedom without having to accept and embrace our brokenness. It's not ever going to happen that way.

Embracing our brokenness begins to shed light on freedom's direction. It's the same process for each of us. It begins in bondage, which for some of us ignites desperation. The energy of desperation moves us to search for revelation. Once we experience revelation it leads to transformation. From transformation we move to liberation.

BONDAGE - DESPERATION - REVELATION - TRANSFORMATION - LIBERATION

SOFTWARE PROTECTION

There's no way around it; we are going to need revelation if we want to experience liberation. We need software protection that offers us objective truths – ultimate truths. The subjective mental filer in our software is highly prone to viruses. It was never designed to be the final authority on right and wrong. We begin to determine our own truth. There is my truth and your truth, my morality and your morality, or what works for me and what works for you. The real truth is – that never works for anybody. The proof is in the number of men behind prison walls in our country. They are people who have chosen their own truths, their own morality, and their own boundaries of right and wrong.

Truthful words stand the test of time, but lies are soon exposed
PROVERBS 12:19

If the conclusions we use to navigate life are to be right as well as sincere they have to come from objective truth. It's the only form of virus protection that exists for the human soul. The same is true of morality; it can only be determined by right mental conclusions that initiate right emotional reactions as your will translates them into actions. A life of freedom requires truth, morality, and disciplined maturity to carry that truth out.

For those whose senses and mental faculties are trained by practice to discriminate and distinguish between what is morally good and noble and what is evil and contrary either to divine or human law
HEBREWS 5:14

Our subjective mental filter is part of our design. We were not created to be clones with no variation in our thinking. Without it there would be no unique personalities, no imagination, or creativity. When the subjective mental filter is in authority we tend to mold truth so that it is convenient and less painful. It seems to naturally protect our comfort zones without protecting our best interests. The answer for us is to refer to the Designer's standard of objective truth. It works by filtering potential falsehoods through a filter of ultimate truth. While sometimes painful and not always easy, it is at the same time life enhancing and self preserving.

All society asks of us is conformity. We are to obey the laws whether we like them or not. Conformity will surely keep us out of prison. The law of the Spirit of life offers us so much more than conformity upon release. It offers us objective truth that points toward a better definition of freedom and liberty. It offers a definition of liberty and freedom that includes inner peace, an unshakable foundation for life, and all the things the rich and famous are still trying to purchase with their money. When we become a united society of truth and morality, we become unique individuals sharing in the joy naturally inherent in the liberty and freedom of life according to the Creator's design.

THE EMOTIONAL COMPONENT

THE ENERGY OF ACTION

Emotions played a role in our incarceration. Likewise, emotions will play a major role in our successful reintegration into society. Emotional responses can make us or break us. They represent part of our unique personal response to experience. We blame the world for them, yet they are uniquely our own.

Early release will mean a flood of emotions – some welcome, some not so welcome. The experience of these emotions can range in intensity from low to overwhelming. Even positive emotions can lead to self-destructive behaviors when experienced too intensely and too long. The important thing to remember about emotions is that they push us to take some kind of action.

The same emotion can produce different behaviors in different people. For example, ambition may cause one person to start his own legitimate business upon release but another will join a crime ring. Fear may motivate one person to double his efforts to find employment upon release and another to not look at all and return to old familiar patterns of behavior.

Reentry in many ways can be viewed as a form of emotional boot camp for life preparation. Adult life is a series of challenges to be solved, and it won't end at successful reintegration. The rest of our lives will mean going into a challenge, being in the middle of a challenge, or coming out of a challenge.

Emotions blend together to produce a richer spectrum of experience. For example, release may cause us to experience both anticipation and joy, which may yield optimism. The experience of being reunited with family may cause us to feel joy and acceptance that fuses into new love.

Surprise and sadness in the midst of difficulty may blend into disappointment to fuse into contempt toward society or the system. When confronted with missed life events – a child born, a family member passed on – we may experience both disgust and sadness that fuses into deep remorse.

No matter what you encounter upon release, hopefully the emotional response of acceptance will be the longest and strongest of emotional experiences when it comes to life's challenges. Acceptance is simply the feeling of receiving what it is as it is. How we experience these emotions, and the choice of actions they move us into, will determine how well we become accustomed to new surroundings and conditions and change or make change as a result of contact with society.

EMOTIONAL INTELLIGENCE

There is no way around it. If we are going to experience successful lives we are going to need some knowledge and skills in the area of emotions we did not have before we came to prison. This means improving our emotional intelligence. Five traits are recognized as contributing to our emotional intelligence (*Primal Leadership: Realizing the Power of Emotional Intelligence*. Boston: Goleman, Poyatzis & McKee 2802):

1. **Knowing one's own emotions.** The ability to recognize and monitor our feelings. This is of central importance to self awareness and all dimensions of emotional intelligence.
2. **Managing one's emotions.** The ability to control impulses, cope effectively with sadness, depression, minor setbacks, and control how long emotions last.
3. **Using emotions to motivate one's self.** The capacity to marshal emotions toward achieving personal goals.
4. **Recognizing the emotions of other people.** The ability to read subtle, non verbal cues that reveal what other people really want and need.
5. **Managing relationships.** The ability to accurately acknowledge and display one's emotions, being sensitive to the emotions of others.

Together these traits define our overall emotional stability – how well we adjust to stress, hostility, anxiety, and vulnerability upon reentry. The practice of these traits can also serve as a form of empathy training which is critical to those who have a history of violating the rights of others. Empathy training means improving patterns of human communication and mutual expectations. It teaches us to share inner feelings and listen to and understand another's feelings. Human conflict and hostility are common, and life provides us with abundant opportunities to encounter them. The amount of empathy we can feel toward other people affects our willingness to validate their feelings, which may be the one thing that prevents us from violating their boundaries.

> *Remember those in prison, as if you were there yourself...*
> *as if you felt their pain in your own bodies*
> HEBREWS 13:3

SOCIAL ISOLATION

Without an operative level of adult emotional intelligence, we suffer from varying degrees of social isolation. The less emotional intelligence we are able to express, the more isolated we become from healthy adult social circles. The more isolated we become from these healthy social circles, the stronger the traits of social isolation become. Due to the isolation and dysfunction of the prison environment, these traits are likely to become more pronounced. These traits share a strong relationship to past as well as future potential anti-social behavior and crimes. Below are eight traits that commonly result from social isolation.

1. Failure to form normal attachments to other mature adults.
2. Primarily non-social in normal adult circles.
3. Difficulty interacting with other mature adults.
4. Problems communicating with other mature adults.
5. Inability to perceive differences between self and others in feelings and needs.
6. Lack of mature adult social instincts.
7. Failure to comprehend emotions of others results in frustration, improper responses.
8. Lack of empathy and sympathy toward others.

EMOTIONS SERVE A VITAL PURPOSE

Emotions are energy in motion. They were designed by our Creator to help us interpret a need, a loss, or fulfillment in relation to Him or others. They are to help us act effectively and take care of ourselves while correctly interpreting reality. When governed by truth they give us important information about what we need to do, what action to take, and how we need to change. Emotions are vital to personal and interpersonal survival. Without them we cannot be fully human.

WHEN EMOTIONS RULE

Although the soul is designed so that our thought life is in authority over the emotions we experience, this has not been the case for us. We have not understood the order of these self governing powers and our feelings have ruled our lives. We have been inclined to base our reality on how we feel or by what we desire, rather than processing emotions through a mind grounded in truth. This has proven to be a great source of pain and tragedy in our lives.

Reasoning grounded in principles of truth should be the final authority on how we navigate our lives. Our ability to reason is the eyes of our will. Without the order of intellect over emotions we make decisions without a clear view of reality. This habit becomes our life pattern, and we live our lives governed by impulse and instant emotional gratification. We develop an unspoken philosophy for life that says, "If it feels good do it." We alternate between short term pleasure and long term painful consequences. We never grow up; we never experience the joy of mature adulthood.

EMOTIONAL MEMORY
Emotional memory is where the human soul again differs from the computer. Each memory is tied to a specific type and degree of emotional energy. If we want to change the memory in a computer we simply push the delete button. The human soul can be resistant to this change due to the emotional energy tied to the information.

Emotional memory means we can store emotional experiences associated with both trauma and pleasure. It can affect our behavior years later even though we have no conscious recollection of the experience. Emotional memories can become pre-set emotional responses triggered by new experiences. Remembered or forgotten, they can impact us all over again with the same amount of emotional energy. It is because of the emotional energy tied to memory files in your soul that you will be aided or hindered in receiving the information in this book. It will determine if you remain the same person you were when you came to prison or are moved enough by the experience to seek instruction and correction.

He who refuses and ignores instruction and correction despises himself,
but he who heeds reproof gets understanding
PROVERBS 15:32

If you are ashamed of your crime and have experienced grief over the losses of your incarceration, you have emotional memories regarding these experiences. The laws of physics tell us it will take an equal or greater force to change the direction of an existing force. This is true in the hidden realm of thought and emotion as it is in the physical world. If your God-given sense of grief and shame are not experienced equally or more intensely than the emotions you have tied to the things that brought you to prison, there is likely to be little change.

A FORCE FOR CHANGE
When you have these experiences of intense grief and shame for your actions and current circumstances, your mind will be ready to receive new information and take new action toward change. This is why people who have failed the most have the potential to serve the best. The emotional energy blindly put into failure is met with the same amount of energy to change and reach out to others.

MY CHANGE
When I first got down on my knees in the county jail, I was horrified at how I had behaved toward others in the actions of my crime. I agonized and cried

out to God about wrecking my own life for the fourth time as well. When the Holy Spirit came upon me there was peace in knowing my life would never be the same. However, God did not remove my sense of remorse right away. The remorse intensified for a period as truth invaded my mind – the truth of what I did and what I had become. Without truth governing our soul, emotional energies will never be cleansing and purifying, and we will have no healing and transformation. Instead of emotional energies enhancing our lives they will destroy us.

So foolish and stupid was I, and ignorant; I was like a beast before you
PSALM 73:22

EMOTIONAL TRANSFORMATION

Emotional healing is the work of spiritual transformation. It is based on our willingness to embrace spiritual principles and disciplines. This involves a lot of work and persistence. It is difficult but not impossible. The difficulty involves the emotional energy attached to releasing our old ways and embracing the truth.

For the fruit (the effect, the product) of the light or the Spirit [consists] in every form of kindly goodness, uprightness of heart and trueness of life
EPHESIANS 5:9

Purifying and cleansing emotions that come from an encounter with truth are like SALT and LIGHT. They can act like irritants to the wounded or those longest in darkness. This may cause us to ward off and avoid any exposure to bring these emotions to the surface. If it may involve pain, why bother? We have set aside our crimes. Are you sure, or is it because prime opportunities don't exist? Does this represent change? Certainly not.

Principles of truth have a way of eating away at old desires. They never look the same again, opportunity or not. Principles of truth shed new light upon old desires, and they lose their appeal. Once truth is the guiding light of our lives, emotional healing begins to take place. Our emotions become healthy responses to the challenges and problem solving we face in reentry.

The fruit of the [Holy] Spirit [the work which His presence within accomplishes] is love, joy (gladness), peace, patience, (an even temper, forbearance), kindness, goodness (benevolence), faithfulness, gentleness, (meekness, humility), self control (self restraint, continence). Against such things there is no law [that can bring charge]
GALATIANS 5:22-23

THE PHYSICAL COMPONENT

THE TEMPLE OF THE INNER IMAGE

There are many analogies used to describe the human body. It has been referred to as a temple. The sanctuary and dwelling place of immortal the spirit.
The body has been called a home the real self resides within. Some call it a
garment covering the real self and will one day be cast aside. The body has been
called a shell; the real self hidden inside will one day leave it behind.

Do you not know that your body is the temple (the very sanctuary) of the Holy Spirit
Who lives within you, Whom you have received [as a gift] from God?
1 CORINTHIANS 6:19

None of these analogies are wrong. The body is all these and more. The
wisdom of God refers to the body as a temple in its most honored analogy. No
other analogy so perfectly describes our responsibility to it and care it should
be given (all temples need a foundation). Its care should be grounded in the
spiritual foundation, navigated by a principle centered mind, and energized
by emotional inspiration. Our physical body is vital to the ongoing interaction between the other parts, but it is the most vulnerable to breakdowns and
problems. If we neglect the primary needs of our body, we will handicap the
function of the other five potential powers we use to navigate our lives.

Unless the Lord builds a house, the work of the builder is wasted
PSALM 127: 1

THE ESSENTIAL SIX:

1. Sleep: Seven to eight hours every night.
2. Food: Three balanced meals each day.
3. Water: Six to eight, eight ounce glasses of water each day.
4. Relaxation: One hour each day.
5. Exercise and recreation: Three hours each week.
6. Cleanliness: Body, oral, clothes, residence each day.

The essential six are primary needs for our physical well-being and have
a pronounced impact on the quality of our lives. Our physical component is
a system within our whole system. How well we manage them will determine
the condition of our trinity of body, soul, and spirit. When they are neglected
the first to weaken are body and soul. If we carry this neglect far enough the
spirit can be broken.

The strong spirit of a man sustains him in bodily pain or trouble,
but a weak and broken spirit who can raise up or bear?
PROVERBS 18:14

THE DEMANDS OF REENTRY

Reentry can place a lot of demands on our body. We face the physical labor of new employment, psychological stress, and many other factors. Early reentry and today's world can exert powerful distraction from our responsibility for caring for ourselves. It is a common response in early reentry to try to meet these challenges by taking care of ourselves less and accomplishing more.

It's almost as if we expect our body to be able to handle not meeting its essential needs – and to what degree we can somehow determines our manhood. Nothing could be further from the truth. This is why the acclimation tool of commitment to truth is so important. Manhood means responsible self management and not the ability to handle pushing our body beyond its limits.

We must begin our journey of reintegration with commitment to the essential six. It will dramatically increase our chances of success. We need solid boundaries and personal management skills when it comes to caring for our physical body. Without them life will be about trying to survive reentry rather than progressing in it.

BENEFITS OF THE ESSENTIAL SIX

1. Reduced Stress
2. Balanced Moods
3. Illness Prevention
4. Prolonged Life
5. Health and Vitality
6. Ability to Function at Best
7. Self-Esteem
8. Sense of Well-Being

MANAGING THE ESSENTIAL SIX

1. Sleep

Inadequate sleep has become a national epidemic for Americans. The average person suffers from sleep deprivation. Many attempt to manage their demanding life on five to six hours of sleep each night. The fast pace of our modern society places great demand on our lives. We are constantly challenged to do more and sleep less. The challenge of family, work, and social agendas tend to have us put sleep as a last priority. It needs to be a high priority and a well-protected boundary.

It is vain for you to rise early, to take rest late, to eat the bread of [anxious] toil –
for He gives (blessings) to His beloved in sleep
PSALM 127:2

We are no good for anyone or anything when deprived of proper amounts of sleep. A lack of sleep can produce the same impairments as alcohol intoxication. People do not adapt to chronic sleep loss. Losing an hour or two of sleep every night impairs our ability to maintain attention and reason. There can be loss of memory recall, reaction time slows, and errors in judgment increase. This is why poor sleep patterns have been associated with an increased tendency to engage in risky behaviors.

Men reentering society after a period of incarceration cannot afford to risk this impairment. People do not always realize they are not getting enough sleep. We can become accustomed to suffering the symptoms and think it is our normal state. It is important to know the signs and not ignore the warnings from others. Warning signs, including those mentioned above, are: anger, aggression, depression, apathy, indifference, and lack of motivation. Research indicates a twenty-minute nap can increase alertness, reduce irritability, and increase efficiency. A one-hour nap leads to even greater increased performance. However, naps can never replace the body's need for proper amounts of sleep.

2. Food

The majority of people today eat for pleasure instead of health. It is important to realize you can do this without sacrificing your health. We can seek out foods that taste good and are good for us. We can train ourselves to eat healthier foods and still enjoy our favorites on the weekend. The key is to survey the need, develop a plan, and take action.

Some estimates conclude 52% of Americans are overweight and 76% suffer from poor diets. If you are one of these individuals you are cheating yourself out of the eight benefits. The Essential Six operate like a system. Getting enough sleep will not provide health and vitality if your diet is poor. A poor diet can even sabotage sleep patterns.

Certain foods provide essential nutrients and vitamins that support health and some do not. You can gain weight from overeating and still be starving your body of nutrients and vitamins. Healthy eating doesn't require you to become a health nut or nutritionist. It does requires some conscious effort. The key is to use a common sense approach by eating foods from all five major food groups in the quantities recommended by the Food and Drug Administration.

I urge (warn, encourage, advise) you to take some food [for your safety]
it will give you strength
ACTS 27:34

Most experts agree on eating a wide variety of living foods. We need fruits, vegetables, nuts, and whole grains, accompanied by small portions of fish and lean meats. Non-living foods are usually bagged or boxed. This includes chips, crackers, Little Debbie's, and so forth. These foods and fast foods are not healthy foods. They are calorie rich and nutrient poor. Remember, your ability to meet life's challenges outwardly is directly related to how you manage your life inwardly.

3. Water

Water is the most important nutrient for the body, yet most are in a state of constant dehydration. This may be due in part because thirst often can be mistaken for hunger. When you should be reaching for a glass of water, are you reaching for a snack instead? The human body is 75% water. We can go up to only seven says without water before we die of dehydration. The right amount of water is serious business when it comes to how well we function.

Water is necessary for muscle contraction and helps prevent stiffness. It increases functioning and stabilizes moods. All your body's major organs are highly dependent on water to function, even your bowel movements. Your entire nervous system is dependent on water to send electrical impulses. No part of your body will work well without water.

4. Relaxation

If you can't relax you will soon be hearing it from everyone else. Sometimes doing nothing is the hardest thing to do but it is the thing we need the most. People who practice this habit are usually more productive than those who never stop trying to accomplish. Employers are incorporating relaxation classes to increase employee productivity, and it works.

Relaxation training is a stress buster. It decreases lactate, a primary chemical linked to stress. It promotes alpha brain waves which activate centers involved in attention and relaxed wakefulness. The regular practice of relaxation techniques help in self regulation of moods and lower heart rate.

Now every athlete who goes into training conducts himself temperately
and restricts himself in all things
1 CORINTHIANS 9:25

Knowing how to relax is just as important as knowing when to relax. It is more than flopping down in front of the television with remote in hand. It requires lying quietly from head to toe. It is the only way to recognize muscle tension. Relaxation training involves tensing each area of the body for a couple seconds and then relaxing it. Breathing exercises can also play an important role in relaxation training. It involves taking two to three deep breaths from the pit of your stomach every thirty seconds for several minutes.

5. Exercise and recreation

Unlike recreation, exercise is a dirty word for many. The hardest part is getting past the idea of getting started. There is one unanimous conclusion among those who have accepted the challenge to get in shape: the reward is worth the effort. Studies show three hours a week can dramatically alter your health and fitness level. Exercise is proven to slow down and even reverse your physical age. It can lower blood pressure and cholesterol, aid in digestion, and costs nothing. For those who are alone upon release, joining a gym can help to meet new friends and provide a safe environment to occupy time.

Whether you see yourself lifting weights, joining a softball team, or taking regular brisk walks, the key is just do it. While variety is always best, doing something you enjoy is just as important. If you enjoy it you are likely to be more committed. There are several factors to consider when determining a personal exercise program. You need to consider your age, abilities, needs, goals, and available time. It is important to get a physical before beginning a rigorous exercise program.

The benefits of aerobic exercise are well established. This could be anything from biking, hiking, jogging, swimming, or aerobic classes. The best exercise programs will include strength, endurance, and flexibility training. All forms of exercise improve our response to stress, how we react to stress, and how we recover from stress. Exercise is loaded with benefits. It can reduce depressed feelings and increase confidence. You are likely to feel more vigorous, more energetic, less anxious, and less irritable. It can reduce aches and pains, lower the risk of colds, and improve sleep.

When it comes to recreation it may or may not involve physical activity. If you are into sports, your recreation is likely to involve physical activity. On the other hand, sometimes we need to just disconnect from the business of regular life. It may save your life. You can disconnect by having a cook out, going camping, or canoeing. You can go to dinner and a movie or go to the park. Recreation is a re-creating and restoring our mental freshness and vitality.

There are many things you can do and it costs nothing. Be creative.

6. Cleanliness

Cleanliness in all areas of our lives has a powerful influence on our sense of well-being. It not only enhances it but projects it to the world around us. Cleanliness can be therapeutic in many ways. It can reduce boredom, elevate your mood, and even lower stress. Taking a shower or cleaning the house can change our perspective on the day.

Cleanliness is a form of preventive maintenance for a large number of health concerns. Health issues can reduce our ability to function and create down time for employment, not to mention they are costly. Showering each day removes bacteria and dead skin from the body. This is why we feel refreshed. Changing clothes daily, especially underclothes, is very important. You have two types of sweat glands in your body. One is for perspiring to reduce body heat, the other is to expel waste from the body. The areas undergarments cover are the areas that dispel waste products from the body. A lack of oral hygiene can lead to gum disease which has a relationship to heart disease. Start reentry clean and present how much you value yourself.

FAITH IN DESIGN FOR REENTRY

We don't worry if the sun will shine or if the spring will come. God is faithful. His designs work within His principles. Our personal lives are no different than the coming sunshine or spring. If we operate within the principles of God's design, life will always work for us in reentry.

- What has represented the foundation of your life, principles or self interest?
- If you could push a button, which program files in your mind would you delete?
- Is your level of emotional intelligence prepared for reentry? Why or why not?
- What are your strengths and weakness in regards to the Essential Six?

The next chapter will reveal the underlying issues of why we choose which behaviors we believe are correct and best suited for how we manage our lives.

CHAPTER FIVE

Psycho-Social Development (Part One)

—∞—

THE PATH TO ADULT MATURITY

We are all somewhere on the maturity progression shy of perfection in regard to resolving psycho-social conflicts. Our private character and social personality depend on what degree we have experienced and resolved these conflicts.

This is very important because they will determine how we process rules regarding which behaviors are correct and best suited for personal and interpersonal success.

If we do not resolve these conflicts, we are set up to develop personality and social problems that lead to antisocial behavior

and crime.

— THE AUTHOR —

It was expressed to me by a spiritual mentor and pastor that men read many books but do not change. I had to agree with his insight. The same had been true in my own life. The truth is, our personalities are fairly consistent and stable throughout our lives, and only slightly refined and modified in most instances. This is unless we experience something with sufficient impact to significantly alter it. I am confident the psycho-social stages I have outlined in later chapters can create the corrective experience to do just that. They can produce the corrective experience because they operate within the natural laws of human growth and development.

The law of the Lord is perfect, converting the soul
PSALM 19:7

Unlike other theories and self-help philosophies, natural laws do not change. They are consistent and reliable. We can depend on and use them to our advantage anywhere – validating them by our own experience – and succeed time and again. Natural laws are design laws operating through the power of divine law.

Psycho-social development, like all natural systems of life, is based on the super intelligent design of relationship, wholeness, order, and balance. These natural laws are tightly interwoven chords of strength running with precision through the foundation of all life. We could say these natural laws are the foundation for all life development.

Unless your law had been my delight, I would have perished in my affliction
PSALM 119:92

Since these natural laws under-gird every dimension of life, we are able to use them in this chapter to chart out the process of human development on what we might call the maturity scale. A simple glance at these laws in this chapter, and how they apply to our development, can give us a complete and accurate map of a life where all the principles fit together and are properly related to each other.

We need to see the problem clearly and recognize its seriousness so that the solution will matter to us. In order to do that, I will discuss the following questions in the next two chapters.

What is psycho-social development? How do these natural laws apply? How does this relate to crime and incarceration? Finally, how can the application of these natural laws assist in the corrective experience and reignite our psycho-social development?

WHAT IS PSYCHO-SOCIAL DEVELOPMENT?

Psycho-social development looks at how we develop mental and emotional skills that allow us to interact with progressively higher levels of mature social environment, from childhood to adolescence, and on to adulthood. At the same time we develop mentally and emotionally we develop socially. Both psychological and social development, from the immaturity of childhood to the maturity of adulthood, are long and complicated processes. They are influenced by a vast number of mental, emotional, and social factors. This is not to say we need to become professors in the field of human development. The pattern of God's design was that we would experience them ourselves through competent models of manhood, so that we could pass them on naturally yet intentionally.

Train up a child in the way he should go: and when he is old, he will not depart from it
PROVERBS 22:6

1. **Mental development** involves progressive skills in our reasoning, judgment, and perceptions which determine our world view and decision-making skills.

2. **Emotional development** involves progressive achievement in our ability to perceive emotions accurately, both our own as well as others. It means to take emotions into account when reasoning, while learning to understand and manage them.
3. **Social development** involves progressive achievement in social skills important to our interactions, such as intimacy, boundaries, and social norms.

Together these three determine how we develop a sense of self and our position in a world full of others.

LEARNING HUMAN BEHAVIOR
1. The law of relationship
Practice what you have learned and received and heard and seen in me,
and model your way of living on it
PHILIPPIANS 4:9

The more intelligent a creature is the more complex its development. The more complex its development the longer the nurturing process is to reach self-sufficiency. Psycho-social development for humans requires growth in multiple stages and multiple levels within those stages. This lack of development is significant to our incarceration. Some estimates are that 85% of those incarcerated were fatherless. Some statistics state that children raised by a single parent are three times more likely to grow up with emotional and relational problems.

Humans are the most fragile and easily flawed of all creatures and necessarily require the longest period of guided development. The nurturing process for humans to reach self- sufficiency is twice as long as any other creature, requiring at least eighteen years and often longer.

No one comes through this development process unmarked by some degree of error. Our ability to learn is vastly larger than any other creature. Psycho-social development can occur throughout our lifetime and can be re-ignited at any point. We have the capacity as humans to learn what was left unresolved through the corrective experience. This means all of us can have hope for a better future. We are not shackled by our past conditioning or present circumstances.

Unlike any other creature, learning how to function as a fully developed human being is not a naturally resulting process. We must learn to be fully functional human beings through the process of mentoring and modeling from others. In my early years of college, I remember reading two profoundly sad stories that illustrate this point.

The first story was about a young boy abandoned in the wilderness. He spent the most important developmental years of his childhood alone and without human contact. He survived but when found he was crawling on all fours and grunting like an animal. He survived by eating nuts and plants and crawling into holes for shelter. His scars indicated he had been bitten by several wild animals. As a result of intense work and reigniting the psycho-social process of mentoring and modeling he made profound progress. He learned to walk upright, dress, and eat with a spoon. However, due to the lack of human contact and learning in those early formative years he never became totally self-sufficient.

The second story is just as tragic – if not more so. It's about a thirteen-year-old girl who had been locked in a closet her whole life. She suffered total sensory deprivation for the first thirteen years of her life. Her fragile brain was not stimulated by sight, smell, touch, and rarely taste or sound. The only time the closet door opened was for feeding or to empty the tin pot she used for a toilet. Once discovered, she lived only into her twenties. She never experienced the vital psycho-social process of learning to initiate action to thrive and care for herself. If the basic life skills of caring for herself were not done by others, she would not take the initiative to do them. Initiative is one of the eight conflicts we will look at.

These are truly profound examples. They show us how successful psycho-social development is largely dependent upon learning everything it means to be human from others. Nothing will have as great an impact on what we choose to become. We will be as healthy and well-rounded in our wholeness as we are connected to other healthy human beings. And so God declared, you will become social creatures.

THE LAW OF THE SPIRIT OF LIFE IS LOVE
The most profound bonding adhesive for human development at every stage of the process is love. When we plant seeds of unconditional love in other human beings it encourages their natural growth process. Love expressed without self-centered conditions helps children and adults to feel safe and secure. It provides an environment to learn and grow. We validate and affirm their God-given identity and worth, and what they learn bonds to them in proportion to their sense of value. I wonder what role the absence of love played in the two sad stories I illustrated?

Above all...[put on] love and enfold yourselves with the bond of perfectness
[which binds everything together"...]
COLOSSIANS 3:14

When we live within the primary principles of love (2 Corinthians 13:4-8) and make deposits of unconditional love, we encourage others to live by the law of the Spirit of life. They will be inspired to express and pass on the love they have themselves experienced. That's what the law of the Spirit is really all about. It becomes the fruit of the seed and manifests in cooperation, contribution, and integrity. Unconditional love inspires people to discover and live true to the highest potential for good within them. It offers freedom in the environment of nurturing relationships to focus on growth and maturing, rather than spending energy trying to survive the environment. I wonder what impact love has had and is having on your life?

By mercy and love, truth and fidelity [to God and man...]
iniquity is purged out of the heart
PROVERBS 16:6

You can't change the seed without changing the fruit. When we violate the principles of unconditional love it places conditions and limitations on a person's basic value. This encourages others to violate the law of the Spirit of life. It teaches others to live in a defensive-reactive and manipulative position in relationships, where people feel they have to prove they matter as a person. These are not the seeds of unconditional love, and the fruits will not be the qualities expressed in the law of the Spirit of life. They will be performance centered counterfeits.

When love is conditional and performance centered the focus of life will be to produce evidence of worth at any cost. This can prove fatal to human potential. When their God-given and God-honored identity and value are not unconditionally affirmed, it does not offer people the freedom to adjust their learning and behavior to that position. It encourages defensive rebellion and a walled in heart. The result is trust issues, intimacy issues, lack of empathy, antisocial behavior, and crime. The law of relationship according to God's design cannot be broken. The result is only broken people.

2. The law of wholeness

So that the man of God may be complete and proficient,
well-fitted and thoroughly equipped for every good work
2 TIMOTHY 3:17

PSYCHO-SOCIAL CONFLICT RESOLUTION
The law of wholeness requires that the necessary conflicts are successfully negotiated so that the end result is mature adulthood. As we progress through the natural stages of childhood, adolescence, and adulthood, we engage specific

conflicts at each level. If we resolve each potential problem as it arises, we acquire skills that prepare us for the next level of maturity. If we do not resolve the conflict, it keeps repeating itself throughout our lives and manifesting in various experiences.

For example, intimacy requires trust. Once the conflict of trust is resolved, genuine intimacy is possible. Those who never resolve trust issues often live out the rest of their lives in a prison of suspicion and fear. Part of enjoying other people is the bond of intimacy we share with them. Without trust we build walls of isolation in mainstream society rather than bridges of intimacy. We become blocked in our ability to function in the reality of adulthood that requires mature trust and intimacy in reentry. Below are the psycho-social conflicts that determine our mental, emotional, and social levels of maturity.

THE CONFLICTS OF PSYCHO-SOCIAL DEVELOPMENT

1. Trust
2. Intimacy
3. Attachment
4. Ego Boundaries
5. Integrity
6. Autonomy
7. Initiative
8. Identity

1. **Trust** comes from resolving the conflict of faith in our relationships with other people. We either discover people are dependable and we can place confidence in them, or that they are not deserving of this confidence.
2. **Intimacy** comes from resolving the conflict of developing an inner regard and affection for others. It involves the familiarity of very long and close associations that allows us to open up and fully reveal ourselves to other human beings.
3. **Attachment** comes from resolving the conflict of being able to develop binding affection that allows us to associate ourselves with other personalities. We learn to establish a special regard and empathy for others.
4. **Ego boundaries** come from resolving the conflict of being separate from others. My thoughts, feelings, and desires are mine and separate from yours. I am responsible for them. Ego boundaries operate as a conscious mediator between self and the world. They distinguish what's mine versus what's yours, what I like versus what you like, and helps us to see moral and legal boundaries as fixed limits.
5. **Integrity** comes from resolving the conflict between inner morals and values and outward behavior. It is an unimpaired condition of soundness in private character and public personality.
6. **Autonomy** comes from resolving the conflict of becoming self-governing. It means to be capable of living a self-contained and independent life. I can live on my own and separate from the guidance of an institutional

setting that ensures the care of my life in all areas.

7. **Initiative** means to resolve the conflict of needing others to take action for us. I can initiate action using my own discretion outside of the control of others.

8. **Identity** is resolving the conflict of conformity and stepping into our own uniqueness. This identification not only distinguishes my personality and character as different from others but what it means to be human.

We are all somewhere shy of perfection on the maturity scale. We all have various conflicts to resolve. Our private character and social personality depend on what degree we have experienced and resolved these conflicts. This is very important because they will determine how we process rules regarding which behaviors are correct and best suited for personal and interpersonal success. If these conflicts are unresolved, we are set up to develop personality and social problems that lead to antisocial behavior and crime. These social symptoms are an outgrowth of being frozen in our development.

FROZEN IN OUR DEVELOPMENT

Our lack of wholeness means we remain egocentric and frozen in various stages of childhood and adolescent maturity while living out our lives in adult bodies. To be egocentric is to be overly concerned with self, rather than how we might affect others and society. It is a limited and immature outlook of excessive concern for our own activities and needs. The theme of this adult immaturity is to see ourselves as the starting and stopping point of all thought process. It is to remain selfish and self-centered, from childhood to adulthood, to the point of self obsession.

Let no one then seek his own good and advantage and profit, but [rather] each one of the other [let him seek the welfare of his neighbor]

I CORINTHIANS 10:24

The excessive concern for self and the belief self-interest is a valid end of all actions are natural occurring conflicts for children and adolescents. For an adult it means to struggle with destructive lifestyles based on pleasure and desire that eventually lead to conflict with other people and society. The missing essential conflict resolution and lack of wholeness comes at a great price. Mature self love and self discipline cannot manifest without resolving these conflicts.

Without this self-love and discipline we cannot develop personal and interpersonal skills necessary to be partners with society in adulthood.

Diagram 1:

Psycho-social	conflicts	=	Self love/Discipline	=	Personal/Interpersonal skills
1. Trust	5. Integrity				1. Delay gratification
2. Intimacy	6. Autonomy				2. Problem solving
3. Attachment	7. Initiative				3. Coping
4. Boundaries	8. Identity				4. Decision making
					5. Communication
					6. Courage
					7. Commitment
					8. Consistency

PRINCIPLE CENTERED
MATURITY BASE

PARTNERS WITH
SOCIETY

3. The law of order

God has appointed and arranged [in divine order]
ROMANS 13:2

THE STAGES OF OUR DEVELOPMENT

There are progressive stages as well as basic conflicts on the maturity scale of growth and development. If the path we traveled was in harmony with the natural design of growth and development, we will have resolved the basic conflicts that lead to wholeness. As we resolve these conflicts it builds a series of bridges that move us on an ordered maturity progression from dependence to independence, and ultimately interdependence. Each stage is a platform for the next. Our personal and interpersonal skills are learned and perfected from dependency through interdependence.

Diagram 2:

Basic conflicts		Personal/Interpersonal skills	Progressive stages
1. Trust	5. Integrity	1. Delay gratification	Dependence-outer directed
2. Intimacy	6. Autonomy	2. Problem solving	
3. Attachment	7. Initiative	3. Coping	
4. Boundaries	8. Identity	4. Decision making	Independence-inner directed
		5. Communication	
		6. Courage	
		7. Commitment	Interdependence-inner directed/other connected
		8. Consistency	

1. **Dependence** is the (other dependent) I-Self-Me.
2. **Independence** is the (self dependent) I-Self-Me.
3. **Interdependence** is the (self dependent/other connected) We-Us-Ours.

THE TWO LEVELS OF MATURITY

It is impossible to ignore or violate the development process by jumping from the dependence of childhood to the liberties of independent adulthood. Ten-year-old children who are still dependent on others for survival do not pack up one day and announce they are moving out on their own and entering the work force. It is clearly contrary to our design and would only result in frustration and disappointment.

We understand these laws of development in physical skills for basic survival in living alone and employment. What happens if we fail to resolve the natural conflicts of growth and development that secure our psycho-social maturity upon reentry? Are our chances really any better? The mass presumption and unspoken expectation is that we will grow mentally, emotionally, and therefore socially, as we go through life and grow physically. Our "coming of age" falsely assumes that since we have acquired the necessary skills to take care of ourselves physically; we will have become inner directed and self-reliant – mentally, emotionally, and socially.

As men returning back into society, we must connect the relationship between character development and successful reintegration. It is the resolution of our conflicts, the bonding agent of unconditional love, and our personal and interpersonal skills that move us along the maturity scale from dependence, to independence, and on to interdependence. We may be strong, skilled, and capable men physically, but we must be equally capable mentally, emotionally, and socially. Diagram 3:

Maturity scale **Mental -Emotional – Social**
1. Dependent people -Need others to get what they want and need
2. Independent people -Get what they want and need by their own inner-directed efforts
3. Interdependent people -Combine their efforts with others for best results

DEPENDENT PEOPLE

The dependency problem with adult males is the problem of personal maturity. We come to prison with, and often leave with, unresolved conflicts of trust, intimacy, boundaries, and others. We suffer from a lack of communication skills, struggle with an inability to delay gratification, and lack other personal and interpersonal skills of adulthood. There are struggles that result from our failures to include others in our self-obsessed thought processes. We are driven by a hundred forms of self-centeredness and self-seeking that bear witness to our self-obsession.

The profound consequence is that we suffer from major relational issues that prevent success in many aspects of adult social reality. To avoid the pain of facing these issues, along with our lack of understanding of them, we turn to subcultures, gangs, and compulsive/addictive behaviors. Even when we are "in the game" with our illegal activities, we are unable to see that we still rely on the mature adult society we prey upon to get most of our needs met. It is their committed and consistent level of principle centered interdependence that makes a structured society possible.

Adult reality can only be navigated from a character base of principle centered maturity. This center becomes the guide for our decisions, actions, and responses for success in the everyday life of adulthood. Dependent people lack this inner-directed character base from which to operate. Like a physical handicap, nature will seek to compensate for survival.

EMOTION DRIVEN SURVIVAL

Dependent people compensate for a lack of principle centered maturity by operating from emotion driven survival. This method of survival means to make decisions, take action, and respond through a point of reference where desire, pleasure, and impulses are the ruling authority in our lives. The head is placed above the heart for a reason. It symbolically represents our design, that proper thinking governs healthy emotional responses. Without this design, society as we know it could not exist.

For people will be lovers of self and [utterly] self-centered, lovers of money and aroused by an inordinate [greedy] desire for wealth, proud and arrogant and contemptuous boasters. They will be abusive [blasphemous, scoffing] disobedient to parents, ungrateful, unholy and profane. [They will be] without natural [human] affection (callous and inhuman), relentless (admitting of no truce or appeasement); [they will be] slanders (false accusers, troublemakers), intemperate and loose in morals and conduct, uncontrolled and fierce, haters of good. [They will be] treacherous [betrayers], rash [and] inflated with self-conceit. [They will be] lovers of sensual pleasures and vain amusements more than rather than lovers of God

2 TIMOTHY 3:2-4

Without mature reasoning, emotions will always relate to coping, problem solving, and decision making through the path of least resistance called shortcuts and quick fixes. There are times when even the most mature and disciplined minds hear the loud and clear call of their emotions to take the easy way. It's called temptation. Emotions are not logical or moral. Their only goal is to feel good and avoid discomfort. If we lack mature and principle centered reasoning, our relentless and powerful emotions will dominate our decisions. This is emotion driven immaturity. Since the goal of emotion driven immaturity is pleasure and desire, any emotional discomfort is avoided at any cost. The path of shortcuts and quick fixes often means choosing illegitimate methods to deal with legitimate problems. We violate the laws of society and other people to avoid the pain of problem solving the normal challenges of adult life. As we have come to experience, in the end it creates more traps and trouble than anything else.

COMPULSIVE/ADDICTIVE BEHAVIOR

Life is all about relationships. As a result of the arrested development, we are set up for problems with people and addictions. Meaningful relationships with others help to create a psychic balance in our lives. The inability to relate to others in meaningful ways has created a psychic imbalance, a psychic wound, nothing outside of self can fill. Addiction is an attempt to medicate this psychic imbalance and nothing works. The pain and emptiness always returns.

This psychic imbalance and our attempts to heal the wound creates a chronic obsession for more. Whatever it is, we want more of it. The chronic pain of the wound and the constant psychic imbalance will never let us rest. There is no escape except in brief moments found in mood altering chemicals or a variety of mood-altering experiences. We will never "out do" the sense of longing, that sense of being driven, and the emptiness will remain, because it is an illness of separation from God and others.

Addiction is an unhealthy relationship to any mood-altering chemical or experience that has life damaging consequences. It could be anything we develop a relationship with outside of ourselves to escape the pain of our lack of healthy connection to God and other adults, and our inability to relate to them in meaningful ways. The relationship to our addiction is set up by our unhealthy relationships to people, our inner barrenness, and our lack of wholeness that results from our arrested development.

The world has defined this chronic obsession for more as the addictive personality. I call it self-inflicted replacement therapy. We replace our trust and intimacy void in relationships with our emotional connection found in our addictions. We want more sex, more drugs and alcohol, more money, power, control, and more social status. Too much is never enough because the attempts to mood alter are a quick fix and a short cut that cannot permanently fix the problem.

Nothing we attempt can create the long-term fix. In the end, we trade long term memorable relationships for soon forgotten short-term pleasures. We trade homes for prison cells and freedom for bondage. The obsession for more and its accompanying addictions, narrows our lives until it finally destroys it. Prison is a safety net that saved many of us from ourselves. In some instances, failure is a second chance. Sometimes you've got to lose so you can win.

THE CYCLE OF ADDICTION

We can often live for years without suffering the effects of our lack maturity and its resulting mismanagement of our lives. We vaguely feel uneasy when not mood altering. When the pain intensifies we take steps to temporarily ease the pain. We get used to the pain and uneasiness because it is chronic, and we believe it is our natural states. We learn to live with it as it takes us from one devastation to another – one incarceration to another.

When we have problems in our interactions with others and society, our chronic pain is intensified by the acute pain of those interactions. That's when we treat the symptoms (people, circumstances, situations) with the quick fixes and short cuts of addiction. We cannot see that the momentary pain of the symptoms is an outgrowth of our deeper chronic problem of immaturity. Diagram 5:

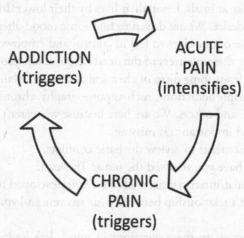

ADDICTION
(triggers)

ACUTE
PAIN
(intensifies)

CHRONIC
PAIN
(triggers)

The acute pain (people problems) intensifies the chronic pain (arrested development) which triggers a desire to mood alter and self medicate with addiction. The recklessness and unmanageability of the addiction triggers more acute pain and the cycle repeats itself. The addiction is the result of continually self medicating a pain we cannot name. We keep doing the same things that never worked before and expecting different results in each attempt.

The loss of choice inherent in the arrested development is multiplied by the addiction. It further narrows those choices. Consumption addictions such as drugs and alcohol have their own unique and inherent biological addictive qualities that must be addressed before recovery can be lasting. However, if the chronic pain of immaturity is not addressed through the corrective experience, we simply trade less socially acceptable addictions for more well hidden and socially legitimized addictions. This is an especially common practice for men while incarcerated.

Addiction is not just about drugs and alcohol, sex, gambling, and pornography. Addiction is about the things of everyday life. It is about how we eat, how we work, how we love, our religion, social status, and even exercise. It 's about how we practice recovery, our perfectionism, our sense of self righteousness, and moral superiority. These addictions are more acceptable but certainly no less damaging. The chemical changes in the brain are similar to those of consumption addictions like drugs and alcohol. It is still self medicating an inner psychic wound – the self rupture of an arrested development with replacement therapy.

The arrested development and the psychic imbalance that results violate our will, our rights, our boundaries, and our needs. Our attempts to replace meaningful relationships with a mood altering relationship to our addiction violates our true self and our rightful place in maturity. They force human beings to become like animals, living their lives by their lower drives and impulses, pleasure, and desire. We are driven to find some mood-altering chemical or experience outside of ourselves to feel in control and empowered, whole, and worthwhile. Over three-quarters of the nearly 2.3 million people in U.S. prisons are suffering from some form of chemical addiction. Many of them are in the bonds of multiple addictions, such as pornography, chronic masturbation, tobacco, caffeine, and others. We are here because we weren't all there; something of profound importance is missing.

Take a few moments to review the basic conflicts.

- Which ones have you resolved the most? The least?
- Which personal/interpersonal skills have you developed most? The least?
- Can you find a relationship between your answers and your incarceration?

With the answers to these questions in mind, let's look at part two and discover a deeper relationship between our psycho-social development and our crimes.

CHAPTER SIX

Psycho-Social Development (Part Two)

—ᴍᴍ—

Liberty is options.
The choice of options will determine your freedom.
The options do not represent freedom,
only the potential to attain it.
Freedom belongs to the man who chooses the right options.
All others are not free; they are just in the land of options.
— THE AUTHOR —

We will either be partners with society or we will be predators and parasites. There are no other categories that define our relationship with our community. What category we represent is largely determined by the outcome of our psycho-social development. It is not the result of bad breaks, lack of opportunity, the behavior of others, or the unfairness of life.

Their consciences (sense of right and wrong) also bear witness;
and their [moral] decisions (their arguments of reason,
their condemning or approving thoughts) will accuse or excuse [them]
ROMANS 2:15

These challenges may provide good opportunity to create excuses and generate blame. However, most people who experience them do not end up in prison. Three hundred million people in America experience the unfairness of life, only 2.3 million of them are in prison. How we deal with these challenges expresses our level of maturity to cope and problem solve.

Problems and trials draw out and reveal the maturity of our character. Predators and parasites are dependent people who fail to solve the problems of life and choose instead to prey on the legitimate success of other people.

The **predator** is defined as one who shows a disposition to commit crimes that injure or take advantage of others for one's own gain. The predator expresses (overt) violent behavior. It is observable, without concealment, and with evident intent.

1. Murder   4. Carjacking   7. Kidnapping
2. Rape   5. Home invasion   8. Arson
3. Robbery   6. Assault   9. Extortion

The **parasite** is defined as one who shows a disposition to commit crimes that bleed others of life and sustenance for one's own advantage. The parasite expresses (covert) non- violent behavior. It is manipulative, concealed, or disguised.

1. Drug trafficking   4. Writing bad checks   7. Identity theft
2. Theft   5. Internet fraud   8. Fraud
3. Stolen property   6. Embezzlement   9. Illegal weapons

UNHEALTHY SURVIVAL BEHAVIORS

There are strikingly common characteristics between adult males with an arrested maturity and incarcerated adult males who are predators and parasites. The common characteristics they share reveal an underlying connection between the disorder of an arrested development and its social symptoms of anti-social behavior and crime. They both represent people who have learned to survive by developing and refining a lifestyle that involves a predictable pattern of maladaptive behaviors.

Maladaptive behaviors are behaviors that fail to help us adapt. They are unsuited and inadequate for adult society and result from our faulty adjustment to adult maturity. These behaviors are our survival behaviors which we attempt to use to manage our lives. We have perceived them as helpful and protective but, in reality, they have been very destructive. They feel normal to us since we use them every day and are drawn to people who operate in the same way. This helps to make them all the harder to give up. Over time they become a recognizable pattern of fixed personality traits.

However, unpopular it may sound to us as men, what we have been reacting to is the trauma of an arrested development. We have also been dealing with the trauma of the maturity issues, relational issues, and compulsive/addictive issues that result. We are men with an arrested level of conscious maturity trying to relate to an adult world through maladaptive survival behaviors. In the end, they have left us shackled to extreme self-centeredness, powerlessness, spiritual bankruptcy, and incarceration.

But this is a people robbed and spoiled; they are all of them snared in holes, and they are hid in prison houses: they are for a prey, and none delivereth, for a spoil, and none say restore.

Who among you will give ear to this? To open the blind eyes, to bring out the prisoners
from the prison, and them that sit in darkness out of the prison house
ISAIAH 42:22-23, 7

I am not at all implying there are no evil people or that evil does not exist.
We can be sure that evil is alive and well in humanity. Evil is one of the most
obvious facts of human existence. There are truly bad people. However, there
is a difference between truly bad people and people who do bad things as a
result of an arrested development.

I am confident evil people are the exception and not the rule, much like
the wild boy described in part one was an exception. They represent extreme
examples of unhealthy psycho-social development as a result of neglect, abuse,
or organic causes. My purpose here is not to discuss the exceptions but rather
to point out the fact that the exception merely proves the rule.

I have briefly outlined some of the maladaptive personality traits, following the chart on the arrested psycho-social development. I have created
a checklist of some of the most common traits using each letter in the words
"predator," "parasite," and "offender status." These traits can give us a clue to
understanding the issues behind our crimes. From the chart and the checklist
it's clear that we as offenders are not just products of social and economic disadvantages or other outside influences, nor can we be labeled as just bad seeds.
But rather our evolution into the predator and parasite that led to our offender
status is rooted in our arrest psycho-social development.

THE ARRESTED PSYCHO-SOCIAL DEVELOPMENT

Unresolved Conflicts	Lack of Personal/Interpersonal Skills
1. General mistrust of people	1. Poor impulse control/pleasure seeker
2. Absence of genuine intimacy	2. Poor problem solving/confusion
3. Unhealthy or lack of attachment	3. Poor coping/compulsive-addictive behavior
4. Blurred moral/legal boundaries	4. Poor decision making/emotional/comparing
5. Integrity issues	5. Poor communication/isolation
6. Dependent personality	6. Fear/self-obsession
7. Lack of responsible self-discretion	7. Poor commitment/compromising
8. Unresolved identity	8. Consistent only when convenient

Egocentric Personality	Dependent Predators/Parasites In Society

PERSONALITY TRAITS OF THE PREDATOR AND PARASITE

Poor modeling experience

Remiss neglect of developmental needs

Early childhood symptoms

Delinquent criminal behavior

Abandoned inner child

Trust issues

Overly dependent

Repressed/internalized emotional coping

Offender/victim ambiguity

False self

Fixated personality development

Employment related issues

Now phobic

Defenses

Extremely Controlling

Rigid/measured/judgmental/perfectionistic

Psychologically split

Addictive/compulsive

Reactive rather than proactive

Acute intimacy problems

Submarginal boundaries

Inability to initiate/problem solve

Thought disorders

Express faulty communication

Subjective reality/little objectivity

Tailored truth

Abnormal fear

Typical low self worth

Underlearning

Spiritual bankruptcy

P: Poor modeling experience. You have never learned how to do many of the things necessary for a fully functional adult life. Your methods of problem solving do not work, but you continue to use them over and over. You learned ways of caring for your developmental wounds that actually make them worse. There is a whole set of models of what's normal you have never seen. You often guess at appropriate behavior. You have no real knowledge of what is normal. Your bottom line tolerance and coping is very low.

R: Remiss neglect of development needs. You have an inner psychic wound that feels like a hole in your soul. You never seem satisfied. No matter how you anticipate something, soon after it is over you feel restless, irritable, and discontent. You are childish in specific ways and often feel like a child.

E: Early childhood symptoms. As a child you expressed dramatic mood changes, aggression, and sudden, unprovoked behavior. You expressed age inappropriate talk and behavior. You expressed over-attachment or under-attachment to other people.

D: Delinquent criminal behavior. You were aggressive and destructive as a child. You set fires, trespassed, and destroyed private property. You had problems with fighting, curfew, and early alcohol/drug use.

A: Abandoned inner child. You have an unsatisfiable child living inside of you. You put your needs ahead of everyone else's. You look like an adult and talk like an adult, but you respond to stress and the challenges of adulthood like a child. You are very impatient.

T: Trust issues. You trust no one completely. When you risk trusting your judgment is bad. You believe everyone operates with ulterior motives. You are not attracted to those who are truly trustworthy.

O: Overly dependent. You have a childish sense of entitlement. You are constantly irritated because people do not adequately respond to your needs. You are demanding and impatient. You expect others to see that your needs are met. You blame others for everything that goes wrong in your life. You feel you are not responsible for what is happening. You stay in relationships that are life damaging (male/female), and severely dysfunctional. You are possessive and suspicious in relationships. You believe others are responsible for your feelings and happiness.

R: Repressed and internalized emotional coping. You are controlled by your emotions and at the same time completely out of touch with them. You never quite know what you feel. You don't know how to express your feelings. You are an angry person. Your emotions do not rise and fall like spontaneous emotions but function like an "on" button waiting to be triggered. Your emotions have become a state of being: anger, fear, shame, guilt, sadness, and joy. You may be one or more of these.

P: Psychologically split. You often feel like you have two personalities. You are one way on the outside (public personality) and another way at home (private character). You think everyone behaves that way and it's normal. You are confused about your real identity. No one can believe how different you can act at times.

A: Addictive/compulsive. You are or have been in an active addictive/compulsive pattern of behavior. You have experienced multiple addictions.

R: Reactive rather than proactive. Your life is one overreaction after another. You realize it and others have brought it to your attention. You feel powerless to stop overreacting. You feel things that are disproportionate to what is going on. Your words and actions are disproportionate to circumstances.

A: Acute intimacy problems. You have trouble in relationships. You have had multiple marriages. You are attracted to emotionally unavailable and unhealthy partners. You are attracted only to partners who are dependent on you or allow you to be dependent on them. You are not attracted to partners who are kind, stable, reliable, and interested in you. You feel "nice people" are boring. When you start to get close you sabotage the relationship. You confuse closeness with compliance, and intimacy with enmeshed boundaries. You confuse lust with love. You view people in your relationships as objects to meets your needs, rather than equal partners with the same life goals.

S: Submarginal boundaries. You lack healthy legal and moral boundaries. You tolerate dangerous, unhealthy, and inappropriate behavior. You guess at where you end and others begin. You live within enmeshed boundaries (no lines) or walled boundaries that keep others completely out. You have tolerated in your life what you never thought you would tolerate. You believe all life is relative – there is no absolute right or wrong. You manipulate to get around the boundaries of others.

I: Inability to initiate or solve problems. You get frustrated about getting started because you have trouble planning. You can't see alternatives and often feel lost and confused. You believe your problems are unique. You constantly seek ways to avoid the pain of problem solving.

T: Thought disorders. You obsess about things you can do nothing about. You obsess about the little things until they appear bigger than your ability to solve them. You worry a lot and repeat things over and over in your mind. You stay in your head and constantly intellectualize. You think at polar extremes and constantly fantasize or focus on catastrophe.

E: Express faulty communication. You have had trouble communicating in every relationship. You avoid deep and personal communication. Goal-oriented communication bores you. You feel no one really understands you. You are often highly emotional and confused when communicating with others. You don't listen well to others, and you form your answers before the person is finished speaking. You try to dominate conversations, interrupt, and rarely allow the other person to talk or finish a thought.

O: Offender/victim ambiguity. You have been in trouble with the law. You have an "us versus them" mentality. You feel the law and the system are oppressive, yet you have been labeled an offender. You have broken the law without regard to how it might affect others. You have little empathy or sympathy. You feel you have been a victim of the law. You are defensive when you experience interactions with the police. You believe your sentence is not fair. You focus more on how you believe you have been victimized by the courts than you do the victims of your crimes. You spend your time trying to escape consequences rather than changing yourself for the better. Your expressions of remorse are more about consequences than the violations of others.

F: False self. You pretend a lot. You gauge your behavior by how it looks and by the image you believe you are presenting. You wear a mask, play a role, and constantly work to conceal what is on the inside. Your self-worth depends on externals: image, success, power, prestige, reputation. You calculate, manipulate, and play games. You are so lost in the mask of the false self you have no idea who you really are.

F: Fixated personality development. You look like an adult, but you think-feel-operate much like a child. You are extremely needy. You have impulse control problems. It is impossible to satisfy your need to be recognized.

E: Employment related problems. You have never been full-time employed. You have rarely or never held a job over one year. You change jobs frequently. You have inconsistent work ethics and struggle with commitment and consistency. You have authority-related work problems.

N: Now phobic. You feel extreme remorse about the past and constantly wish you could do it over. You create fantasies about your future but make no effort at personal growth to make them a reality. You live in the past or in the future, but rarely in the now. Memory and imagination are used to avoid present feelings and reality.

D: Defenses. You use dissociation, displaced feelings, depersonalization, delusion, denial, and psychic numbness to avoid the impact of your current state of affairs and all the pain you have caused in the past. You create fantasies about yourself and your life that exclude the total view of reality. You idealize how things used to be.

E: Extremely controlling. You have very little internal control over your impulsive and compulsive behavior, yet you try to exert extreme control over people, places, and things. The less inner control you experience the more outward control you try to exert. You try to control what cannot be controlled and pay little attention to the things you can control. You control others by manipulating (helpful/needed) or you control with anger, rage, and oppression.

R: Rigid, measured, judgmental, perfectionistic. You have unrealistic expectations of self and others. You are rigid and inflexible. You are always comparing yourself to others to see if you measure up. Your judgment of self and others is rigid. You are stuck in rigid attitudes and behaviors even though it hurts to live the way you do. You expect people and things to be a certain way and when they are not you walk away or throw in the towel.

S: Subjective reality with little objectivity. You are very opinionated. You have no in- depth understanding of normal adult reality. You find it hard to understand why other adults are interested in the things they are interested in. Mature interests are square and boring. If you attempt those interests you quickly lose interest. Your belief system conflicts with adult society. It is inconsistent and self-conflicting because it is built on self-serving myths and falsehoods.

T: Tailored truth. You are a talebearer. You believe it impresses and influences people in their opinion of you. You impulsively embellish or twist the truth concerning just about everything. You find yourself lying when you could just as easily tell the truth.

A: Abnormal fear. Your fear is a fantasy in reverse. It is false evidence appearing real. You live in constant fear about everything. You fear not getting your needs met by a seemingly unreliable and unpredictable society. You fear anyone different. You fear anything you don't understand. You fear anything you cannot control. You fear what most adults trust will work out.

T: Typical low self-worth. You are dominated by your social environment, at the same time preying on it in rebellion. Your self-worth and value is dependent on conditions and people outside yourself. When these variables respond to your physical pleasures and desires you feel well, appear agreeable and in partnership, and your self-worth and value are high. You explain your life by conditions, circumstances, or someone else's behavior. Since these elements are impossible to control, you often feel like a victim and it helps you to better reason and accept your predator/parasite offender status. Your level of self-worth does not aid you in being inner-directed and validated from within. In response, you spend your time and energy manipulating, controlling, and dominating these conditions as a predator and parasite.

U: Under-learning. You keep repeating the same mistakes over and over. You keep making the same poor judgments and decisions without really learning from them. You lack a mature level of self-awareness that would allow you to connect your inner life with your outer circumstances. You rarely plan your future. You believe you can still do the same old behaviors that led to incarceration if you manage them right.

S: Spiritual bankruptcy. You have no spiritual life. If you have a spiritual life it is based on head knowledge, church attendance, ritual, and mantra. You relate to your spiritual life through ecstatic emotional experiences. It's still all about being recognized. You believe you have the market on understanding spiritual truths. You refuse discipleship. You are extremely self-righteous, judgmental, and unloving. You hold others to a higher standard than you hold yourself. It is more important for you to be right than to know the truth. You use your religion to alter the way you practice being a predator, or manipulate as a parasite. You have not experienced genuine brokenness that leads to real transformation.

THE MOST COMMON HUMAN ILLNESS

This recognizable pattern of fixed personality traits are chronic patterns that block the potential of spontaneous free choice. The traits we have adopted mark the places our development is arrested, and we have become functionally disabled. It is here we first lost our freedom. See if you can identify yourself with the traits in this checklist. I can identify with them having been present in my own life. It is crucial to experience the powerlessness and unmanageability that results with the traits you can identify with. If you do it is likely you will better see the level of impact of your own arrested development. If we do not outgrow them they will continue to sabotage our lives in reentry.

The arrested development is the most common human illness and was initiated at the fall of man. We can be very talented, intelligent, and religious while remaining extremely immature. God repeatedly appeals to man to seek maturity in His word. No matter what else we might be, we still have to grow up and develop the maturity that resembles God's original design of manhood. The spiritual life is not based solely on supernatural deliverance. It provides the life, the power, the relationships, and the disciplines to enter the path to adult maturity. We are the ones who must weed out the thorns and work toward the harvest.

The seeds that fell among the thorns represent those who hear the message, but all too quickly the message is crowded out by the cares and riches and pleasures of this life. And so they never grow into maturity
LUKE 8:14

We have been unaware of our God-given endowments that have the potential to connect us to our Creator and other mature adults. Our life of substandard maturity and social reality has led us to compensate by entering subcultures full of substandard relationships. Only those who own enough of themselves as mature adults can operate as partners with society. All others operate through the alternating obsessions of predator and parasite. People who live at these levels are not living anywhere near the full scope of life.

SUBCULTURAL INFLUENCES

There is little question, the people we associate with will influence us for the better or worse. It is also a natural tendency to associate with other people who generally think and act like we do. We share with them a general agreement of reality concerning the beliefs, rules, and needs we use to govern our lives. This general agreement is often unspoken and unconscious and is called a consensus reality.

If we are working toward change and higher levels of maturity, we will naturally be drawn to groups and organizations that are helpful, constructive, and accomplishing things for each other that are life enhancing and beneficial to all. This is because their level of maturity will provide a consensus reality for them as to the beliefs, rules, and needs best suited for a successful adult life. The belief is that the group exists to make a better individual. They are independent adults uniting to produce an interdependent force greater than themselves.

On the other hand, if we suffer from an arrested level of maturity, our connection to others will be very different. We will naturally bond with others as a result of our common immaturity and remain bound by our common unhealthy survival behaviors. The belief is that the individual exists for the group, and are likely to require you share in the same anti-social behaviors and crimes. They are dependent people uniting to be legitimized by numbers. The more of them there are, the more their consensus reality is strengthened and legitimized in their eyes.

Walk with the wise and become wise; associate with fools and get into trouble
PROVERBS 13:20

These groups form strong barriers and walled boundaries that not only keep the "outsiders" out, but the "insiders" in. No information gets out and at the same time, no new information gets in. This creates the perfect environment for the group to shape their own belief systems and codes of behavior that are at odds with the beliefs, rules, and needs of mainstream society. The end result is the formulation of subcultures such as gangs, codes of prison, crime rings, and the drug culture.

Each of us has a powerful need to belong. The problem is, the price of becoming part of these groups will always cost us more than we can afford to pay, with little or no rewards. No one grows and becomes mature and independent. To be accepted will cost you your individuality, your identity, your future, and in all likelihood your freedom.

A major factor for maturing out of these associations is an awareness of our true value and potential. What helps to keep us stuck is the lack of new information and modeling to break out of the old beliefs and behaviors we remain bound in. These associations, like the unhealthy survival behaviors we share with them, are all forms of compensation to survive an adult world we do not know how to relate to.

There are several dynamics that must take place to move us away from subcultural influences and toward a successful life of maturity:

1. Grasp the consequences of staying where you are
2. A desire for something more in life
3. Identify with the unhealthy survival behaviors
4. Exposure to new information that challenges old beliefs
5. Exposure to models of genuine manhood and maturity
6. Involvement in groups working toward growth
7. Awareness of your value and potential

PRETENDERS ARE NOT APPREHENDERS

We can pretend for a while. We can wear the mask of the false self-image and pretend what we represent is mature manhood. The prison environment can be used to aid us in our false pretense. We can pretend to be anything we want and be anybody we want to be. We might even deceive ourselves, because we have played the role so well for so long.

We have made lies our refuge, and in falsehood have we taken our shelter
ISAIAH 28:15

No matter how hard we work at the art of compensation on the outside, the truth of what we are on the inside always gets pressed out when squeezed under the pressures of adult life in society. Our efforts will forever be counter-productive until we stop treating our issues of immaturity with quick fixes and shortcuts in an effort to escape them. This only builds weaknesses into our character because it reinforces inappropriate responses rather than building effective life skills.

The myth of massive appeal (the trap and the trouble) is the belief there exists some quick and easy way to achieve quality of life. There is the belief that somehow, some way, we can experience personal success, rich and strong relations with others, without going through the work of the maturing process that makes it all possible. Our maps must be drawn from reality – roads that actually exist. Our destinations in reentry must be practical and realistic, and we need a principle-centered compass to hold us on course. Leaving prison and experiencing reentry with unresolved issues of maturity and a tool box of quick fix schemes won't work. It's like leaving California for Hawaii in a canoe, blindfolded and without a map. It means having the wrong tools for the journey and a lack of proper navigation.

PRISON: THE SUBSTITUTE PARENT

When there are no skills to resolve the challenges of adult life, the transition from the dependency of the prison environment to the independence of society will be too difficult and problem oriented. If life consisted of no more than our wants and desires, choices and decisions would be easy. The only basis for these choices and decisions would be urge and impulse. As we have come to experience, it is the consequences of these type of choices that are the most difficult. Due to our inability to choose wisely and maturely as adults in society, the prison system becomes our substitute parent. The "parent institution" (as it is rightly called) provides the outer controls for us who still lack the inner controls that mark the character of adulthood.

The prison experience is a period in our lives defined by an almost total loss of choice as a result of our inability to choose maturely. We are told what to wear, when to eat, when to sleep, and even to stay in the yard. In prison our lives are totally dependent on the system. Like children, all the details are thought out and managed for us. The parent institution employs high-priced babysitters who monitor the social controls we should already have in place within ourselves. Like children, our primary focus is playing our pretend roles, eating our meals, and enjoying recreation.

RELEASE IS A TEST OF MATURITY

Eventually we are released back into society as part of a mature, interdependent adult world; one we must relate to every day. The naturally occurring problems of reentry and everyday life can both conceal and reveal our arrested development. The daily problems of living in a free society easily conceal the character causes of repeated incarcerations because there is a degree of legitimacy to the limitations and barriers incarceration can create. We attribute them to employment issues, yet unemployed mature adults don't use their unemployment as an excuse to engage in illegal activities. We attribute them to lack of family or social support, not acknowledging our lack of interdependent maturity to form and sustain healthy relationships.

We are more accepting of the possibility of potential handicaps in the realm of external causes. We have yet to accept and relate it to the problem of personal maturity and our own moral character. It is far more painful and far less common. Even if we understand this concept in theory, to accept it in our own lives, and then the work it requires of us, is much more difficult.

But let endurance and steadfastness and patience have full play and do a thorough work, so that you may be [people] perfectly and fully developed [with no defects], lacking in nothing
JAMES 1:4

On the other hand, the natural occurring problems of reentry and everyday life can reveal our arrested development to both ourselves and others. We cut corners, avoid the pain of problem solving, take short cuts, and engage in illegal activities that provide quick fix solutions for our problems that require long-term commitment and consistency. Others see us struggling and complaining about reentry. From the right distance they could easily conclude we are going through a lot of re-adjusting. Our inability to cope tries to get others to believe we are suffering and struggling deeply.

In an attempt to keep our inadequacy concealed, we refuse to seek out the all-important help we need. The inability to make progress through legitimate methods with patience, without complaining and blaming, reveals our lack of skills to cope in an adult world. These efforts to conceal and legitimize our problems create an effective disguise but only for those too close to us to see the bigger picture.

INDEPENDENCE

As we reach out toward independence from dependence on state institutions it is easy to see that independence is much better than dependence. Achieving independence after release from prison is a major accomplishment in itself. However, true independence of character (personal maturity) can take us further than independent living skills. It is the only element of independence that can sustain the ground we gain. Independence of character frees us from mental and emotional dependence on others. It is truly a worthy and liberating goal of reentry.

If I am mentally and emotionally independent I will have forged a principle-based center from which I can think my own thoughts. My emotions, desires, and impulses will be governed by that thinking. I can validate myself from within and therefore become inner directed. As I gain principle centered, independent thinking, I become more value driven and less driven by desires and impulse. I am now able to organize my life and execute reasoning and judgment around my new priorities of life with a high degree of personal integrity.

The integrity of the upright shall guide them, but the willful contrariness and crookedness
of the treacherous shall destroy them
PROVERBS 11:3

True independence comes from dominion over self, and provides a platform for real value based self respect. Unless we are willing to do the work disciplined, principle centered maturity requires, it is worthless to try and develop independent living skills. We might try to achieve reintegration – and have some degree of stability when times are good. But in difficult times there won't be a solid guidance center of principles to keep things together.

Successful reintegration into society is all about successful relationships. The most important ingredient we can put into our relationships is our character, not our personality. The skills that make for success in human interactions are the ones that flow naturally from the maturity of an independent character. True independent maturity empowers us with human relationship skills that create a platform for effective interpersonal relationships with other mature adults. If our independence does not flow from the core of our character, but rather from a mask of a shallow personality, others will eventually see our lack of integrity and our missing genuine independent empowerment.

INDEPENDENT EMPOWERMENT

Independent Living Skills	Independent Character
1. Employment skills	1. Conflict resolution
2. Education	2. Self-love/Self-discipline
3. Financial management	3. Personal/interpersonal skills
4. Housing	4. Dominion over self
5. Paying Bills	5. Principle centered
6. Consumer information	6. Value based self-respect
7. Insurance/Investments	7. High level of self-awareness

If we hope to remain free we must travel from dependence to independence, both in living skills and character. However, we can get so caught up in our quest for independence that we begin to glorify it as the ultimate goal, which is beyond its natural and rightful place. If independence is not seen as a platform to prepare us for interdependence, it leaves us to believe a life of interdependence is an option. We are left to believe communication, teamwork, mentorship, and social unity are optional for life in society and successful integration.

> *Two people are better off than one, for they can help each other succeed. If one person falls, the other can reach out and help. But someone who falls alone is in real trouble*
> ECCLESIASTES 4:9-10

The dependent person who has not attained independent empowerment lacks the ability to understand genuine interdependence. The concept of mature interdependence can only be understood from a conscious maturity level of independence. To this dependent person who is still self-absorbed and self-obsessed, interdependence sounds like another weak form of dependence. We often lack the capacity to see it in ourselves that the push to avoid interdependence and glorify independence is our defensive reaction to mask our own inability to function on that level. Self-awareness and self-obsession are not compatible; we are unlikely to be able to discern our own arrested development, let alone its severity.

More times than I can remember, I have been listening to my fellow inmates talk about how they just want to get away from it all when they are released, and find a place far away from everything and everybody. I have been guilty of this unrealistic fantasy in the past. The desire is to become liberated from all outer controls. The idea of "be your own man," "do your own thing," and "avoid the rat race of society," often reveals deeper levels of dependency hidden behind the concept of independence.

How wonderful and pleasant it is when brothers live together in harmony
PSALM 133:1

We can run but we can't hide, because what we are running from is not external but rather internal. They are maturity issues, such as feeling victimized by people and environments that hold us accountable, or because we do not have total control over them. The issues behind the obsession of total independence from others has little to do with "being your own man" and at its core is a maturity issue.

INTERDEPENDENCE: PARTNERSHIP WITH SOCIETY

The goal of mature independence is to discover that the highest parts of our potential have to do with our relationships with others. Dependent immaturity sees the goal of independence as a means to not have a need for others. Nothing could be further from the truth. Our increasing independence allows for an increasing awareness of all life, including human societies, is governed by interdependence. As we grow and mature as adults, we realize greater and greater levels of success within our society result from an increasing awareness of the interdependence of everyone in society.

We begin to see with greater and greater clarity that there is cooperation, unity, and partnership that governs society. It is from this level of maturity we begin to see how our interactions affect our community. We further discover the highest reaches of the quality of our lives has to do with our active participation in our community's interdependence.

THE PARTNER OF SOCIETY

1. Independent/interdependent
2. Conscious maturity of we-us-ours
3. Cooperation, unity, partnership
4. Legal boundaries-tradeoff for success
5. Recognize personal impact on community
6. Enhance quality of community
7. Meaningful connections with community
8. Life of purpose and meaning

Interdependence is a far more advanced level of reintegration than independence. Independent people still suffer from many of the same problems of reintegration as dependent people. The decision to work toward a more complete level of reintegration and embrace interdependence is where much of the self-awareness, healing, and personal growth takes place. Self help groups like Alcoholics Anonymous are possible through interdependence. It is the platform that makes it possible to win a Super Bowl, to become a highly skilled technician in a field of interest, or fulfill any dream of great achievement.

Live in harmony with one another; do not be haughty (snobbish, high-minded, exclusive), but readily adjust yourself to [people, things] and give yourself to humble tasks. Never overestimate yourself or be wise in your own conceits
ROMANS 12:16

Complete reintegration is made possible by a level of awareness that realizes "WE" working together can accomplish far more than "I" could, even at my very best. Mature interdependence realizes that in order to experience these social benefits I must act within the moral and legal boundaries of that social system. They also realize it is a more than fair trade-off and choose to act within that framework that makes society possible. Interdependent mature adults can choose it because they are principle-centered, self-reliant, and capable. They have the character and own enough of themselves as mature adults to have the inner controls in place to properly govern themselves. Reintegration moves from dependence, and on to independence, and then interdependence by reaching out to other competent, caring adults in our local community.

PRINCIPLE CENTERED MATURITY

Each of us has a center from which we operate. We are either self-centered or principle centered. It determines our level of maturity and expresses the resulting degree of harmony and balance in our lives. It determines our level of dependence, independence, or interdependence. Each of us uses our operation center to chart and navigate reality, and it determines how clearly we see everything else in our lives.

1. **Principle**: A complete and most basic law. A rule of conduct. The laws or facts of nature. A divine principle. A testable truth.
2. **Center**: A thing most important or crucial to an indicated activity, interest, or condition. A source from which something originates or operates.
3. **Balance**: A position or state of harmony. To stabilize, regulate. Mental/emotional stability. To settle.

Our operation center functions as a lens through which everything we experience is filtered and forms our view of the world. We use this lens to form our most basic perceptions and ideas about life's meaning. Our operation center determines our motivations, our values, and our purpose. It is the resource center from which we make our decisions, problem solve, interpret our interactions with others, and even define ourselves. It is the standard we use to categorize past experience (hindsight), to define our current circumstance (insight), and how we view our future (foresight).

Our operation center is the place where we made the maps that led us to our current environment and will determine our destiny. If our operation center has not empowered us to live the life of success, stability, and freedom we had hoped for, our current circumstances are more than likely challenging us to change the center from which we operate. It has become necessary for our effectiveness to make a move to a new center of operation that will bring this harmony and balance into our lives. If our operation center does not change, we are destined to keep operating the same way and experiencing the same outcomes. It is a basic law of life. If nothing changes, nothing changes.

Stand by the roads and look; and ask for eternal paths, where the good, old way is; then walk in it, and you will find rest for your souls
JEREMIAH 6:16

If we look at the world from an operation center of principles, what we will see through that lens will be dramatically different from what we see through a self-centered life. A principled centered person thinks differently, sees things differently, and therefore acts differently. A life of principle-centered maturity offers us an operation center of truth from which we can describe the realities before us, and make the best possible choices to navigate our way through them.

Get the truth and never sell it; also get wisdom, discipline, and good judgment
PROVERBS 23:23

An operation center based on principles of truth is the only lens that will allow us to accurately determine our current position and map out our direction and destination. When our lives are centered on proven and enduring principles we can live our lives in a wise and balanced way. We can better define and avoid the extremes that always create our detours, traps, and troubles. It not only establishes our freedom through right choices and sound decisions but secures it.

WHERE TO FIND PRINCIPLES OF MATURITY

The best place to seek out principles of human conduct is the principle maker Himself. If you want to understand the best possible operation of a design, you read the operation manual provided by the designer. Widely misunderstood, God's word is often viewed as a book of restrictions we could just as easily live without. Biblical principles are guidelines that offer everyone the potential to experience the best of life's rewards. Principles are no respecter of persons. They point to success and warn us against our own self destruction. We make the choice. We don't choose the consequences of those choices.

I will meditate on your precepts and have respect to your ways
[the paths of life marked out by Your law]
PSALM 119:15

Biblical principles align us with genuine manhood and maturity for at least two important reasons. First of all, only the designer has the patent on defining what manhood really is (Genesis 1:26-27). Do we really believe there could be seven billion definitions of manhood? Then which one is correct? How has your definition worked out for you so far? Second, the practice of these principles in all our affairs evokes a level of self-discipline that leads to a degree of maturity with which we can all agree.

For example, we can all agree on the importance of being in touch with truth (John 8:32), and the importance of strong relationships (Proverbs 11:14). We can all agree on the importance of accepting responsibility for ourselves (Galatians 6:5), and for us to have some ability to examine ourselves (Lamentations 3:40). We can all agree life requires that we face challenge (Romans 5:3-4), and if we are to ever learn anything from others we need to be open to the examination and challenge of others (1 Peter 5:5).

We know these things are necessary and admit they make sense, even if we don't like to practice them. What we may not see as clearly, or like to admit, is our level of personal discipline to operate within those principles. Self-discipline is self-management. We get the word discipline from the word disciple – a person who adheres to a set of principles that has become their own set of values. When we place our value on the principles that govern human life, a function of our self-discipline is to align our thoughts, desires, and impulses to those principles.

Those who love your instructions have great peace and do not stumble
PSALM 119:155

Self-discipline is a common denominator all successful men of maturity share. They are people who have a habit of doing what others don't like to do. Men of maturity often do not like to break out the tools of discipline either; they do it anyway. Dislike is made submissive to the value in the principle, and the strength of the purpose found in a clear sense of direction that defines genuine manhood. A set of mature values on the inside makes it possible to say no to other things on the outside.

Principle-centered maturity is aligning our values to a set of truths and choosing not to be governed by desire and impulse at any given moment. While principles based on enduring truths point out our direction, it is the value placed on them moment by moment and day by day that keeps them first in our lives. Discipline is merely the self-love of carrying them out.

MY QUEST FOR PRINCIPLE CENTERED MATURITY

He who will not examine his thought life will remain forever shackled to the center from which his sorrow originates. He will never be able to change his reality and its consequences and will never make any progress. I was alone in prison and in the presence of my own sorrow when I sought answers to my freedom. I poured myself into the Bible. I wrapped myself deeper and deeper into its truths until I was wrapped in it like a cocoon. What did I have to lose? My real hope was what I might have to gain.

His delight and desire are in the law of the Lord, and on His law
(the precepts, the instructions, the teachings of God) he habitually meditates
(ponders and studies) by day and by night
PSALM 1:2

I meditated on it day and night and was profoundly moved by how it spoke to my own past experience. I discovered reading it was not the same as letting it speak to me. It was there in the refuge of my cocoon that I discovered I couldn't change my life with the same mind that created it. I couldn't hope to change until I gave up my own opinions and armed myself with the truth. I realized I survived living with myself all those years by redefining everything. I created my own definitions for manhood, love, courage, for right and wrong, and even for God. The truth opened the door to a whole new level of self-awareness I had never before experienced.

Their purpose is to teach people wisdom and discipline, to help them understand the
insights of the wise. Their purpose is to teach people to live disciplined and successful lives,
to help them do what is right, just, and fair
PROVERBS 1:2-7

I learned to step back from myself and see what did and did not benefit my life. I discovered ineffective but deeply embedded habits that were in total opposition to my freedom and the things I valued most. What mattered now was whether I was responsible enough to move to a new governing center of principles, one where all the parts worked together instead of against each other in self-defeating ways.

I could continue to add to the volume of battle scars on my soul from a life of quick-fix skirmishes, or I could end it right here and right now! I was determined to tap into the potential of my maturity instead of clinging to my severely limited immature past. The question that could only be answered by action was, did I value myself enough to do this work?

I am absolutely certain that without competent, caring people in my life to guide and direct me I would not have stayed on course or be the man I am today. I have been blessed with wise and mature mentors who continually mirror to me the unconditional love I have described in part one. Dramatic changes took place when I began to accept the value God placed on me in His Word, and the constant unwavering affirmation of that value from others. This confirmation of value opened the door for me to walk out the psycho-social stages I have outlined in later chapters.

Admonish and train one another in all insight and intelligence
and wisdom in spiritual things
COLOSSIANS 3:16

I began to practice what I learned and realized if I could win enough battles, in time I could win the war. I could have a new life, because I had a new level of maturity defined by a new way of thinking governed by higher values. I went from living out my present bondages and sorrows day after day to writing a new script for my future. It meant walking away from a self-centered life of careless living to a principle centered life of maturity, manhood, and freedom.

Principle centered maturity was not a momentary choice for me but rather a process. It involves hard work and the practice of new disciplines. Nor was it an entirely painless process. It takes deep inner self searching and careful analysis, as well as thoughtful practice. The process is just as important as the final product. It forces us to think through our priorities deeply and carefully, and to align our resistant habitual patterns of behavior with our new found principles.

FREEDOM REQUIRES PRINCIPLE CENTERED MATURITY

We are not expected to deny things that hurt us emotionally and cause us great pain and sorrow, but our value-based self-respect does not have to be hurt at all. Our painful experiences can become the resistance training that forges our mature character when our self value comes from the right source, and we respond to these challenges with principle centered maturity.

Whatever you are now facing or face in reentry, don't just go through it, grow through it. Most won't, but you can if you will learn to understand you are worth it; life is worth it.

As I sit here writing this today, I listened to the news tell a story about a young man who just left prison recently. He was being arraigned for aggravated robbery with a gun. If he valued his freedom at all he had no principled centered discipline to secure it. He simply didn't own enough of himself to own his freedom. His choice was governed by extreme self-centeredness and the fleeting desires of the moment. Now he will spend another one to two decades in prison to get it right and start all over again. That doesn't have to be you and me, but it will be us if we don't move from self-centered immaturity to principle-centered maturity. Until then we will never realize our own value or own enough of ourselves to remain free.

Let our lives lovingly express truth [in all things, speaking truly, dealing truly, living truly]. Enfolded in love, let us grow up in every way and in all things
EPHESIANS 4:15

Principle-centered maturity never puts self or what we desire in supreme authority. It doesn't have to like those driven and controlled by their own self-obsessed immaturity. It offers the freedom to handle the difficult circumstances and conditions of reentry, instead of being destroyed by them. It starts now, before we are released, or it doesn't start at all. We gain our freedom before we gain our liberty, or we will never attain either one. Liberty is options. The choice of options will determine your freedom. The options do not represent freedom, only the potential to attain it. Freedom belongs to the man who chooses the right options. All others are not free, just in the land of options.

YOU CAN BE THE ONE WHO REMAINS FREE
The accounts of ex-prisoners who have been able to develop principle centered maturity and express it in difficult circumstances was made possible by how they chose to define themselves before they left prison. It is what raised them above their circumstances and is an inspiring testimony for us all who hope to remain free. The powerful character of principle-centered maturity expressed by those who never return to prison is hope for the rest of the prison culture. It answers the most important question for the rest of us. It is the HOW of the few who remain free, not the WHY of so many who do not.

This is the manhood and character we all envy, the type we lay on our racks and watch movies about. Some individual in very difficult circumstances and under severe handicaps who refuses to take the easy way out based on desires and impulse. He holds to his principles at all costs. Nothing has greater impact on us and longer lasting inspiration than the story of the one who overcomes – the one who transcends his suffering and his circumstances, lifted above by the principles he stood for.

We don't call them men or make movies about their character because they get into the blame game or because they argue circumstances and conditions. People who exercise this liberty day after day will, little by little, expand their freedom as they continue to live by principles. People who do not exercise this liberty will find it withers away until they behave like the man I heard about on the news. He is on his way back to prison. Why? Is it conditions or circumstances; the economy? No – for poor choices in the misuse of his liberty of options.

Wise choices will watch over you. Understanding will keep you safe
PROVERBS 2:11

A CHANGELESS CORE CAN HANDLE CHANGE

The society we must reintegrate ourselves into is changing at an ever increasing pace. Reentry itself is characterized by a series of rapid and successive changes. The key to our ability to deal with this change is to have a changeless core of principle centered values and a changeless sense of who we are, what we are about, and what we value. These changes overwhelm ex-prisoners reentering society who have no changeless principles on which to stand. They feel they can't handle conforming to society's standards. Soon it becomes too hard to cope. They become emotionally reactive. Eventually they give up, hoping on whatever occurs by chance or the throw of the dice of compromise, hoping everything will work out right. It doesn't have to be that way.

Short cuts and quick fixes driven by desire and impulse just get us to the wrong place faster, costing us our freedom once again. The principle-centered maturity we need helps us to better understand we are the ones responsible for where we are now and empowers us to choose differently and change direction. Such empowerment gives us the capacity to make dramatic changes in our lives rather than remain submissive to past memories and past behaviors. It instills a framework for a new way of thinking so we can become inner directed and self-governed in light of our new found maturity.

For only the godly will live in the land, and those with integrity will remain in it
PROVERBS 2:21

Take a few moments and reflect on how your crimes represented a predator or parasite.
- In what ways has your life represented partnership with society?
- Which traits in the checklist can you relate to as having been present in your life?
- Are you willing to do the work that disciplined principle-centered maturity requires?

With the answers to these questions in mind, let's look at the next chapter and discover how the self-obsession of the arrested development leads to a predictable pattern of returning to prison, called the unconscious mental progression of recidivism.

CHAPTER SEVEN

Psycho-Social Stages of Reentry (Part One)

—⚬—

THE UNCONSCIOUS MENTAL PROGRESSION OF RECIDIVISM

*Freedom is a process established over time
through right choices and sound decisions made
within the ranges of socially acceptable standards
which secure individual liberties.*

— THE AUTHOR —

When almost every detail of your life suddenly changes it is a traumatic experience. Trauma is said to be an agent or force of stress that produces a heightened emotional response. According to researchers, certain traumatic experiences involve a common yet wide range of mental and emotional responses. For example, the loss of our freedom is a form of trauma, and it will trigger a grief process which involves a natural set of mental and emotional responses. The grief of incarceration commonly begins in shock and denial. It proceeds to a kind of bargaining, then anger, guilt and remorse, sadness, and ends in the healing and resolution of acceptance.

We most often associate trauma with experiences of loss and tragedy. However, traumatic experiences do not always have to come from negative experiences. For example, promotion in the military has such a high rate of producing trauma that military psychiatrists gave this experience its own diagnosis – promotion psychosis. It is a disordered behavioral state resulting from severe mental and emotional stress. The trauma of promotion would often trigger the most irrational, illogical, and life damaging behaviors.

Likewise, just as the sudden loss of our freedom triggers trauma and the grief process, suddenly regaining our freedom produces a form of promotion trauma and triggers a common set of mental and emotional responses as we attempt to negotiate our freedom. The highest risk of recidivism for us as ex-offenders occurs within the first twelve months after release. On average nationally, ex-offenders have a one in three chance of getting through the first three years without being re-arrested. Half of all who make poor decisions and are re-arrested will do so within the first six months. Thirty percent of those will be for serious crimes. After five years of crime free living (not five years without being caught), the probability of returning to prison is very low.

What's interesting is that these common mental and emotional responses I have outlined show a promising relationship to the time frames and rates of recidivism found in early, middle, and late reentry. This chapter will map out this unconscious mental progression. If we can identify these responses we can abort them and choose an alternative set of responses geared toward successful reentry transition and permanent reintegration.

The most common mistake ex-prisoners make is to define release as freedom. Freedom is not defined by the momentary event called release or the starting point of the gate. Freedom is a process established over time through right choices and sound decisions made within the ranges of socially acceptable standards which secure individual liberties.

Anything short of this definition threatens the goal of freedom. Freedom is not free for anyone. There is always a price to pay in regard to conduct. Freedom is not given to us as the right to do as we please but instead the liberty to do the right thing and reap the benefits. Once these liberties are established, they can only be maintained through the sober watchfulness of self-restraint.

Those who are released on parole or post-release control still have an active prison number upon release. In these cases, release should be viewed as though you still have a bunk with your name on it. You simply have been given an opportunity to prove you are no longer in need of it. For example, one reentry study found the rate of re-arrest was especially high during the first few hours and days following release. These findings clearly demonstrate freedom is indeed a process of right choices and sound decisions. These individuals were not free at all.

They were simply released and then necessarily re-arrested.

The wise are cautious and avoid danger; fools plunge ahead with reckless confidence
PROVERBS 14:16

MORE OPTIONS REQUIRE CAREFUL DECISIONS

The moment you are released and step out of the gate you will be faced with a multitude of potential options. Many of these options are dangerous and downright destructive. The liberty of options can produce intense frustration and confusion for us as newly released prisoners. We may feel a sense of shock and embarrassment as we realize how dull our skill of deliberation has become. Having spent years or even decades without the liberty of options, it is not surprising so many newly released prisoners make the wrong choice. You can't afford to be overconfident of your ability in this area.

All the available options will present us with a lot of decisions to make. After possibly years of having every minute of your daily routine controlled and dictated by prison authorities, this period of time in early release can be the most stressful and challenging. You can easily feel overwhelmed by the accumulation and concentration of the many large and small decisions faced in early release. You will be in a position where every decision is met with several options. How to choose between these options and make the best decisions can be confusing. Even minor decisions can prompt feelings of intense stress and anxiety.

IT HAPPENED TO ME

I can relate my own experience as a good example. Within five minutes of completing seven years in prison, I was sitting in a restaurant staring at a menu. I was with my mother and two other relatives. The waitress came over to take our orders. Everyone quickly told the waitress what they wanted, but my eyes kept racing up and down the columns of choices. I knew it was my turn to order but the number of options overwhelmed me, and I was literally paralyzed.

The silence grew heavy, and I felt all eyes on me. I thought they might be wondering if I was all right. In an instant I began to panic. I was absolutely shocked that I was paralyzed by such a thing as a menu. I did everything I could in prison to keep my mind sharp. Now I was having a hard time deliberating over a breakfast menu, something people negotiate with little effort. I ended up just ordering anything to ease the anxiety and embarrassment.

For seven years I was not allowed to make very many decisions about what I ate. There wasn't any huge list of options to sort through and deliberate, only minor commissary lists and an occasional special order. I went to the chow hall and ate whatever they put on my tray most of the time. Later we laughed at the event in the restaurant. What I couldn't see was how this event became a warning for some of the challenges ahead of me. I truly understand how ex-prisoners who lack a strong support system and the guidance of a reentry mentor make poor choices and end up back in prison. I've really been there. If you add alcohol, drugs, or a highly charged emotional relationship to this scenario it can become impossible.

Wise people think before they act
PROVERBS 13:16

EQUIPPED FOR RELEASE

Poor decisions led to incarceration. More of the same poor decisions after release can only lead to re-arrest. Aimlessness and lack of direction are major culprits in poor decisions. You will need an accurate map of reality, a designated destination, and a moral compass if you plan to remain free and succeed. Doing what you "feel like" won't cut it anymore. It's time to put principles before preferences. Going to prison is about preferences that led to poor decisions. A map, a destination, and a moral compas lets us know where we came from, where we are, where we need to go, and what road to stay on to get there. Having a reentry mentor is critical. Rules, restrictions, and even incentives are not enough for us to succeed. Only people can love and care about people. You need someone who can support you in those first few critical hours, days, and months that follow release. A mentor can help you think through your options as you navigate the challenging psycho-social stages of reentry.

There is a path before each person that seems right, but ends in death
PROVERBS 14:12

Whatever visions you have of life after release, nothing will be exactly like it was. Our survival depends on recognizing the way things "used to be" and the "good old days" are outdated and no longer work for us. The only option is adapt and live in a new way that establishes our freedom. Release is not freedom. It only offers us an opportunity to develop it. What release does do is trigger the psycho-social stage of reentry called the Euphoric Response stage you will need to navigate.

The reason so many are re-arrested within the first few hours, days, and months after release is in part due to a lack of understanding the dangers and vulnerability created by the Euphoric Response stage of reentry. The mental and emotional responses experienced in this stage help to shed light on why half of all of who are re-arrested within the first three years have it happen within the first six months. To understand how the Euphoric Response stage can affect you, it is necessary to discuss ego boundaries and how the trauma of negative and positive experiences can affect them.

In chapter five, The Path of Adult Maturity, we looked at ego boundaries as a potentially unresolved conflict. Outside of any forms of trauma, mature adults know and accept they are individuals confined to the restrictions of their own identities, boundaries, and limits. Healthy ego boundaries help us to understand our limits in regards to others, thriving and remaining free only by our cooperation within a group of fellow human beings called society. Ego boundaries help us to distinguish what's yours and what's mine, what I like or dislike versus what you like or dislike. They allow us to define all that separates us and makes you-you and me-me. Ego boundaries provide the incentive to protect "mine" and respect "yours."

WHEN BOUNDARIES BECOME WALLS
When an experience has a huge impact on us it will alter our ego boundaries in ways that have a powerful effect on us. The difference in our reactions to these

events determines the way our ego boundaries respond. The sudden loss of our freedom will cause our ego boundaries to close in, become more restricted and more distinct. It is a natural defensive reaction to protect ourselves from further loss or threat.

You suddenly see yourself as less connected and more contrasted and separate from the world around you. Your limits become more clear and your actions more carefully planned and calculated for your safety. You become more aware of the rules and the boundaries of others around you and more inhibited about expressing yourself. Basically you have become less open and more on guard to the world around you. Everyone who has suffered the trauma of incarceration has temporarily experienced these reactions within themselves.

WHEN BOUNDARIES COLLAPSE

Suddenly regaining your freedom can have the opposite effect on your ego boundaries.

The Euphoric Response stage of reentry is described as a sudden release of euphoria triggered by a partial collapse of ego boundaries as a result of release from the isolation of confinement. It is an explosive outpouring of powerful emotions, an exaggerated sense of well being, coupled with a type and degree of stress.

This sense of elation is experienced by us as overwhelmingly positive, and in many ways, it is. The intent here is not to say the joy experienced as a result of being released from prison is invalid or unnatural in and of itself. There are few experiences as positive and rewarding as being freed from the confinement of prison. This is especially true when we gradually and consciously choose to EXTEND our boundaries to include the larger world into which we are released.

For most of us it is lonely behind our ego boundaries. This is especially true for the ones we erect while incarcerated. People normally feel their ego boundaries to be more isolating than they wished. There is a natural yearning in all of us to escape from behind the walls of our ego boundaries to a condition more unified and connected to the world outside of ourselves. This is why the Euphoric Responses stage of reentry can feel so right and not at all potentially dangerous.

Let us be sober, (calm, collected, and circumspect)
1 THESSALONIANS 5:6

However, it can produce a disordered behavioral state when boundaries suddenly COLLAPSE and create a state of euphoria. Our boundaries become blurred and our limits are no longer clearly defined. The limits of our power, and where we end and others begin, become uncertain. Our actions become impulsive, less self-restricted, and less carefully planned out.

The result can be the most illogical, irrational, and life damaging behaviors. If you have blurred boundaries as a result of there being an unresolved conflict, the loss of control can be greater. The unreality of these feelings of euphoria are essentially the same as the non-reality of an intense chemical high. The difference is that it is created by an experience and not man-made chemicals.

The pleasure related chemical changes in the brain during the euphoric response are powerful enough to impair judgment, create distortions in perceptions, and influence our decision-making process. This is why some are re-arrested before they make it home or even out of the parking lot of the prison. We have heard the stories and wonder how anybody could ever be so foolish. Whether you do not make it out of the parking lot or you are re-arrested in the following weeks or months, there is little difference. Freedom was never established. No one should consider themselves beyond these dangers. The nature of the Euphoric Response is what causes us to feel unrealistically secure and in control, leaving us vulnerable to outside influences and poor decisions.

Wise choices will watch over you. Understanding will keep you safe
PROVERBS 2:1

For example, it can create the illusion of an exaggerated ability to overcome familiar temptations, leaving us vulnerable to them. The neuro-chemical changes in the brain related to the euphoria can trigger cravings from previous addictions that have been inactive for some time.

It has the potential to leave us unable to perceive potential dangers that may compromise our freedom. The exaggerated sense of well being can cause us to feel we are not in need of any development and move us to rebel against necessary reentry supportive programming. The ex-prisoner in this stage may feel their only need was to be released. They have little or no perception of the work ahead of them that must be done to become free and remain free.

Fools think their way is right, but the wise listen to others
PROVERBS 12:15

CONSIDER THE FOLLOWING SCENARIO
You made it past the initial impact of release without any legal problems. During this period you have been called by a prospective employer. You were surprised and happy to get the call, and you accepted the job you were offered. It requires long hours, and it's hard work. Fresh out of prison, you are just hap-

py to be working. In a short time you are able to purchase a modest car. It's not a new car and it needs a little work, but it's reliable and in decent shape. You have already started doing little things to give it your personal touch. Next, you are finally able to rent your own place. Again, it's modest but it's yours. You pick up some furniture and other things you need as time passes. At this stage of your journey, if you perceive any faults with your circumstances, you perceive them as minor and insignificant.

If you decide to enter into a relationship in this stage of reentry, it brings a whole new set of complications and challenges into rebuilding your life. The sole focus of your reentry is no longer following your mission statement, mapping out your restoration, and protecting the progress you have made. These most important aspects of your reentry may even become secondary to the intense emotional high of the new relationship. Nothing could be more dangerous. No one intends for it to happen that way. It happened because of the attention new relationships require. Even if you try to reassert your boundaries in the name of personal progress, the lines become thin and blurred in the heightened emotions of the relationship.

Charm is deceptive, and beauty does not last; but a woman who fears the Lord will be greatly praised
PROVERBS 31:30

If you perceive any faults with the circumstances of the new relationship, they are perceived as insignificant. The relationship has increased the collapse of your ego boundaries and intensified the euphoria. The relationship seems perfect, and there are no shortcomings or faults that you can see.

Due to the unreality created by the Euphoric Response stage, you are unable to see that your progress toward reintegration has slowed and in some ways it has stopped completely. Life is good. You are riding the wave and enjoying the high. You feel no need of development, and you are content with what you have achieved. The euphoria is real. The perception of the world the euphoria created is not.

THE RETURN TO REALITY

What goes up must come down. Sooner or later, in response to the problems of daily living the Euphoric Responses stage passes. One by one, gradually or suddenly, your ego boundaries snap back into place. The intense joy and emotional high of early release wears off. Once again, you are just another person struggling in a life full of problems and challenges. You have entered the Return to Reality stage.

You once perceived everything in your life as right and any faults as insignificant. Your perceptions of everything somewhere along the line has changed. Nothing is as joyful and rewarding as it was at the point of release. The routine and pressures at work cause you to want to move on even though you lack a full year of employment. You are no longer doing little things to your car; it has become no more than transportation. Your place of residence is no longer your castle. Sometimes it feels just like another prison, and you wonder if you will be stuck there forever.

Each heart know its own bitterness, and no one else can fully share its joy
PROVERBS 14:10

If you have complicated early release with a relationship, it is beginning to present its own set of challenges. The honeymoon ends and the bloom of romance fades. You no longer agree on everything or like all the same things as before. You both begin to see the human imperfections and faults of each other and naturally begin to wonder if you have chosen the right person. The relationship now requires the real work of sacrifice and compromise.

The return to reality from the high of the Euphoric Responses stage has left you feeling disillusioned. You begin to question all your choices and wonder if things will ever change for the better. What your life now represents no longer feels like enough. You no longer feel you are where you should be. Your life no longer feels like a self-enlarging experience.

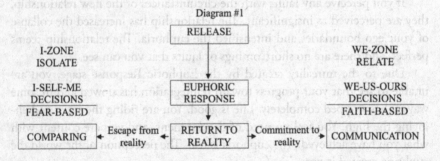

Diagram #1

ESCAPE FROM REALITY

At this point in the Return to Reality stage you will choose one of two ways from which you will attempt to deal with reality. You will either choose to begin the real work of commitment to reality or you will seek alternatives to escape from reality. The Return to Reality from the Euphoric Response stage does not guarantee your view of reality will be accurate. You can really struggle to see the world accurately when making the transition between these stages. The less clearly we see the reality of the world, the more our perceptions can be distorted by falsehoods and misconceptions. Without an accurate view of reality, we will be less capable of determining the correct course of action or be able to make wise decisions.

The prudent understand where they are going, but fools deceive themselves
PROVERBS 14:8

One poor decision and incorrect course of action ex-prisoners commonly make in the Return to Reality stage is the decision to make up for lost time. It is the result of our inability to accurately see where we are in relation to the world we have returned to. If we are unable to accurately see where we are, we will generally be unable to see where we need to go. Without a clearly defined path to move us toward a commitment to reality in reentry, we will become vulnerable to the temptations to escape certain aspects of the realities we face.

The decision to make up for lost time in any area of our life is an attempt to escape from some of those realities. The danger is that it sets us up to move into a progression of mental stages that lead to catastrophe. It naturally involves the desperation and the inclination to become attracted to the path of least resistance and the short cuts that put our freedom at risk. There is one all important truth we must come to terms with when returning to society: There is no such thing as making up for the lost time.

Good planning and hard work lead to prosperity, but hasty shortcuts lead to poverty
PROVERBS 21:5

The desire for progress is a noble human trait. It drives us and in some ways defines us. Genuine progress made from right choices and sound decisions is necessarily slow, so we can manage it. In order to make up for the lost time we must exceed the natural timetables of legitimate progress. This requires we bypass right choices and sound decisions. We begin to lose sight of our promise and obligation to ourselves to never again put our freedom at risk.

This obligation is bullied into submission by our inclination for faster progress. Wanting too much too fast and too soon – and then acting on it – is an immature and undisciplined desire for unreasonable progress. We are carried along by the current of its power, and in our restless striving we trigger the thirst and itch of self obsession. We return to using the maladaptive behaviors we are so familiar with. To move from one stage to the next in this progression only requires that (I-Self-Me) become the primary consideration in our decisions. If others are considered at all, it is only how they can serve as a benefit in the obsession of self.

This isolates us from the life-saving relationships necessary for successful reentry, especially in times of struggle and uncertainty. It fails to see our deep need for God and others who can help us commit to the realities of reentry. We will reach a point where we are imprisoned in our own narrow perspective, or we will reach out and welcome the supportive input of others. We will RELATE or we will begin to ISOLATE. The desperation secures the secrecy. The secrecy secures the isolation. The first stage in our attempt to escape from reality is called comparing.

COMPARING

Comparing begins when we move from measuring our progress by the standard of where we have come from to measuring our progress by the standard of examining the lives and progress of others. Gradually we begin to take notice of the wealth, the richness, and the fullness of the lives of others and we begin to compare it to where we are at right now. We take notice of the old friend's house and the co-worker's car. Our standard of progress becomes the job, the money, the house, the family, the possessions, and the social standing of those around us.

Pay careful attention to your own work, for then you will get the satisfaction of a job well done, and you won't need to compare yourself to anyone else
GALATIANS 6:4

Comparing is not in any way harmless. Left unchecked, comparing is the fuel which feeds our obsession and triggers an unending want that will eventually control our lives. The more we compare, the more everybody seems to be where we need to be and the more restless, irritable, and discontent we become. What we seek to possess as a result of comparing slowly begins to take possession of us before we even acquire it.

COMPARING INCREASES TO COVETING

The self-consuming nature of comparing causes us to place everything we are, our self worth and our self esteem, on acquiring what we believe we need in order to be happy. Once comparing has reached the point of affecting our personal value, it has progressed into the highest level of obsession and the potential danger called coveting. What began as a seemingly harmless admiration toward others for their progress and success has slowly turned into a full-blown lust to posses. Admiration is replaced by frustration.

Coveting arises from comparing when it progresses into a perverted desire for something that does not belong to us. To covet is to set our heart on something we have no legal right to possess, because we have not rightly invested the time and requirements to earn it. Coveting deals with people, places, and things. It is a type of "forbidden fruit" that has always found a way to conquer the hearts of men who stumble into the path of comparing.

Many will believe they are above this gradual slide into self obsession that is so destructive. This stems from false pride and lack of genuine humility towards the real power and potential dangers of the human desire and lust to possess. Pride in this area appeals to the empty head that says, "I deserve it." The lust to possess in this area appeals to the empty heart that says, "I need it." In combination, they are extremely self destructive. Together they secure the irrational belief that we can keep the fires of coveting contained. All the while we keep pouring the fuel of desire on the flames until it consumes us.

Pride leads to disgrace, but with humility comes wisdom
PROVERBS 11:2

America has modeled this thirst for more and lust to possess for the rest of the world. This makes the obsession of comparing and coveting more severe here at home. We are constantly bombarded with advertisements designed for the sole purpose of stirring up a lust for things. It is extremely hard not to compare and covet when you are released from prison. The ex-prisoner who is in this stage is painfully aware of his missed opportunities and material handicaps. It can be completely overwhelming.

Comparing that leads us to covet is so destructive that God spoke against it in His tenth commandment. It is so dangerous because it's not about what we don't have outwardly but what we lack inwardly. It is the empty head and the barren heart that create the distorted desire for the counterfeit things in life. They are counterfeit because they cannot fulfill us.

The barren heart supplies the thirst which supports the irrational belief that more will satisfy the need for importance, value, peace and happiness. This longing has no real connection to things outside ourselves. Since there is no real connection, the more we accumulate, the more we want, the emptier we become. In the end, we don't stop at the neighbor's house and the co-worker's car. It escalates to their wives and their possessions.

You shall not covet your neighbor's house, your neighbor's wife…
or anything that is your neighbor's
EXODUS 20:17

We don't understand that others with whom we compare ourselves can take or leave these things we crave without feeling empty or obsessed. They acquire them as a natural consequence of right living over a substantial period of time. These things are not what controls or defines them. The more we compare, the more we covet, and the further we move away from an accurate map of reality and into a state of confusion.

CONFUSION

The position you now hold in society as a result of the legitimate progress you have made would have been impressive to you, looking at it from the position of your prison bunk.

However, you are no longer connected to the reality of that humble perspective. Confusion that results from comparing has blocked your power of hindsight and will not allow you to see it.

Your current position is no longer accepted as a place of progress. The self obsession that builds momentum in the stage of confusion only allows you to see what you believe is missing.

Reality demands the capacity to strike and re-strike a delicate balance between hindsight (past), insight (present), and foresight (looking ahead). This allows us to develop a flexible response system that aids us in navigating our way through conflicting needs, desires, duties, and responsibilities. The more we are crippled by confusion as a result of comparing, the less flexible we are able to be. Insight is not available to help us maintain an accurate map of the present reality. We are unable to see that our current position has no logical point of reference in the life of others.

For wherever there is jealousy (envy) and contention (rivalry and selfish ambition), there will also be confusion, (unrest, disharmony, rebellion) and all sorts of evil and vile practices
JAMES 3:16

Without a flexible response system, foresight is not available to help us map out a realistic plan of progress. We cannot look forward to the prospects and potentials that belong to us while looking into the lives of others. Without the foresight to move forward, we cannot stop obsessing on the belief we are stuck where we are long enough to see where we need to go. As confusion increases, so do the anxiety, insecurity, and fear that leaves our response system completely inflexible. Comparing and confusion leave us unable to accurately perceive and respond to the world around us.

While you have not yet isolated yourself physically from others, your thought life has increased in isolation since entering the stage of confusion. You dare not let others know what is going on in your head for fear of being exposed. If you are a drug and alcohol user, at this point you may use them to replace the emotional connection you are moving away from in your relationships. This intensifies the confusion and lessens the ability to manage it.

In spite of the secrecy and isolation in your thinking, your comments and conversations expose your confusion as you begin to use words that have no connection to reality. You focus on the way you believe things should be, could be, would be, ought to be, and if only. Such words demonstrate the self image of one who, as a result of confusion, has unknowingly surrendered their power of choice. They are the words of a person who is completely directed by external forces beyond their control.

Guard yourselves and keep free from all covetousness (the immoderate desire for wealth, the greedy longing to have more); for a man's life does not consist in and is not derived from possessing an overflowing abundance or that which is over and above his needs
LUKE 12:15

Since we are unable to recognize comparing and confusion as the source of our restlessness, irritability, and discontent, we are unable to see ourselves as the source of the problem. We fail to recognize the need for self examination. Instead, we initiate the blame game. When we blame someone else, the system, racism, the spouse, and bad breaks for our problem, our problems persist. Casting away our responsibility may momentarily ease the pain, yet we cease to solve the problems of living and we cease to mature and grow.

Our obsession for the way things "should be" in our lives will not accept the timetables required to get us there through legitimate means. Left uninterrupted by the relationships that can help us abort this process, comparing and confusion lead us to a point where we become open to whatever means necessary to get us to the way we believe things "should be." We are about to become a liability as we cast our pain on society through compromise.

Compromise is defined as the unwillingness to suffer now in faith of future satisfaction, and opting for short cuts and quick fixes, in the hope that future consequences can be avoided. The willingness to compromise is a defective approach to problem solving. All plans and decisions are based on (I-Self-Me) without regard for others. This selfish and destructive approach is an impatient and inadequate attempt to find instant solutions for problems that require long term answers.

Compromise begins when we experience so much discomfort as a result of comparing, coveting, and confusion that we demand an immediate solution. We are not willing to tolerate the discomfort long enough to analyze the problem. Instead of representing sound and mature reasoning, the solutions we devise for problem solving only represent gratification of some irrational need. The result is our solutions are grossly inappropriate and illogical, even while they appear as a reasonable calculations to us.

Those who crave to be rich fall into...a snare and into many foolish...and hurtful desires that plunge men into ruin and destruction and miserable perishing
I TIMOTHY 6:9

Compromise always requires a major investment on our part. What we fail to see is the investment on our part is always far greater than any potential return on that investment.

Webster's Dictionary defines compromise as to expose to danger, loss of reputation and disgrace. The word danger in Webster's definition means to expose ourselves to the loss of life, liberty, freedom, rights, choices, and all the invaluable and irreplaceable things those represent. Friends, it's a sad state of existence to be in when we think there is any "thing" out there worth a risky investment of these most precious possessions. Yet this is exactly what we do in the stage of compromise.

Compromise begins in the little details of how we mismanage the use of our precious liberty and accelerates into bigger things. Compromise is the ex-drug dealer who decides to deal a little on weekends or shoots for that one big deal; the ex-thief that sees what he believes is the perfect heist laid right in his lap. It is the ex-robber who lays out that one big score to get him where he believes he needs to be. You name the act of compromise. They are as endless as the limits of the human obsession to covet, lust, and possess.

[Live] as free people, [yet] without employing your freedom as a pretext for wickedness;
but [live at all times] as servants of God
1 PETER 2:16

COMPOUNDING FORCES

Comparing, confusion, and compromise are destructive forces in which each adds momentum to the other. They are oppressive forces we invite into our lives in an attempt to avoid the pain of reality. These forces compound in their destructive power, and together they nudge us to the jumping off point of "all or nothing."

Diagram #2

Comparing		Confusion		Compromise
	X		X	Instant Satisfaction
Coveting	FEAR	Hindsight	FEAR	Drugs/Alcohol (if use)
Jealousy		Insight		Physical isolation
Envy	No=	Foresight		Criminal behavior
Restless		Should have		
Irritable		Could have		
Discontent	Non-Reality=	Would have		
		If only		

Compromise is an act of desperation to avoid the conditions that exist. It is an attempt to avoid the pain of assuming responsibility for our own conditions. We paint ourselves into a corner with justification. We claim life isn't fair. We say we are not getting a fair chance. We protest no one is helping us in the way we feel we deserve. These voices determine our choices by creating a sense of helplessness and hopelessness. It is an inner conviction of being unable to cope and to change things through legitimate methods. By doing this we create a sense of powerlessness for ourselves. We feel powerless because we have, in fact, given away our power the moment we started on a path to escape reality.

Greedy people try to get rich quick but don't realize they're headed for poverty
PROVERBS 28:22

It is no doubt painful to watch others in a place we have not yet reached. It is a place we consider in this stage of life we might have been "if only". There are not many happy and content people in the land of "if only". This pain is a result of the choices we have made. We can't afford to let this pain move us into more bad choices that end in the same old consequences. Yet this is where compromise always takes us.

There are indeed oppressive forces at work in the world. No one is immune to these forces. We have the freedom to choose how we respond to these forces every step of the way if we are willing to face reality with the weapon of truth. To compromise is to forfeit this freedom. Compromise sets us up to sacrifice all our freedoms. It sets us up for the final stage of this progression called catastrophe.

CATASTROPHE

In our defective approach to problem solving called compromise, we become willing to ignore all that is rational, reasonable, and logical in order to avoid the pain of problem solving. We take drugs and drink alcohol to assist us. We lie, cheat, betray, and manipulate. We build the most elaborate fantasies to the total exclusion of reality in order to avoid the pain life's challenges and struggles present. Problems compound as a result of avoidance, and we turn our problems into trouble. The drugs and alcohol, the quick fixes and the short cuts, become more painful than the reality they are designed to avoid.

Here on earth you will have many trials and sorrows
JOHN 16:33

In desperation and without discipline we try to apply the same remedy to our new trouble as we did our old problems. Since avoidance didn't work with our original problems, it is irrational to think it will work with our new found trouble: the lost job, relationship problems, the drugs and alcohol, and the illegal activity that is increasingly difficult to keep hidden and secret.

In our attempts to escape reality and the pain of problem solving inherent in it, we build layer upon layer of trouble into our lives until it explodes into the sudden and terrible event called catastrophe.

Problems and trouble represent something potentially manageable and correctable in size. Catastrophe, on the other hand, represents something that cannot be managed or fixed as it occurs due the immensity of its impact. The loss of life, liberty, and freedom are major catastrophes. Like a tornado it cannot be stopped. All we can do is hold on until it passes. Once it passes we can clean up the mess and put our lives back together if we survive the self-inflicted storm.

When the storms of life come, the wicked are whirled away,
but the godly have a lasting foundation
PROVERBS 10:25

There is an important difference between problems and trouble. Life is naturally a continual series of problems that require solving. Trouble is something we create as a result of our unwillingness to address problems before they turn into trouble. Life is naturally a never-ending series of struggles and conflicts that create fear, anger, anxiety, and frustration. We call these struggles and conflicts "problems" because the challenge of solving them evokes these painful emotions.

Since life is a never-ending series of struggles and conflicts we call problems, life will often be painful and no one who steps out to involve themselves in the world is immune to it. The very act of stepping out into the world and facing these unending series of struggles and conflicts are what gives our lives meaning. In some very real ways, facing them not only defines us but reveals us to ourselves through the character responding to them.

Struggles and conflict create challenge with the potential prospects of success as well as failure. The challenge of problems and their prospects of success and failure depend on our discipline. They call forth and enlarge our discipline through the actions of facing and resolving them. It is only by accepting the challenge of problems and suffering through their pain to resolve them that we mature and grow. They encourage the growth of our spirit and the growth of our character. No honorable challenge – no character.

Dear friends, don't be surprised by the fiery trials you are going through,
as if something strange were happening to you
1 PETER 4:12

For some of us, success is more fearful than failure. We know failure. It is not only familiar to us but seems expected of us by others. Somewhere along the journey of life some of us may have convinced ourselves it is easier to remain a failure than to attempt success and face the pain of new failure. This is not how life works. It is illogical to think so. If we choose to remain in failure and opt not to try and solve life's problems, failure in larger degrees and greater intensity just keeps coming at us.

We continue in this pattern of trying to escape the reality of our problems until it wears us out mentally, emotionally, and physically. We reach a point where we can go no longer maintain the false pretense. Catastrophe hits like a tornado roaring through our lives and the lives of those involved with us. It destroys everything we have built. There is little of anything left to show we existed in the free world as we are carted back to prison. It was a storm brewing in the distance a long time, but we refused to acknowledge it was coming.

In the wake of our storm are the devastated lives we've left behind – the family, friends, and many victims of our crimes. We leave broken hearts, broken dreams, broken families, broken promises, broken trust, lost hope, and broken lives that others must rebuild once we are gone.

Without even realizing it, we head back to prison still caught up in the self obsession of the old self. We are often never required to look back – which is unfair to everyone. We hide in a familiar place of responsibility – free living with three hot meals and a bunk. We hide in our domino and poker games, our commissary lists, and our recreational activities. We still live our lives avoiding reality and the emotional pain of problem-solving.

The challenge lies not in the difficulty of facing reality, but in the willingness to suffer through the problems reality creates. When we avoid reality and the natural pain involved in problem-solving we also miss out on the necessary growth we need to remain free. To learn to live free is to suffer and grow. It is the only way to remain free.

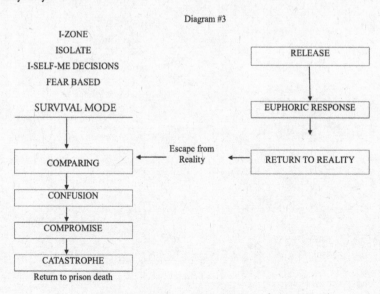

Diagram #3

Take a few moments to consider the newly discovered challenges developing your freedom may present.

- How has this chapter changed the way you will monitor your adjustment upon release?
- What role will relationships play in your ability to overcome the challenges presented in this chapter? What other tools can you incorporate?

With the answers to these questions in mind, let's look at the next chapter and discover the most important tools for developing our freedom.

CHAPTER EIGHT

Psycho-Social Stages of Reentry (Part Two)

———~~~———

THE PRINCIPLES OF ACCLIMATION

*Acclimation: the process of becoming accustomed to a new
climate, surroundings, or conditions of a social system.*

*"A principle – as its very name implies – is something
which comes first. A principle is a master key which opens a thousand locks;
a compass which will guide you, even on an uncharted sea."*
— E.M. STANDING —

The issues we suffer from that have sabotaged our lives do not just go away with the time we serve. They must be worked through or they forever remain a barrier to our freedom. The return to reality from the Euphoric Response stage involves aspects of our reentry that are painful. Our natural tendency may be to take the path of least resistance and attempt to escape from painful aspects of that reality.

Just because something is a natural tendency doesn't make it right, or even inescapable. In order to move away from the direction of our natural tendencies upon release, we must incorporate a set of acclimation principles. These acclimation principles are, in reality, tools of discipline. These tools of discipline are what we use to build a series of bridges from one stage to the next in a consciously chosen path from release to freedom. These stages are revealed in the next four chapters.

Without these acclimation principles, called tools of discipline, it will not be possible to enter these stages and transition from one stage to the next. These acclimation principles are requirements for our freedom. A life of freedom always requires discipline. Little discipline means little freedom. Total discipline means complete freedom.

COMMITMENT TO TRUTH
[THE FIRST REQUIREMENT FOR FREEDOM]

And you will know the truth, and the truth will set you free
JOHN 8:32

A total commitment to truth is the first and most important principle for establishing our freedom. Truth allows us to navigate through every aspect of reality we encounter upon reentry. Without truth we lack the ability to deal with reality, and we are powerless to solve life's problems. When we have no map to navigate the realities we face, we will attempt to escape a crisis when we feel lost. The challenge is, however, that the truth we need to navigate us through the realities in our lives can be just as painful as or more painful than the realities before us. Without a willingness to face the pain of problem solving, we will attempt to escape both truth and reality. Either facing or attempting to escape truth and reality is often extremely painful. The only difference is not so much the pain but the outcome.

DEVASTATING WRONG TURNS

Most of us realize deception flourishes at every level of human existence. Deception on the journey of life, whether temporary or for our entire lives, is always a form of being lost. No one likes to admit they have been deceived because no one wants to deal with the terror and vulnerability of being lost. The idea of being lost, and therefore vulnerable, creates intense fear because survival is about knowing where we are at all times.

In many ways, prison is the land of the lost. They put people there who have lost their way. The hope is that by the time they are released they will no longer be lost. They will better understand their way and where they need to go in order to survive. In our search for happiness we have bought into deception, and we have become lost. We have chosen paths we thought would give us everything we wanted. Instead they took everything we had.

The way of peace they know not, and there is no justice or right in their goings. They have made them into crooked paths; whoever goes in them does not know peace
ISAIAH 59:8

The loss of human life we call incarceration results when we base our choices on unreliable sources of truth. We trust our own uncensored logic, our feelings, or even the influences of others. As a result, we inaccurately read the reality before us, and we navigate ourselves into a devastating wrong turn.

THE PERFECT LAW OF LIBERTY

The most important decision we can make is to be willing to investigate the Word of God with our reentry mentor and other men in a fellowship group. Over time, we can decide through actual experience if its principles are the perfect standard for manhood and for ultimate authority for navigating reality. Through research, reflection, and application, we can come to our own conclusion that it is an illuminating light revealing "the perfect law of liberty."

But he who looks carefully into the faultless law, the [law] of liberty, and is faithful to it and perseveres in looking into it, being not a heedless listener who forgets but an active doer [who obeys], he shall be blessed in his doing (his life of obedience)
JAMES 1:25

I ask you, was it not liberation we sought in all the things that promised much and provided little? You know it was. We sought what we thought were increasing levels of liberation and freedom. Our penalties show that our logic has been terribly wrong and reveals our desperate need for truth. We thought liberty and freedom came from abandoning the law. The exact opposite is true. Our own experiences show, and "the perfect law of liberty" testifies, that liberty and freedom come through the law, not apart from it. Without a map and a perfect standard for truth, we incorrectly navigated this reality and became its prisoner.

TRUTH OVER COMFORT

Learning how to live free in society requires that we make revisions, sometimes major revisions in our view of truth. In order for our revisions to be accurate, we must first decide to be totally committed to truth whatever the cost. We must determine to hold truth to be more important than any personal comforts or interests. In pursuit of freedom and success, our personal discomfort upon release must be held as relatively unimportant. Without this type of commitment and determination upon release, we will gravitate back to the familiar and return to manipulating the world around us to conform to our inaccurate view of truth. We can never afford to forget; actively clinging to an inaccurate view of truth and our inability to accurately navigate reality has been the basis for all our problems.

COMMITMENT TO HEALTHY RELATIONSHIPS
[THE SECOND REQUIREMENT FOR FREEDOM]

There is safety in having in many advisers
PROVERBS 11:14

Nothing shapes our lives more than the relationships we make, because there is nowhere else to learn how to live, relate, and love. Our ability to accomplish these tasks is determined by the sum total of our relationships, past and present. It cannot be found in the books we read, the courses we take, or the information we accumulate. It cannot be found in the isolation of our own efforts, because the lifelong process of learning how to live, relate, and love is the process of growing and maturing. The relational qualities and their dynamics that nurture this process can only be experienced in the environment of healthy relationships.

It requires the environment of relationship to learn and then practice the qualities of trust, honesty, integrity, accountability, and other qualities that guide us into new levels of maturity.

They are not qualities that naturally come with age, nor are they a normal part of every adult relationship. They must be sought with conviction and intention and can only be found in the right type of relationship – a relationship of morality and virtue and the mutually shared conviction of their value for success.

> *So that you may surely learn to sense what is vital, and approve and prize*
> *what is excellent and of real value*
> *[recognizing the highest and the best and distinguishing the moral differences]*
> PHILIPPIANS 1:10

THE COST OF RELATIONAL IMMATURITY

Relationships are also the environment that puts these qualities to the test. Our broken relationships, unhealthy relationships, and lack of relationships are convincing and convicting testimonies to our lack of maturity and relational issues. Our separation from society and incarceration should provide the final personal conviction.

If we are willing to be honest with ourselves, our lives didn't just fall apart as a result of poor luck or bad circumstances. The truth is, in our relationships we have perfected the art of selfish concealing instead of unselfish revealing, selfish hiding instead of unselfish confiding, and selfish repressing instead of unselfish confessing. The necessary qualities that lead us to learn how to live, relate, and love have been more of an ideal than an actual meaningful experience in our lives. Our lives of pretending the ideal while avoiding or longing for the real is evidence of our need for growth and healthy relationships.

> *Let us not become vainglorious and self conceited, competitive and challenging and*
> *provoking and irritating to one another, envying and being jealous of one another*
> GALATIANS 5:26

We have chosen our relationships out of comfort and convenience rather than conviction. These types of relationships offer us the best relational environment for avoiding and concealing who we really are. Relationships that are chosen out of comfort and convenience are immature relationships, and do not foster the qualities that challenge us to mature and grow. They teach us little or nothing about how to live, relate, and love. They operate under the dynamics of shallow, self-centered convenience and protecting one another's comfort zones. Relationships help develop us, or they help destroy us, either way they will define us. There is an old proverb that says, "Show me your friends and I will tell you who you are."

We have been prone to what I call "selective isolation." Our natural tendency has been to "SELECT" relationships out of comfort and convenience and "ISOLATE" ourselves from the kind of people who could really help us grow and mature. Selective isolation allows fantasy to play a big part in our daily lives. We can be anybody we want to be – without being challenged, questioned, or confronted. This possibly more than anything else helps to keep us locked in a world of extreme self-obsession. Breaking out of this selective isolation, however painful and unnatural for us, is a crucial step to a life of growing, maturing and bringing lasting freedom.

THE NEED FOR RELATIONAL MATURITY

On the other hand, when relationships are chosen out of conviction, the very foundation of those relationships is the shared values and qualities that foster growth and maturity. There is a strong conviction of faith that there is a mutually shared value placed on the inner qualities of a strong and mature character. Not only do you have a strong conviction of the importance of morality and virtue for your own welfare, but a strong sense of conviction that the other person shares in these same convictions as well. When these are the dynamics of choosing our relationships, we are choosing relationships out of deep conviction, rather than any comfort, pleasure, or convenience it may provide.

The dynamics of mature relationships present the exact opposite of those shared in immature relationships. The mutual agreement is that the value placed on these qualities is above any personal discomfort or inconvenience. There is mutual trust, mutual honesty, authenticity, and integrity, regardless of the discomfort or inconvenience it might create. The mutual honoring of these relational values is, in reality, a mutual honoring of each other for the purpose of growing and maturing.

Don't just pretend to love others. Really love them. Hate what is wrong. Hold tightly to what is good. Love each other with genuine affection, and take delight in honoring each other. Be happy with those who are happy, and weep with those who weep. Live in harmony with each other. Don't be too proud to enjoy the company of ordinary people. And don't think you know it all!
ROMANS 12:9-10, 15-16

Learning how to live, relate, and love will never be possible until we humble ourselves, open our hearts, and become transparent to God and others who have no other interest than helping us to become what we need to become. It is one of the most difficult things that must be done on this "wilderness journey," but it must be done. Hiding and masking our true inner person by avoiding healthy relationships will only keep us locked in perpetual immaturity. Our immaturity will keep us in perpetual opposition to the beliefs, rules, and needs our society holds sacred. You may institute all the other principles and disciplines in this book into your life, but if you fail with this one relational principle, all your efforts are likely to be in vain.

If you are wearing state blues or have worn them, you need the help of other people.

There is simply no way around this. If you could have handled it on your own, you would have already done so, before it led to incarceration. But we can't. Some of our problems are deeply ingrained. They have become part of our identity and are simply too big to solve on our own. We can only remain committed to truth and navigate the realities of reentry by being deeply involved with others who are totally committed to truth. The journey from release to freedom is a journey of never ending commitment to healthy relationships.

COMMITMENT TO PERSONAL RESPONSIBILITY
[THE THIRD REQUIREMENT FOR FREEDOM]

For we are each responsible for our own conduct
GALATIANS 6:5

Men often believe they know something and can claim it as their own if they understand it conceptually and can regurgitate it verbally. "I am personally responsible for my life upon release from prison." In asking many inmates this question for the purpose of this chapter, everyone of them understood their personal responsibility in this area in a general sense. The truth of the matter is, we can only claim a meaningful experience with personal responsibility if we are consistently living it. If we are consistently living it we will find our personal responsibility is affecting the hundreds of decisions we make every day.

For years, maybe even for our entire lives, we have been consistent in shaping and perfecting a lifestyle of avoiding personal responsibility. We have accomplished this by developing a lifestyle of instant gratification and selfish indulgence while avoiding meaningful commitments and the pain of problem solving. It would be safe to say we know these things and can claim them as our own. This doesn't mean we have never had an encounter with personal responsibility or never experienced discipline. What it does mean is we cannot claim a lifestyle of personal responsibility as our own because it has not been a consistent part of our life and molded into the shaping of our character.

Those who are wise will find a time and a way to do what is right, for there is a time and a way for everything, even when a person is in trouble
ECCLESIASTES 8:5

You would think it would be obvious to us that we cannot get out of prison and cast the responsibility of remaining free on society and the circumstances life offers us. Without even being aware of it, I was guilty of this on more than one release from prison. I have talked with countless others who have shared the intimate details of their return to prison as a result of casting responsibility of remaining free elsewhere. It's not a matter of conscious choice but rather a lack of commitment to truth. Without this commitment we are unlikely to see just how inappropriate this is.

The relationship fails, so we turn back to the drugs and alcohol. We lose the job and we return to dealing and stealing. The demands at the halfway house are tough so we walk away. We thought things would go according to our preconceived visions and plans upon release. We envisioned exactly how things should go with the family or the business venture but they didn't work out that way. We had expectations and if we managed it just right, things would go exactly like we planned. When things don't always go well we blame life and throw in the towel.

Behind every one of these stories is an unconscious choice to cast our responsibility of remaining free on these sources. When we do this we cast away our power. The attempt to cast responsibility for our lives anywhere besides ourselves is an attempt to escape from freedom, and it always works.

We have been especially drawn to the things that require little and promise much. It never really works out and we still don't get it yet. The inability to see beyond what is easiest and most rewarding at the present moment is one of the most consistently grounded elements of our character. Our lives have been governed by short term thinking. We have paid severe penalties for our inability to think of end results and the long term. Focusing on pleasure and avoiding the pain of problem solving has been our greatest enemy of accepting personal responsibility.

Once we are released we can only act out of the substance of what we consist of as men. The less responsible and the more undisciplined we live, the more our character is stripped and gutted of anything of real substance. Sadly, there are many who will never accept personal responsibility for their lives.

They will never see that they are constantly being held accountable because they are personally responsible for their freedom.

No problem we face upon release can be solved until we solve it. Responsibility is simply respond-ability. The ability to respond, but also the willingness to respond in the most appropriate manner that protects our freedom. No one is exempt from distinguishing between what we are and what we are not responsible for, as well as determining the best possible method for meeting our responsibilities. These are two of the greatest challenges of human existence.

Throughout our entire lives we must continually assess and reassess where our responsibilities lie in the ever-changing course of events. It is only through a willingness to accept personal responsibility for our lives, a commitment to truth, and our relationships with others who are committed to truth, that we gain the capacity to see the world accurately and access our responsibility to it. A life of freedom is a life of personal responsibility.

COMMITMENT TO SELF EXAMINATION
[THE FOURTH REQUIREMENT FOR FREEDOM]

But let every person carefully scrutinize and examine and test his own conduct
GALATIANS 6:4

At some point in life we have to give up our delusions of self importance and of having it all together if we want to grow up and experience our own mature and authentic self. These issues are at the core of our criminality, and we have lacked the self awareness to recognize it.

The fact that we would strongly defend our maturity and our ability to manage our lives in light of having to be removed from society for its security and order shows the tremendous lack of self-examination in our lives. It is only through a continual, never ending self-examination that we discover who we are and where we are at on our journey in life.

DEFENSES THAT BLOCK SELF EXAMINATION
About the time of adolescence we discover that examining certain aspects of the reality of the world are painful. We also discover that self examination is even more painful. To avoid this pain we began to censor certain realities about the world – and even more realities about ourselves. For a long time we have built up the emotional energy that thickens the walls of our denial and delusion about ourselves. We have refused to accept certain realities about ourselves and have created false beliefs that have no basis in reality.

This emotional wall created by our defenses has left our self-awareness severely limited.

We are in a very dangerous position. We cannot see who we are and where we are in our development and our defenses will not allow anyone to tell us. The most powerful way to remove the block of emotional energy that holds up the walls of our defenses is through pain and suffering. Without it, we are unlikely to see a need for a level of self-examination that looks at the harshest realities about ourselves.

When the pain and suffering are intense enough, they instruct our awareness in ways with which we cannot argue. If we begin to experience pain and suffering from our denial and delusion that is greater than the painful truth we have avoided, the walls of our defenses come tumbling down. We can no longer hold up our defenses against our inner pain. What hurts gets our attention in a way nothing else can.

THE BIRTH OF SELF EXAMINATION

If the pain is strong enough to completely break down our defenses, the sudden impact brings us face to face with a willingness to examine ourselves. Something quite revolutionary is taking place on the inside of us. We experience a tremendous upheaval of our inner world. We have come face to face with the self-obsessed beast within, and we are repulsed by our own immature selfish nature. For the first time in our lives we feel profoundly defiled by it in ways we cannot describe. We are completely disgusted over the hidden levels of our selfish depravity and totally shocked by our ignorance of our own true inner condition.

Our prideful self-obsession is dealt a severe and precise blow by a genuine remorse that penetrates the deepest regions of our hardened heart. We have been pierced to a level never before reached, and we become horrified by the enormity of the inner self violation that has taken place. We have an overwhelming sense of being utterly undone by the betrayal of our own hands and the enemy within. We now hate what we have become more than we hate being locked up.

We begin to experience a change of heart that has, at its genesis, the potential to transform our entire life. Like many in that same jail cell before us, we no longer avoid the concept of God, but cry out to Him, hoping He is there and listening. This level of self-examination has led to true poverty of spirit. This is the painful birth of self-examination that a man – who has been removed from society for its own welfare, will necessarily need to experience.

I am glad now, not because you were pained, but because you were pained into repentance [that turned you to God]; for you felt a grief such as God meant you to feel. For godly grief and the pain God is permitted to direct, produce a repentance that leads to and contributes to salvation and deliverance from evil, and it never brings regret. For

[you can look back now and observe] what this same godly sorrow has done for you and
has produced in you...
2 CORINTHIANS 7:9, 10, 11

ADMITTING AND SOCIAL COMPLIANCE

If immediate action does not follow our self-examination we run the risk of
falling into complacency. Awareness without action – complacency at any level – gives our strong emotional defenses time to rebuild their energies and
bounce back. When this happens, we usually make it no further than admitting our problems, which leads to some form of social compliance. This is a
common but serious problem among incarcerated men.

Admitting a problem exists and social compliance result from guilt, and
allow us to acknowledge the harmful yet obvious consequences without having to accept the destructive underlying causes. Guilty people fear punishment
and try to escape it in the most creative ways. I have misled many counselors, judges, and parole board members through admittance and compliance.
I completed all the programs and even worked as a program aid. I had the
appearance of all the right actions without any real and significant change. It
represented my covert methods of fighting against consequences in a totally
self-referential way, while still preserving their causes in my heart.

A level of self-examination that only leads us to admitting our problems
and compliance is not the same as a level of self-examination that moves us
into change. A level of self-examination that moves us into change means that
we are beginning to let go of our childlike illusions that tell us we know it all
while still believing in nothing. It means we are willing to listen to someone
else and do it their way, rather than our way, which may continue in a cycle of
incarceration.

ADMITTING VERSUS ACCEPTANCE

There are profound distinctions between admitting and acceptance. Admitting
something is a form of mental reasoning that allows us to conclude that a problem exists. Acceptance carries the same mental conclusions as admitting but
carries with it an emotional awareness that continues to carry us into deeper
levels of self examination and change. Acceptance is therefore often described
as a feeling of knowing in our hearts that moves us toward the self preserving
actions involved in change. It could be said that acceptance is motivated by
a level of emotional awareness that leads us to surrender to a specific type of
authority. What have you admitted to – yet still refuse to genuinely accept?

Consider your ways (your previous and present conduct) and how you have fared
HAGGAI 1:7

For example, we can admit there are laws that govern our society without accepting them and obeying them. We can admit there is a God without accepting His principles for living and His authority. We can admit we have committed crimes against society without accepting the underlying causes that led to incarceration.

While it is often painful, acceptance that results from self examination breaks down all barriers of delusion and denial. It puts us in touch with our healthy, God-given sense of shame that lets us experience that we are finite and limited; that we need God and others. Acceptance puts us in a state of willingness to embrace the root causes of our incarceration, and even embrace our punishment. Without self examination that leads to acceptance, we will never be able to embrace the pain of growth and change. We won't make self examination a part of our daily lives nor welcome the level of intimacy with God and competent caring men who can help us get there. My hope is that we can all get there.

Let us test and examine our ways, and let us return to the Lord
LAMENTATIONS 3:40

If you have experienced self-examination that gives birth to acceptance, you are already a work in progress. It means self-examination is a part of your daily life. A commitment to truth, our relationships with others who are committed to truth, personal responsibility, and self-examination will lead us to a profound revelation. We come to realize the sources of danger and failure lie more within us than around us.

COMMITMENT TO CHALLENGE
[THE FIFTH REQUIREMENT FOR FREEDOM]

Let us exalt and triumph in our troubles and rejoice in our suffering, knowing that pressure and affliction and hardship produce patient and unswerving endurance. And endurance (fortitude) develops maturity of character...
ROMANS 5:3, 4

If we are to remain committed to truth in our pursuit of freedom, we will remain committed to challenge. Life is full of challenge for those actively involved in it. The more actively involved we are, the more challenge we will encounter. The truth is, we are faced with an enormous amount of challenge coming into prison and in returning to society. Our level of commitment to the challenges we face coming into prison will determine how well equipped we are to face the challenges in our return to society.

To attempt to avoid challenge is to attempt to avoid life. The very reason we call something a challenge is because it stretches us mentally, emotionally, and spiritually beyond our current measure. It is because of the pain involved in this stretching that we seek to buffer or completely avoid challenge. When we attempt to avoid challenge, we are, in effect, attempting to avoid the growth that life is offering us.

CHALLENGE AND THE CROSSROADS OF INCARCERATION

Our incarceration represents a very real crossroads in our lives. We can stay on the old road, or we can take the new road – the high road which means fighting the right wars and choosing the right battles, that all exist within us, not around us. All we need is enough fear and we will fight any battle around us. There is nothing impressive or manly about that. However, when it comes to facing our transgressions against God and others, our defects of character, and our addictions that brought us to prison, the journey can only begin with real courage to commit ourselves to these challenges.

Everyone has problems. Everyone! The difference for us is that our unwillingness to face the challenges inherent in them have caused us to be removed from society. It's time to take off our mask and stop pretending we have it all together as we walk around in state blues. It's time to face the real challenges we conceal deep within us and step into healing and freedom.

Pride is a stern master. It demands we hide our faults at the expense of our freedom and project an image of having everything under control. False pride and the courage we need to be committed to life's challenges are absolutely incompatible. This crossroads asks each of us daily, "Which one will you choose, pride or courage?"

Humility and courage are closely related and are part of a mentally healthy person. Humility lifts us above the barriers that hold us back from the best life has for us, because humility builds relational bridges over the barriers and helps provide support and answers to the challenges we face. When we have some degree of humility we realistically see our prison experience as a need to accept the challenge to grow into greater levels of maturity.

Do nothing from factional motives [through contentiousness, strife, selfishness, or for unworthy ends] or promoted by conceit and empty arrogance. Instead, in the true spirit of humility (lowliness of mind) let each regard the others as better than and superior to himself [thinking more highly of one another than you do of yourselves]
PHILIPPIANS 2:3

Growth and maturity are naturally a lifelong experience. No one is "already" matured. It is an endless continuum of progress that provides greater freedom with greater levels of maturity. No matter how far we travel on this road, there is always more road to travel. It is important to understand, then, that it is all about the journey. Without our total commitment to challenge, we cannot travel very far on this journey. With our total commitment to challenge, with God's help, and other competent caring men, we can continue to evolve the way we think, develop new habits, and little by little, put our defects and barriers to freedom behind us.

Pride and humiliation are closely related, and are not part of a mentally healthy mind set. They are based on a deadly combination of an exaggerated level of self importance that simply does not exist and fear. Pride builds thick walls around us and between us and other people – and denies our need to change. It continues to fight the battles around it in order to avoid the challenges within.

Pride ends in humiliation, while humility brings honor
PROVERBS 29:23

Few experiences we encounter in life are as humbling or as humiliating as incarceration.

It is humiliating if pride is part of our mind set. We feel humiliated when we believe we are experiencing something beneath us or that is unjustly administered. The focus of pride is self-centeredness and self obsession, and anything that gets in the way of these is unjustly administered.

Incarceration is a humbling experience when we relate it to our actions toward others and society. Contrary to pride's belief, humility is not thinking less of yourself. It is thinking of yourself less and thinking of yourself realistically. What was your incarceration experience, humiliating or humbling? If it was humbling, you are humbled by it daily.

CHALLENGE AND THE CROSSROADS OF REENTRY

No areas of life are exempt from challenge because no areas of life are completely free from learning and problem solving. Unfortunately, there will be many who will face reentry without being aware of this simple and essential truth. If we do not expect challenge and even welcome it upon release, we will be ambushed by it. Unexpected challenge is likely to be unwelcome challenge and perceived as an attack or threat. In such cases, we will not be able to see how we can grow from it and become more as a result, and ready for bigger challenges in the future.

We can never afford to begin reentry harboring some irrational belief that our challenges are unique, unfair, or especially burdensome. It is as if we believe life should be easy and when it's not, it's simply unfair. Since life is full of challenge for those actively involved in it, nothing could be further from the truth. We cannot always pick and choose what challenges we fill face upon reentry. Without remaining committed to challenge in reentry, we will take the path of least resistance instead of the path of freedom and growth.

In the cycle of our lives there will be periods of intense challenge. Reentry is likely to be one of those periods. It is a natural part of rebuilding our life in a completely different environment than the one in which we have been living. For this reason, we need to constantly remind ourselves in reentry, "My challenges are average."

COMMITMENT TO THE EXAMINATION AND CHALLENGE OF OTHERS
[THE SIXTH REQUIREMENT FOR FREEDOM]

Likewise, you who are younger and of lesser rank, be subject to the elders
(the ministers and spiritual guides of the church) –
[giving them due respect and yielding to their counsel]"
I PETER 5:5

A life of freedom and truth also means a life of commitment to the examination and challenge of others. For many of us, this is likely to be the hardest tool of discipline to sharpen and the toughest step to take. The tendency to avoid the examination and challenge of others has been present in human beings since the fall of man. It is one of the major traits of our fallen human nature but calling it part of our nature does not mean that is beneficial and life enhancing. There exists in each of us a potential to overcome negative and destructive tendencies and replace them with habits that truly benefit our lives.

If we are not willing to use the wisdom and the eyes of others to help us see who we are, where we are, and where we need to go, our chances of freedom are less than promising. The only way we can be certain that a chosen perception about the reality of reentry is accurate is to expose it to the examination and challenge of others who are committed to a life of truth.

However, the potential pain involved in exposing our thoughts and desires can lead us to avoid any challenge to their validity and exposure. We will often choose to live more and more in an isolated world of self delusion rather than face criticism, even at the ultimate cost of our freedom.

If you listen to constructive criticism, you will be at home among the wise
PROVERBS 15:31

Sharing our deepest thoughts is risky. It always involves the potential of our ideas being rejected as wrong. It may mean stepping down from the false pretense of "King in control" and into the role of the confused common man. Isolated within the confines of our own mind, we build layer upon layer of falsehoods and misconceptions about ourselves and the world. We can pretend anything we want in there. We use it to protect us from the harsh realities of life we would otherwise be forced to face. It's no wonder so many avoid the examination and challenge of others.

While we play the role of "king of control" on the stage of life, the realities that seek our attention begin to devour us. Without honesty it's the worst that remains hidden. That which remains hidden defeats us. When we live a lie we are already defeated. It's just a matter of time before the man who is prisoner on the inside is once again a prisoner on the outside.

Whoever stubbornly refuses to accept criticism will suddenly be destroyed beyond recovery
PROVERBS 29:1

BLINDSIDED BY BLIND SPOTS
The examination and challenge of others will begin to shed light on the blind spots of our character that we cannot see. There are always aspects of our character that others can see that we cannot see, and aspects we can see that they do not. There are aspects that we all see about our character, and aspects that no one sees and are yet to be discovered together. Since we all have blind spots, the examination and challenge of others can dramatically enhance our level of self awareness, revealing both our strengths and our weakness. This will prove vital in our reintegration into society. It is likely to mean discovering who we really are for the first time in our lives.

We are naturally prone to overlook the deeply embedded defects in our character that have continually sabotaged our lives. Our defects have an extremely deceptive nature that allows them to blindside us. The deeper they are embedded, the less we are aware of them and are able to see them, even when pointed out to us.

The person who has dealt with their personal issues the least in the past is likely to see their behavior as helpful in an area that keeps creating problems around them. They will attribute those problems to outside sources and will never resolve the real issue. For us, it may be the primary issue that sabotaged our freedom the last time and is waiting to blindside us again.

THE CONVICTION OF PERSONAL VALUE
People who welcome the examination and challenge of others are stronger people. They are stronger people because such openness with God and others

153

develops strong relationships that create a deep conviction of being valuable. The conviction that, "I am valuable person" is critical to successful reintegration into society. This self caring is in reality self disciplining. No matter how intelligent or how educated we are, if we lack a realistic assessment of our own value, there will be no self discipline. It is the examination and challenge of others that provides us with the ability to make a realistic assessment of our value and our potential. Outside of these relationships and disciplines we may learn survival but understanding our genuine value will be impossible.

Take a few moments to reflect on these six principles of acclimation.

- Consider experiences where you applied them. What was the reward?
- Consider experiences where you failed to use them. What was the penalty?

Now that we have the tools, let's build some bridges across the stages that secure our freedom. As you read about these stages, consider the importance of these principles for moving through them.

CHAPTER NINE

Psycho-Social Stages of Reentry (Part Three)

—∙∙∙∙—

COMMUNICATION

Those who are willing to step into our fragmented and broken lives and give us their valuable time, attention, and direction in the act of goal oriented communication are expressing a profound act of love.

In time, we reach a major turning point where this value given to us by god and expressed by others is reflected in our own self-love.
The self love that results will liberate us and allow us to radically depart from lifelong patterns of the old, the known, and the familiar that we used to escape in the face of harsh realities and intense struggles.

— THE AUTHOR —

Communication is the first stage we enter on a consciously chosen path to establish our freedom. It must be consciously chosen because it won't happen by accident. Communication that is goal oriented is different from casual conversation. It often requires a tremendous amount of energy and effort. Goal oriented communication has intention and purpose. There is something specific to be accomplished. It is a form of concentration that can often require hard work. Communication that is valuable and productive is truly a difficult skill for most people to develop. There are only two reasons we would consider engaging in this kind of effort. First, we must have a strong interest in the subject and second, we must see the value in the content of the communication.

The more knowledgeable people desire to be, the more likely they are to engage in goal-oriented communication. They are regularly willing to engage in the effort of communication for the sake of their own personal progress. No matter how much they already know, they are able to engage with people who have wisdom they find value in. People who engage in this kind of communication are success oriented. They keep their eye on the goal of expanding their world view in order to increase their potential for success.

Successful people have learned an all-important truth. Success is not possible without valuable and productive goal-oriented communication. For this reason, they learn to develop this skill and continue to practice it the rest of their lives. This includes sports stars, businessmen, doctors, scientists, and all the way down to you and me; the common man with the common goal of life, liberty, and the pursuit of freedom.

Get all the advice and instruction you can, so you will be wise the rest of your life
PROVERBS 19:20

The question we need to ask ourselves is this: Do we have enough interest in the subject of our own lives, our future, and freedom to engage in serious goal-oriented communication? If the answer is yes, we will be willing to show a deep interest in the wisdom of those who can provide us with insight on how to accomplish these goals. We will acknowledge the value and content in what they have to share with us. If there are people who value us enough to give us their time, attention, and direction with no thought of reward, it's time we value ourselves at least as much.

THE ART OF LISTENING

We can hardly discuss communication without mentioning the topic of listening. Few of us are really talented speakers. There are times we can really struggle to clearly explain our ideas. Most of us are aware of this challenge and are patient when others struggle to communicate. What we are not usually aware of is how poor of a listener most of us are. Since listening is an art in its own sense, it requires practice to develop skill.

In the act of communication, both parties are senders and receivers of information.

Attention determines the strength of the connection between the two people communicating, which makes it critical to effective communication. The most important way we can exercise attention is by listening. God gave us two ears and one mouth because effective communication requires that we listen twice as much as speaking.

Let every man be quick to hear [a ready listener], slow to speak
JAMES 1:19

All that we learn from others is through listening. If we listen twice as much as we speak, we will learn twice as much as we are trying to inform. Hearing is not the same as listening. The art of listening requires that we work against trying to develop an answer before the speaker is half finished. The result of this is that we hear only a little over half of what the speaker is saying. This is what's called jumping to conclusions. Miscommunication usually results in misunderstanding. The work of attention and the skill of listening requires the effort of total concentration. We cannot listen to someone and do anything else at the same time. Listening requires that we put aside all self-preoccupations.

THE FOUNDATION FOR FREEDOM

For ex-prisoners reintegrating into society, communication is the foundation stage upon which the other stages are built. No other foundation can be laid that will be strong enough to support our journey to freedom. We build our reentry upon the foundation of communication or what we build upon crumbles in the right storm. The time to begin laying the foundation of communication is not at the Return to Reality stage after our release. If we decide to wait until then, we will not take the time to lay a solid foundation. What we will do is take the less honorable path of least resistance and attempt to escape the pain of problem solving. The foundation stage of communication is best started long before our release date.

When a builder lays a foundation there is always a lot of time and care put into it. The builder knows it will be what sustains the weight and pressure of everything else built upon it. The more time and effort we put into laying the foundation of communication before release, the more secure we will feel in the first initial days, weeks, and months of release. The goal is to begin to develop trusting relationship before we face the challenges waiting for us on the other side of the gate. Once these challenges come – and they will come – we will have practiced and developed the skill of communicating for the goal of problem solving. We will have learned to trust it enough to utilize it to its fullest potential in a time of crisis.

THE ART OF SECRECY AND SILENCE

Most of us were not effective communicators before we came to prison. It was not because we lacked ability or potential, but practice. This is especially true when it comes to sharing the weight of our problems. What we perfected was secrecy and silence. Since the prison is full of people who have perfected these two skills, we are likely to have continued this pattern of behavior in prison.

Where there is no counsel, purposes are frustrated,
but with many counselors they are accomplished
PROVERBS 15:22

Prison is a place where we tell few what we think and even fewer what we feel. In prison this may have represented a method of survival. On the journey of reintegration it will secure our failure and possible destruction. We can hardly expect to live a life of severely limited communication in prison and suddenly reverse the process during reintegration when necessary. It just won't happen. We are creatures of habit, both in our personal lives and our social lives. These defenses of secrecy and silence will follow us out of prison unless we deliberately begin to sharpen the skill of communication before we are released.

CHOOSING CONTACTS AND GETTING STARTED

The most important contact for goal-oriented communication – next to God – is our reentry mentor. He will be a man who is dedicated to truth in his own life and will be fully committed to truth for your life. We will look at this subject in great detail in the chapter on the reentry mentor, but for now, begin to open yourself up to this vital need. However, he is not the only contact we have as we begin laying the foundation of goal-oriented communication. We may also include our clergy and members of our church. If we are involved in a recovery support group we may want to add our sponsor and other members of our support group. The goal is simply to seek the guidance of competent and caring people.

Those who listen to instruction will prosper; those who trust the Lord will by joyful
PROVERBS 16:20

The most important thing right now is to get started laying the foundation of honest and open goal-oriented communication. The sooner the better, whether you are years or even weeks from release. This kind of communication does not come easily or quickly, so it is never too soon to get started. The more trust develops in these relationships, the deeper the communication can go. Once trust begins to develop it is important to begin opening up concerning our goals, plans, hopes, and fears about our return to society. Any time we can look at something with more than one set of eyes, there are more angles to see it from. This book can help facilitate discussions, and later we will be able to get more specific and personal as trust develops.

If you stop listening to instruction…you will turn your back on knowledge
PROVERBS 19:27

Many of the unknowns about reentry can lose some of their mystery through honest and open communication. First we learn to be fully open and transparent about what we think about these topics. If we are willing to do this, in time we will be able to share what we really feel about them as well. This is very important. Unresolved emotional energy can create confusion, cloud our judgment, and interfere with our decision making.

Our efforts will provide us with an objective look at what we will face upon reentry. We will gain more insights to fine tune our specific plans. This communication will help us to release any rigid expectations that can set us up for failure. Rigid expectations are always dangerous because they lack flexibility. For those who have not given reentry any real thought, goal-oriented communication will help you begin this process you cannot afford to avoid.

Partnership in goal-oriented communication can reduce the initial impact of release. It can help reduce the vulnerability and dangers of the Euphoric Response stage. This partnership is invaluable in helping us resist the pull and tendency to escape reality once we enter the Return to Reality stage. Overall, this early preparation through communication will provide a sense of readiness to change worlds: a readiness to leave the prison world and enter the world of liberty and freedom.

CHANGING WORLDS REQUIRE PREPARATION

I remember when I went to the Philippines for two weeks. There was a tremendous amount of preparation and communication involved. It was a twenty-two-hour flight to the other side of the world, to a people and land I knew only little about. As I look back, I realize I spent months preparing for that brief visit. I read books on their customs and culture and listened to language tapes to gain a few basic words. I met with a young couple who had made the trip a few times. They shared advice and stories with me and provided information about the currency exchange. They helped me to line up a driver over there that would pick me up at the airport. I had to investigate air flight prices, departure and arrival dates. Finally, I had to go to the health department to get a series of shots. While I was there they provided me with a safety packet on where and what to stay away from.

Once I arrived I felt like a fish out of water. No amount of preparation and communication could totally prepare me for the impact of changing worlds. The impact was lessened by my preparation and communication, and the people there waiting to guide me. All this was extremely important. In some ways my life was at stake in preparation and communication. There was no room for overconfidence in my intelligence or life skills.

All their sources of confidence will fail them
ISAIAH 28:20

If we value our freedom we should be no less willing to prepare and communicate for reentry. We will be changing worlds, and our survival is at stake. Most importantly, we will need to change in order to survive or we won't survive. Changing worlds sometimes means changing our world view.

REENTRY AND OUR WORLD VIEW

However accurate or inaccurate, everyone has a set of beliefs about the essential nature of the world. That view dramatically affects the way we respond to the world upon release. Most people are not fully aware of their world view. This causes us to operate from a frame of reference that is far narrower than which we are actually capable. Our old methods of survival become outdated and no longer work under our new circumstances and conditions of reentry. We fail to see alternative choices to our decisions and potential paths to overcome our limitations.

We pay too little attention to our world view before we are released. Once we are released, we have no time to examine it because our focus is on how to survive it, enjoy it, and progress in it. Let's take a look at a few basic world views to see how they might affect our lives.

If we view the world as chaotic and without any real meaning, it will make sense to us to live from one fleeting desire to the next – grabbing whatever pleasure we can, whenever and wherever. If we view the world as survival of the fittest, a dog-eat-dog place where ruthlessness is essential to survival, we will view ruthlessness as the path to success and will respond ruthlessly to the world. We may view the world as a place that owes us a life no matter how we conduct ourselves. We will then expect reward without sacrifice, and we will remain angry and resentful when the world never pays up.

If we perceive the world as dangerous and frightening, we are not about to pass up any quick fix or short cut that may provide security in the present. We will not have faith that future rewards will be greater than any short cut, especially since the future seems so uncertain and unstable anyway. On the other hand, we may have matured enough to see the world as a sort of nurturing place in most ways, designed to reward us for our positive efforts and require a price for destructive actions. In such a case, we are not likely to fret about the future but focus our efforts on how we act and respond to the world.

Whatever a man sows, that and that only is what he will reap
GALATIANS 5:7

Whatever our world view upon release, if it has not changed while incarcerated, we will be released with the same view of reality that has already been proven by experience not to work for us. Our world view determines that we will represent one of three types of people to the world: predator, parasite, or partner. It is likely we will be accurately perceived as a predator or parasite and have to work toward proving we can be a partner.

The partners of society remain free. Predators and parasites are re-arrested and re-incarcerated. Our very survival depends upon our goal of partnership being genuine and not of false pretense. It begins with honest and open communication. Goal oriented communication pierces our world view with the truth to better see it, and helps us mold our world view into one that works for us instead of against us.

The wise are mightier than the strong,
and those with knowledge grow stronger and stronger
PROVERBS 24:5

TRUTH AS A COMPASS

Communication has a broad range of purposes, but they all require the truth.

Communication must always be based on truth or it is meaningless and of no profit or value. Goal oriented communication is for the purpose of clarifying truth and to gain true direction. Once communication has helped to arm us with the truth, we can use it to navigate our lives, excel, and protect ourselves.

A compass is a device that allows us to plan or direct our course. It helps us determine where we want to go. A compass doesn't tell us where we were, only the direction we are traveling. This is important. While where we came from may have some degree of significance, it's not nearly as important as the direction we are heading. A compass works simply by having a needle that is magnetized so that it points true north. The idea is that if we know one way for sure, we can find our way in or out of anywhere. A compass is used primarily in the wilderness where there are no road signs to follow.

To reenter society we need a moral compass that continually points in the direction of the truth. It is not because there are no signs or roads to follow, but rather that there are so many that point away from the truth. There are far too many roads and signs that point in the wrong direction and towards the land of the lost we call prison and self-destruction. We need only look around and listen to the stories to know that this is absolutely the truth.

Consider well the path of your feet, and let your ways be established and ordered aright
PROVERBS 4:25

Few if any would deny that the Bible is a great moral compass. The Bible is the guidebook of human operations. Its principles are a guiding light for human conduct that are proven to have enduring, permanent value. They are essential, central, and basic to human activity. It is fair to say they are essentially undebatable because they are self evident in all human experience. One way to grasp this self-evident nature is to consider the absurdity of attempting to live a life of freedom and effectiveness based on the opposite of its principles.

161

For example, I doubt any reader would consider a life of selfishness, lies, bitterness, fear, and hatred to be a solid foundation for lasting freedom and enduring success. Even though we seem to have basic conscious awareness that this is true, this is exactly how we have behaved. In our distorted world view we thought these methods in our particular circumstances would provide the payoff. It was a philosophy for living that exacted a heavy, long term payment plan.

The Bible is a written form of pure reality and absolute morality that points out truth. When we are lost all paths look alike. The Word of God is a discerner of paths (Proverbs 3:6). Every word of God proves true (Proverbs 30:5). His desire is to provide us with good counsel (Psalm 33:11). He sent His word to heal us and deliver us from destruction (Psalm 107:20).

Presidents for generations have prayed openly in front of our nation and requested that God would bless America. They knew that if God did, America would be protected, prosperous, and successful. It is a book that can do for any man what the president hopes for the entire country. The outcome of our country begins with the principles that govern every man.

DECEPTION PREVENTION

What we fill our hearts with will determine the quality of our communication. If the hidden man of the heart is still full of deception, our communication will be deceptive. If the hidden man of the heart is renewed with truth, our communication will be true. From the hidden man of the heart, to the head, to the mouth; that's how we function. When the hidden man of the heart is full of deception, people and even God can grow weary of our words and manipulation (Malachi 2:7). If we wear a mask when we enter into these relationships it will be almost impossible to take it off and reveal ourselves later. The mask will destroy the trust and the goal of honest and open communication. Be natural; let God be supernatural.

For out of the fullness (the overflow, the superabundance) of the heart the mouth speaks
MATTHEW 12:34

If we hope to avoid truth as the main ingredient in our foundation of goal-oriented communication, it will be like building on sand without mortar or metal. If we reject the truth we will embrace a lie. If we reject faith we will embrace fear. We will either defeat deception in our life or deception will continue to defeat us the rest of our lives. The choice is always ours but before we decide we need to look around. The consequences are real. The beauty of harsh consequences is they have the ability to bring us to the end of ourselves, where life can truly begin.

Then there is the other side of the coin. We cannot decide to embrace truth and reject or avoid communication. Isolated in the world between our ears, if we say something is right, then it's right. If we say something is wrong, then it's wrong. If we say something is unfair, then it's unfair. You get the point. There is nothing to protect us from distorting or misunderstanding truth; nothing to protect us from the isolation of our own dysfunction. The only way we can be sure we understand truth is by the feedback from others who are walking in truth.

The way of a fool is right in his own eyes, but he who listens to counsel is wise
PROVERBS 12:15

The world is saturated with confusion and conflicting ideas that can contaminate our world view. It can often be challenging even for the wisest. There are many points on our journey of reintegration where all we know will not be enough. When we don't know what to do or are unsure of which path to take, communication with God and others will always provide the best possible direction. Like the compass that points true north, once we know what the truth is, we can find our way in or out of anywhere and anything we encounter in reentry. When two people communicate from a position of truth, there is growth, change, and progress. The result will be principle-centered maturity.

SELF-LOVE IS ESSENTIAL TO OUR FREEDOM

Those who are willing to step into our fragmented and broken lives and give us their time, attention, and direction in the nurturing act of goal-oriented communication are expressing a profound act of love. In time, we reach a major turning point in our lives. This value given to us by God and expressed by others is reflected in our own self-love. It is only through a relationship with God, and the time, attention, and direction of others that we feel sufficiently secure to defy our old tendencies and desires. The self love that results will liberate us and allow us to radically depart from lifelong patterns of the old, the known, and the familiar that we used to escape in the face of harsh realities and intense struggles.

He who gains wisdom loves his own life...
PROVERBS 19:8

Reintegration is a process that occurs very gradually over time, with little leaps into the new and the unknown. It will often require forsaking whole patterns of life and previously held values. Many will never take any of those leaps. Consequently, they will never reach their full potential or complete the work of maturity because they are the ones who will not remain free. They are the ones who try to go it alone. Self-obsession is not the same as self-love. As we have seen, self-obsession is a form of anti-love.

Such leaps into independence through dependence on God and others can be enormously painful and risky for us. It can require an enormous amount of courage and determination to remain free. Reintegration is a very real challenge and at times, an uphill struggle. It will be at these times that we will have a tendency to want to return to the old, the known, and the familiar.

Through goal-oriented communication we can face reentry and reintegration with incredible bravery to risk an unknown and unfamiliar future. At the same time, we can feel totally free for the first time in our lives as we transition through the stages that secure our freedom. The security of self-love that results through goal-oriented communication not only provides the motive we need for these changes, but also the relationships with God and others provide the courage to risk them. Courage is the next stage we must enter – a consciously chosen path to freedom.

Be alert and on your guard; stand firm in your faith (your conviction respecting man's relationship to God and divine things, keeping the trust and holy fervor born of faith and a part of it). Act like men and be courageous; grow in strength
1 CORINTHIANS 16:13

Take a few moments to reflect on the importance of communication for reentry.

- How have you fared at communication in the past? How about listening?
- Is there anyone you know who could function as your reentry mentor and support team?
- Are you willing to accept this stage and seek them out?

What we are about to discover is that courage is impossible without communication.

CHAPTER TEN

Psycho-Social Stages of Reentry (Part Four)

—◊◊◊—

COMMUNICATION > COURAGE

*Courage is one of two kinds: first, physical courage, or courage in the essence of
danger to the person; and the next, moral courage,
or courage before responsibility, whether it is before the judgment
seat of external authority, or of the inner power, the conscience.*

— KARL VON CLAUSEWITZ —

L ife takes courage. It is as essential as oxygen; without it we perish. For
this reason we must become aware of our special need for genuine courage upon reentry and our quest for successful reintegration. If we are our
own source of courage we are doomed to failure. The communication stage
helps us connect to courage in powerful ways. The relationships, the pursuit
of truth, and the conviction of personal value that result, are the only possible
sources of genuine courage. It is a matter of design, much like nothing comes
from an apple but apples.

Can a fig tree… bear olives, or a grapevine figs
JAMES 3:12

All human qualities begin like seeds planted in our hearts. They must be
nurtured and cultivated to harvest their fruit. Seeds create more. This is true
for the positive as well as the negative qualities. Whatever qualities our life
represents today, some environment we were in planted those seeds. We have
spent years nurturing and cultivating them into what they now are. Uncommon seeds always produce an uncommon harvest.

The potential of the harvest is the seed. Change the seed and you will
change the harvest. The sources in the communication stage result in an alignment with spiritual principles that are the seeds of genuine courage. Likewise,
these sources offer the perfect environment to nurture and cultivate these qualities to produce an abundant harvest of courage.

In whom, because of our faith in Him, we dare to have boldness (courage and confidence)
EPHESIANS 3:12

SEEDS OF:		HARVEST OF:		
1. Belonging	Romans 8:16	Acceptance	Identity	Character
2. Worthiness	Romans 5:6-8	Love	Discipline	Maturity
3. Competency	Philippians 4:13	Security	Courage	Manhood

The environment we come from either instilled the seeds of courage or were harsh enough to prevent them. Whether we want to admit it or not, we all remember the messages that stole or instilled these seeds. If we have not experienced the conditions that plant the seed of genuine courage, it's never too late for us to have this experience. We need only to enter a community of competent and caring relationships that plants and then cultivates those seeds. We will look at these environments in later chapters.

No matter where we came from, who we are, or what our story is, we have all sought acceptance, love, and security in the things that cost us our freedom. We may have put different labels on them, but they are the profound needs we sought to fulfill. The challenge for each of us is that the more brokenhearted or wounded we are the greater our fear will be of taking the first step. We can't get where we need to be until we accept where we are.

CRIME IS COWARDICE, NOT COURAGE

If we are to understand genuine courage we must lay aside our own ideas and examine it through the microscope of truth (Proverbs 30:5). The truth pulls no punches in identifying what courage is, and just importantly, what it is not. If we have learned anything at all from previous chapters, it is that truth is not an optional luxury in life. The truth does not play favorites and shows no partially (Romans 2:11). It is what it is, whether we like what it tells us or not. That's why truth is every man's best friend.

As we have learned, truth is a reliable compass that always lets us know where we are. The more we base our lives on the compass of truth, the further we will travel and the greater will be our success. The more we base our lives on inconvenient lies, the less significant our lives will be and the greater our pain, sorrow, and suffering will become.

But these people scoff at things they do not understand. Like unthinking animals, they do
whatever their instincts tell them, and so they bring about their own destruction.
What sorrow awaits them!
JUDE 10, 11

Pain and suffering have a way of breaking down our well-designed walls of delusion. Suffering has a way of helping us remove our masks of falsehood and aids us in our willingness to see things as they really are. Once enough suffering provides the incentive, we are no longer unwilling to be guided. We will begin to seek out the sources of genuine courage found in the stage of communication who can take us further than we are.

There are two kinds of people reading this book. The first are those who, as a result of suffering, are willing to begin to look at the truth. The other kind are those who still have more suffering ahead of them to create this willingness. Which one are you today?

The hard truth is, no one goes to prison because they had the courage to do the crime they committed. As prisoners of the state, we left society labeled as cowards and society held us in the bitterness of scorn. This label is a result of our willful disobedience of the standards of society, and the open disrespect of the rights, needs, and privileges of others. It doesn't matter what type of crime we committed. I have come to realize, and now maintain, that crime (victimizing) is an act of cowardice. The result of cowardice is always some form of bondage or imprisonment.

Until I was able to see my crimes for what they were, acts of cowardice, I could not move toward a life of genuine courage.

DEFINING GENUINE COURAGE

Webster's Dictionary defines courage this way: "The ability to face difficulty or danger with firmness and without fear." I would like to edit this definition for the purpose of this chapter. I will use two considerations to make this edit. First, courage is considered a virtue (beneficial quality of moral excellence). This means that if our courage is genuine, it cannot be separated from our moral character. Second, fear is considered to be a normal and healthy emotion in many instances that still may require our courage. This means that courage is not always the absence of fear, but rather that courage is the ability to act in the midst of fear. In light of these logical conclusions, allow me to edit Webster's definition of courage to read this way: "The commitment to endure difficulty and danger while standing firm in moral and purpose in spite of fear."

Supplement your faith with a generous provision of moral excellence, and moral excellence with knowledge, and knowledge with self control
2 PETER 1:5-6

The essence of genuine courage flows from inner character. It is the morals, values, boundaries, and priorities that are involved in the small as well as the large decisions of our everyday life. Courage is a virtue of honor among men of character, admired as an advantage, and as a source of power. There is a price to pay for the merit of genuine courage. It is not something that just comes to us. It is only attained by realizing it is something we must work toward. People get physically strong by effort. Likewise, the moral strength of our character can only become strong by exercising it. Courage is to character what maturity is to manhood; they are inseparable. It is a type of inner strength like physical strength to the outward body.

GENUINE COURAGE IS TRUSTWORTHY MANHOOD

If the courage we profess does not affect our moral choices, it's not the virtue of genuine courage. It is counterfeit courage. A counterfeit is something that looks real but in reality is a fraud. Counterfeiters profess courage but they do not possess courage. Counterfeiters never intend to be what they pretend to be. They act out a role they believe others will accept or admire. Webster's Dictionary says it is, "Made to imitate the genuine so as to deceive."

Genuine courage involves a deep and powerful conviction of "I am a valuable person" that transforms our character and therefore our moral choices. The motto is no longer, "What can I get away with and still remain free." Maturity in manhood entreats us to a new level of courage, leading us into actions that are in harmony with building and protecting our freedom. For the first time in our lives, we are able to see that every liberty a free society offers implies a responsibility, every right an obligation, and every opportunity a duty.

Upright citizens are good for a city and make it prosper
PROVERBS 11:11

The man of genuine courage never pretends not to know the difference between right and wrong. Right matters to the man who carries a deep conviction of personal value. His manhood never allows him to blame circumstances or others for poor decisions. He is a man who has moved from con artist to conqueror. The man of genuine courage is not the con artist who seeks liberation from the truth, but rather the conqueror who seeks liberation through the truth.

This admired virtue of character willingly acknowledges that the basic rights of people in a free society are the right of life, liberty, and the pursuit of happiness. When we are released from prison we are offered the same rights. This opportunity comes with a reasonable expectation of us from society: They expect us not to violate them and infringe on their rights.

Courage is learning to be trustworthy in our manhood. Maturity is remaining faithful to our freedom. We will never have one without the other.

Your kindness will reward you, but your cruelty will destroy you
PROVERBS 11:17

GENUINE COURAGE AND THE PAST

Men of courage do not focus on their past handicaps. This inner strength allows them to push on until they excel beyond those handicaps. Hanging on to some hidden visions of failure, being still chained to the things of the past that defeated us, and being haunted by past mistakes, will keep us from genuine courage. These things will keep men returning to prison time and time again. It's not that men of courage never make mistakes. Everyone makes mistakes. In spite of their mistakes, men of maturity never give up and never give in to failure. They are willing to take responsibility for their own destinies. They are able to stand back up, dust themselves off and keep going.

Courage allows us to break away from the old crowd and our old ways, redefine ourselves, and become our own man. It is only genuine courage that allows us to stop being a follower and provides us the freedom to live independent of the old crowd's approval. Courage allows us to resolve the past and turn past liabilities into motivators for change in the present. It doesn't matter what mistakes we have made or what we have been through. In the end, the man of courage will be the man where no one can say, "He could have been so much more but he never really tried."

GENUINE COURAGE AND THE PRESENT

Men of courage don't wait until their youth is gone with four prison numbers (like me) to get a backbone and the wisdom to make their lives count. Truth has allowed us to see there is a better way to live. Faith in the truth has allowed us to believe in that life. Truth and the action of faith will allow us to become barrier breakers instead of law breakers in life. As we attempt to move forward in the action of resolving the past, making changes in the present, and preparing for the future, we begin to wage war against anything that would cost us our freedom ever again.

Be brave and of good courage and let your heart be stout and enduring
PSALM 27:14

All courage is transformed into the energy of action in the present. Discipline is the correct application of courage. The test of true manhood is how a man expresses discipline in his daily life. It is one of the greatest measures of a man; against this, physical strength means nothing. (Proverbs 16:32). The measure of your life will be the measure of your courage.

Courage pushes aside the chilling winds of self doubt as the conviction of value creates a vision of destiny and purpose. There no longer exists a limited mentality in the man of conviction that says, "I can't change," or "that's just the way I am." What we come into prison with and what we let go of while in prison will depend on our courage. Character defects are seen as challenges for self improvement rather than excuses for failure. The focus is no longer on the defect. We wage war against them by focusing on their replacement we are guided toward through the sources in the communication stage. The Master Model of Manhood said that without replacing what we drive out with new things we will end up in a worse condition than before (Matthew 12:45). Let's look at some of those replacements. These are examples of how we can cultivate courage in the present and prepare ourselves for freedom in the future.

COURAGE IN THE PRESENT IS:

Integrity. Character is not the same as personality. Our personality is constructed by what we want people to see of ourselves in public. Character is constructed by what we do in private. No one ever went to prison because of having a bad personality – but because of bad character. When personality slips up, character is revealed. It's what we do when we are alone that determines if we succeed or fail. When our public personality is the same as our private character, we have integrity. A man of courage honors God privately and shows his resulting personality publicly.

Through an alignment with integrity there is unity in public word and private action. The man of integrity is not struggling between two directions. There has been a firm decision to build the type of character that protects his freedom. For example, he will not entertain immoral alternatives when it is convenient because he has become a man of resolve. As old thoughts pass across the screen of his mind, he does not doubt what he needs to do to remain free. If he wavers in thought, he immediately exercises his integrity by sharing these thoughts with his support team who can help him think those thoughts all the way through. Such courage is its own reward. He progressively becomes more and more stable, reliable, and certain in everything he thinks, feels, and does. As a result, maturity in manhood has become faithful to its freedom.

To become different. Boldness itself is not courage. Genuine courage contains a form of boldness that refuses to be silent when asked to compromise. We become bold in our new beliefs and life direction in spite of personal encounters of disapproval and contempt. Courage is not a lack of struggle. It is choosing the right struggles. It means struggling against the talk and the pressure of unpopular change while ignoring the hundreds of suggestions not to do the right thing. An inner boldness through conviction always produces new actions that set us apart from the crowds. It will not allow our maturity and manhood to be determined by the approval of others.

The wisdom and ability to make decisions. Courage is always directed by knowledge. We must have a sound decision making process in order to know what to resist and what to yield to when making decisions. On the path to escape reality, the decision process was based on (I-Self-Me) as a result of fear. On the path of commitment to reality, courage puts self last instead of first in all decisions. As a result of conviction, courage asks four simple questions in all decisions: What would God have me do? What would my mentor have me do? What would my family have me do? Finally, what do I believe I should do?

The ability to make a decision and then stand your ground takes courage with wisdom. Without them we will not put our wants and desires last in our decisions, or we will fail to see the safety and security in such a process. Courage directed by this kind of wisdom always lets us know when to stay and when to leave; what to keep and what to let go of; what to seek and what to avoid. We are no longer basing our decisions on what the world says but on the words of the One who created it.

Where we place our faith. What we hold most in head and heart is what we have faith in the most. Faith is what we focus on, trust in, and believe for ourselves. Our faith could represent fear or courage. We have had faith in many things. What we are and where we are is a result of where we placed our faith. Our incarceration is a result of faith in something that appeared good but turned out all bad. Where we put our faith will determine if we remain free or return as wards of the state.

The voices we listen to will determine our choices because those voices seize our faith. Turning away from the conflicting voices of the world and listening to the unchanging Word of the One who created it means we come to know by experience that every word of God proves true (Romans 3:4). We no longer allow our circumstances to do all the talking, but we begin speaking to our circumstances no matter how they appear. It will determine our conduct and define our freedom. When we let go of artificial securities and put our full focus, trust, and hope in God's promises, the negative self image that made us bullies, criminals, and cowards melts away. Manhood and courage take its place.

Faith is belief in something for ourselves before the evidence (Hebrews 11:1), but it's still not blind faith. We can observe the lives of our mentors and others who built their lives on truth. We can observe the direct evidence of their transformation as we listen to their testimonies of how their faith transformed their lives from cowardice to courage. This is the type of faith that breaks us loose from self doubt and removes the limits on the amount of change that can take place in our lives. We can assume a posture of courageous expectation with new direction, purpose, and vision for our future.

Vision for the future. Without a vision for the future we probably won't have a future (Proverbs 29:18). Positive and successful futures require a vision. Vision is a form of courageous illumination that allows us to see success in our future, and recognizes the provisions for our future that are provided in the present. Vision allows us to plan, prepare, and avoid obstacles that would prevent us from being successful. If we can't see a vision for our future we will see no value in the present. A vision moves us into action in the present, because it shows us that we have something unique to offer life. It allows us to realize our best days are out in front of us.

When our lives have experienced tragic losses, it takes the true grit of genuine courage to see past all the devastation and envision a life of true success. Vision for the future is the courage to see, believe, and then move into the action of becoming that vision. Courage is the vision to see above and beyond what we are going through and focus on where we are going, regardless of the voices and circumstances around us. The future is more about courage than ability.

Identity. It would be completely inadequate to talk about courage and not mention the topic of identity. It is the single most powerful factor in regards to courage. This world will give us many labels and titles. Some of these we would rather not have acknowledged and others we take pride in. Anyone can acknowledge our titles and labels, even those who despise us. When we have our identity affirmed it is much more powerful. It is an expression of value, regardless of title or label given to us by others.

A relationship with the one who created us gives us genuine courage because he affirms our worth in the identity He has for us. It is the greatest "I know who you are, what you are, what your potential is, and what your value is," message the world has ever known. People without identities have problems that often become a crisis because who they are is based on labels and titles that cannot be counted on. When there is a crisis without an identity, there is an identity crisis. There is no identity crisis where there is identity confirmation.

History provides an ultimate example of identity confirmation for us. I do not believe it is coincidence that historical records indicate God affirmed Jesus on two important occasions. The first was at His baptism, just before he began His public ministry.

And there came a voice out from within heaven,
You are my beloved Son; in You I am well pleased
MARK 1:11

This affirmation must have filled Him with incredible courage. Look for yourself. The world will never see you as valuable and with such great potential as the One who created you. The second affirmation for Jesus was just before His journey to the cross.

This is my Son the [most dear worthy] Beloved One.
Be constantly listening to and obeying Him!
MARK 9:7

COURAGE FOR REENTRY

The freedom to choose the direction of your life is the only freedom you now have. Yesterday is history that is forever passed. Tomorrow is an unwritten mystery that is largely dependent on our actions now. To refuse to cultivate genuine courage is a unique form of suicide by selling our future freedoms to the highest bidder of pleasure today. It is maturity that allows us to recognize opportunity in the present. It is courage that allows us to seize those moments and write a destiny of character and manhood that secures our freedom.

Courage expresses a willingness to try new things and to deal with the constant changes and challenges reentry will surely bring. Without this kind of courage we will not remain free. The land of the free and the home of the brave belongs to the men of genuine courage. It involves a deep moral commitment; we endure not because they said we must, but because it is morally the right thing to do. Genuine courage is principle centered courage. This kind of courage not only ensures our own freedom, but helps ensure the liberties of a free society.

GENUINE COURAGE IS

1. Conviction of value
2. Walking in truth
3. Trustworthiness
4. To change
5. Integrity
6. To be different
7. The wisdom to make decisions
8. Where we place our faith
9. Vision for the future
10. Identity

Courage is, "The commitment to endure difficulty and danger while standing firm in morality and purpose in spite of fear." By its very definition courage has a close relationship to commitment. The inner strength of genuine courage is best exercised in our value driven commitments. Without commitment we run the risk of returning to the very things we have worked so hard to move away from. Aligning our courage with value driven commitment is pledging ourselves to be responsible for our freedom. Commitment is the next chapter and third stage we enter on a consciously chosen path to secure our liberty and freedom.

Take a few moments to reflect on how well you have understood courage before now.

- How important do you believe genuine courage is to your freedom?
- What steps can you take where you are to begin the journey toward courage?

Keep in mind how important courage will be to make the right commitments as you read the next chapter.

CHAPTER ELEVEN

Psycho-Social Stages of Reentry (Part Five)

—w—

COMMUNICATION > COURAGE > COMMITMENT

When the morning's freshness has been replaced by the weariness of midday,
when the leg muscles quiver under the strain, the climb seems endless, and sud-
denly, nothing will go quite as you wish — it is then that you must not hesitate.
— DAG HAMMARSKJÖLD —

Anyone who is truly concerned about remaining free can only foster a lifestyle of genuine freedom through a relationship of commitment to that lifestyle.

Commitment cannot be fostered and certified by academic degrees in a classroom. Regardless of our background or talent, the only way to resolve the issue of commitment is to engage the courage to have a meaningful experience with it. Unfortunately, many ex-prisoners have

never had this experience and are unaware of the immensity of the invest-ment required in making meaningful commitments to their freedom. The dif-ference between mere involvement and meaningful commitment is the degree of investment.

For example, if you are going for your first skydiving experience from an airplane, your instructor is involved because he instructs you and packs your parachute. You are the one who is committed because you are the one who must jump out of a perfectly functioning airplane. Even then there is no real commitment until you take that leap of faith. Commitment always means more investment than involvement.

Much like jumping out of an airplane, commitment looks quite different in action and after release than it does in theory prior to release. We can be sure our courage and sense of commitment will be tested by challenges and trials. These tests are likely to come through a variety of ways over the initial weeks and months of early release. Not only must there be genuine commitment on many levels to secure our liberties and freedom, such commitments must grow deeper over time, or they are likely to crumble. When our commitment to that lifestyle ends, so will our freedom.

THE GENESIS OF COMMITMENT

Great truths are always simple truths. The genesis of commitment is to live out the love we have learned. It alone produces the conviction that empowers us to bear, believe, hope and endure all things. It never fails (1 Corinthians 13:7). We first learned about commitment in the communication stage. It is the love mirrored by God and others who invest in us. In time, we begin to reflect it in a return investment toward them. With sufficient commitment from others, we are able to experience a sense of security strong enough to extend ourselves into greater levels of commitment of our own in the other areas of our life. The fifteen qualities of genuine love that make this possible are presented in the next chapter.

Make this choice by loving the Lord your God, obeying Him, and committing yourself firmly to Him. This is the key to your life
DEUTERONOMY 30:20

There is a new type of influence introduced into our lives through our relationships with God, our fellowship, and our mentor. We are gradually immersed into a whole new value system, new principles for living, and a new morality. To be immersed is far more than getting our feet wet. Our commitment literally submerges us in this new environment of competence and maturity. This has a profound effect on us in the following ways. The relationships in the communication stage begin to revolutionize everything about us. All of the commitments we make in every other area of our lives to reintegrate ourselves into society will depend on our commitments to honesty, reliability, accountability, and all that we cultivate in these relationships. Commitment begins to turn undisciplined immaturity into disciplined maturity and failure into success.

The path to genuine commitment involves a willingness to suffer through the discomfort of our commitments. It means to constantly practice the acclimation tools of discipline we discovered in part two without withdrawing when it feels difficult. Without these tools of discipline there will be no genuine commitment to freedom, no willingness to change and none of the growth that freedom requires. As we grow in commitment, we will grow in the exercise of discipline.

People who accept discipline are on the pathway to life, but those who ignore correction will go astray
PROVERBS 10:17

Our commitment and discipline allow for a major expansion in life experiences that are critical to reintegration. For example, we are able to hold down a job and become accountable to an employer and fellow employees. There is an increasing ability to become reliable husbands and reliable fathers. Our financial lives display a high level of responsibility and discretion. Once this level of maturity in commitment takes place we will have reached an invaluable turning point in the stability and predictability of our freedom.

The path of commitment is a path of lifelong learning. It provides us with an understanding of the world and a realistic view of our place in it grows also. It is through meaningful commitment that life begins to make sense to us, and we learn some of life's most important lessons.

COMMITMENT VERSUS INDIFFERENCE

A lifestyle of freedom cannot be fostered in an atmosphere of indifference and instability. We may have lived our lives unwilling to make commitments if we believe that we have not or would not receive any commitment from the world in return. If we have received the message of indifference either growing up or in adult experiences, we may be more likely to live our lives in a state of indifference. Webster's Dictionary defines indifference this way: "Not mattering; unimportant; having no marked feeling or preference; impartial; uninterested." Clearly, indifference is the opposite of commitment.

People who are unwilling to pay the price of commitment are unwilling to change and grow. They are choosing a path of many sorrows and bondage, rather than the many freedoms that commitment will make available to us. Yet due to the indifference we perceived from the world, we were largely indifferent to any specific outcome related to those things. Our way of surviving a seemingly indifferent world was to care less either way, even if we were looking for a specific outcome.

Such a philosophy of life can lead us to become very hard and even ruthless. Crime is an expression of indifference toward the rights of others, the laws of society, and the pain we caused our loves ones. It is an act of indifference toward our own freedom. Nothing could be more ugly and destructive than indifference when it comes to the life of a human being – ours or another's. Indifference to society is nothing short of anti-social and criminal. Indifference to our own welfare is self-annihilating.

The whole of the law can be summed up in this one command: 'Love your neighbor as yourself.' But if you are always biting and devouring one another, watch out!
Beware of destroying one another
GALATIANS 5:14-15

Whatever our past story and circumstances may have been, they are likely to include mental and emotional scars that are still pain-filled. Our scars may remind us where we have been, but they do not have to determine where we are going. Like Mark Twain once said: "History doesn't repeat itself, but it rhymes." If indifference remains an issue, our future may not be an exact replication of our past, but it will closely resemble it. Genuine commitment to a lifestyle of freedom often requires changes in attitude and perspectives we may have carried our entire lives. The degree of discomfort we experience in a commitment to a lifestyle of freedom will depend on our changes in attitudes and perspectives. If we are more committed to our old attitudes and behaviors than we are to a lifestyle of genuine freedom, our past will be what defines us. The sources outlined in the communication stage are invaluable to these changes – expanding our world view to receive them.

COMMITMENT CULTIVATES DESTINY

Nothing forges the direction of our lives more than the commitments we decide to make. Our commitments will send our lives on a path of construction or they will send them on a path of destruction. Either way, they will determine our destination. Show me what you are committed to and I will show you your destination. You really don't need me for that. We are all intelligent enough to make those simple conclusions. The problems is, we do not invest the mental energy to do so.

There are those who believe success can be found even in the midst of conflicting commitments. The idea is that if my life is largely made up of respectful and honorable commitments, I can make a few less than honorable commitments and things will work out and I can still stay on top. We like to think we will abort a risky or dangerous commitment right before we suffer any real consequences, but we never do.

This is just poor logic. There is no such thing as some illusive, just right mixture. The principles of wholeness, relationship, balance, and order directly oppose it. What relationship does stability have with instability without instability in time taking over? A little dishonor in time will dishonor the whole life. What's fascinating is, life has never shown us anything different. Still, we continue to believe we will be the first ones to invent the exception to the rule. We cannot bend or break these principles. We can only break ourselves against them. Nothing we have ever seen in life says otherwise, including our own incarceration.

He gives us more and more grace (power of the Holy Spirit
to meet this evil tendency and all others fully)
JAMES 4:6

There are those who believe success can be found in casual commitment. Actually, there is no such thing as casual commitment in the real sense of the word. We are either committed or we are not. Real commitment means you want to grow, have decided to grow, make an effort at growth, and persist in growing. That's what commitment looks like, and there's nothing casual about it. It requires tremendously mature conviction to whatever the commitment asks of us.

For example, when I was a practicing alcoholic and drug addict I quit more times than I could ever count. I was still unable to completely stop. Why? I wasn't committed to what it required of me. I was involved in recovery programs for fifteen years, but I was never really committed. It doesn't really matter what area of our lives we are talking about, the principle of genuine commitment still applies. It applies to our maturity, our relationship with God, and our freedom. We can spend our lives being involved in these things without much result, until we are committed to what they require of us.

> *Roll your works upon the Lord [commit and trust them wholly to Him:*
> *He will cause your thoughts to become agreeable to His will, and]*
> *so shall your plans be established and succeed*
> PROVERBS 16:3

SHORTSIGHTED VERSUS LONG TERM VISION

Both habits and commitments have one thing in common: they have long-term effects on our lives. What type of long-term effect is likely to depend on if they are honorable or dishonorable, worthy or unworthy. For example, honorable habits and commitments are hard to develop in the short term, but easy to live with in the long term. Dishonorable habits and commitments are easy to develop in the short term, but hard to live within the long term.

When something is "hard to develop" it usually means it involves the pain of problem solving, challenge, and requires a willingness to delay gratification to receive a long-term payoff. There is a relatively short period of discomfort to find employment, learn a new skill, and adjust to new people and a new environment. It is likely to involve a period of problem solving and challenge. However, it will provide a much longer period of comfort in financial security in the long term.

When something is "easy to develop" it usually means it involves a quick route to comfort and convenience, with little or no pain of problem solving. It requires little or no delay to receive the short-term payoff. However, there is a much longer period of discomfort in the long term cost. For example, a life committed to anti-social behavior and crime may provide a quick route to a short-term payoff. However, the legal consequences, sooner or later, will require a much longer period of discomfort when we are held accountable for our actions.

This also applies to the principles of acclimation or tools of discipline we learned about in part two. It is much easier to live with the long term affects of telling the truth than it is to live with a lie. The truth may be more difficult in the short term than the lie, but a life of deception will cost you dearly the rest of your life, no matter how many short-term payoffs it provides.

Our commitment to responsibility may be harder to develop than a life of irresponsibility, but much easier to live within the long term. Our commitment to challenge and self examination may be harder to develop than the habit of avoiding them, but a life full of negative consequences will be harder to live with no matter how many short-term payoffs it provides.

The worthy and honorable commitment of finding a place to belong in the employment world is likely to require a commitment to the principles of acclimation. The unworthy and dishonorable commitment to a lifestyle of anti-social behavior and crime will require that we avoid them at all cost. Which destiny will you choose when you are released?

What man is he who desires life and longs for many days, that he may see good? Depart from evil and do good; seek, inquire for, and crave peace and pursue (go after) it!
PSALM 34:12, 14

As we grow and mature, experience will reveal, with ever increasing clarity, that the principles which govern life do not honor short cuts and quick fixes. We reach a point where we finally understand that a quality return requires a quality commitment, no matter what it is in life. Choosing to embrace a lifestyle that protects our freedom is an honorable commitment that involves a relatively short period of discomfort upon release, and a much longer period of comfort and reward.

COMMITMENT AND DECISION MAKING
Many of the decisions we will make in early reentry will involve reestablishing ourselves in a variety of networks in society, such as employment, housing, relationships, financial investments and others. Many of these decisions, by their very nature, will be major ones. Major decisions require greater levels of commitment. Then of course, the greater the commitment, the more information we must sort through in our decision-making process. The more personal investment a commitment requires of us, the more complex the decision process will become.

Genuine commitment, especially a major one does not mean, "As long as there is no inconvenience," or "As long as it is not burdensome." Commitment means an uncompromising stand, regardless of the inconvenience or burden. This is why the decision process is so intimately related to genuine commitment. When we can understand why we made the decision to commit (reasons discovered in the deliberation process), conviction will hold us on course when things get tough.

Sometimes commitment can seem to exact such a price from us that we need to remind ourselves why we made the decisions in the first place. Making wise and meaningful commitments and then staying the course is the only decent way to live. It is a hallmark of maturity. The conviction we can establish in a sound decision making process offers us an avenue to the life changing experience with commitment we need in order to remain free. A lack of conviction to hold the course on our commitments occurs when we make them immaturely and therefore prematurely. The Master Model of Manhood taught about counting the cost and decision making when it comes to commitments.

For which of you, wishing to build…does not first sit down and calculate the cost [to see]
whether he has sufficient means to finish it? Otherwise, when he has laid the foundation
and is unable to complete [the building], all who see it will begin to mock and jeer at
him saying, This man began to build and was not able (worth enough) to finish
LUKE 14:28-30

We want to be "worth enough" as men to finish what we commit ourselves to. However, decisions and commitments made too quickly will lack conviction. Often that is because hasty decisions and commitments are based on feelings instead of sound and wise reasoning. The result is we end up with unrealistic expectations and are disillusioned by what is actually required of us.

Becoming disillusioned can prove to be a very dangerous mental and emotional state for a newly released ex-prisoner. It can cause us to lose the place in reality we have fought so hard to engage. In a moment we can begin to see everything negatively, unleashing a whole chain of impulsive or compulsive poor decisions. It will be to our advantage to ask ourselves: "Is this an emotional decision? Will I really be better off with this commitment down the road?"

Blessed are those who don't feel guilty for doing something they have decided is right.
But if you have doubts… you are not following your convictions…
ROMANS 14:22, 23

When it comes to the challenge of moral decisions we discovered that we are safest when we put ourselves last instead of first in the deliberation process. Sometimes desire and emotion wants to override our sense of right and wrong. Being the last consideration in a decision helps us play the scene out in our mind all the way through to the consequences. There have been many times we have stopped the deliberation process at the desired reward, without playing it out in our mind all the way to the consequences. We have paid heavy penalties for this. The ability to make sound and wise decisions, even when not a purely moral decision, requires that we slow ourselves down and apply a well calculated deliberation process. A rushed life is never managed well. Wise decisions also require that we willingly allow others to share in that process.

THE DECISION-MAKING PROCESS

Decision making is a special kind of problem solving. The goal is to keep it as simple as possible. We can use three steps to making important decisions in our lives. 1. Name the problem (Survey). 2. Find a solution (Decision). 3. Develop a plan to implement the decision (Action).

This decision-making process can be used for every decision. Early reentry will be a time of many decisions. You can use this simple three stage process when choosing employment, housing, purchasing a car, and every other decision you need to make. The best problem solvers occasionally get stalled when trying to solve problems. Here are a few pointers that can help.

1. **ELIMINATE POOR CHOICES.** First list all possible solutions you can think of, then discard all the solutions that are most likely to have poor results. Examine your list closer and do a second evaluation. Be sure to generate a lot of ideas (brainstorm) before you evaluate them.
2. **VISUALIZE YOUR SOLUTION.** How does your solution look when applied in real life? Is it realistic? Is it really the best way? What are the positives? What are the negatives?
3. **DEVELOP EXPERTISE.** Seek outside help, especially with people who have made this kind of decision before. Make a list of all the people you will talk to and write down their remarks next to their name.
4. **THINK FLEXIBLE.** Don't get fixed on one direction for your decision. Many good decisions require some original and outside of the box type thinking. Be creative in the process.

Our mindset can both help and hinder problem solving. Mindset is in the tendency to perceive and approach problems in certain ways. Two of the most common mind sets are to make decisions impulsively or compulsively. If we make decisions impulsively it means we have developed a habit of deciding things quickly and with very little thought. If we make decisions compulsively it means we have developed a habit of focusing on only one way to solve a problem and excluding all other possibilities. Both of these methods exclude the valuable input of others, result in poor decision making, and are the mindset used in most crimes.

Another important factor is emotional arousal. We must generate a certain level of motivation to make our decisions. Too much arousal can hamper our ability to find the best solution. For example, it is not a good time to make a decision when we are experiencing the powerful influence of H.A.L.T. This stands for Hungry, Angry, Lonely, and Tired. Decisions are best made when we have addressed and recovered from these things. Likewise, even positive emotions can be a dangerous time to make decisions. We have seen this in the Euphoric Response stage of reentry. Emotions distort our perceptions when they are experienced intensely. They interrupt the brain's ability to make logical conclusions that require all the facts. Decision making that is largely emotional is most often poor decision making. Emotional decision making is also a culprit in many crimes.

THE 3 STAGE PROCESS OF DECISION MAKING

1. **SURVEY.** Name the problem (interpretation). The first step in making a decision or problem solving is defining the problem. Write it down. Ask yourself, "Is this really the problem?" We may often find what we first thought was the problem is not the problem once we look at it closely. Seek input from others. Be specific and concrete in naming the problem.

2. **DECISION.** Find a solution (evaluation). The goal is to identify the best available decision based on all the options generated. Involving others in this process reduces the stress of the decision. Investigate, communicate, and then pray and meditate about your final decision. Do not allow yourself to be rushed.

3. **ACTION.** Develop a plan and steps to implement your decision (strategy). The more complicated the decision, the more likelihood that there will be more steps to implement the plain into action. Do not look for short cuts and quick fixes in your action steps. The goal in a good decision-making process is to avoid these methods. Discuss your plan of action with those involved in the previous steps.

Even with a responsible approach to decision making, the commitments we make will not always be the absolute best choice one-hundred percent of the time. We certainly don't lose faith in, or abandon the process just because we are not completely satisfied with an outcome. This is life and this is how we learn. Practice means progress that translates into wisdom. At least we can be assured that such a process will prevent our decisions from being self destructive.

Whatever the outcome, we must always avoid blame that will push responsibility elsewhere. When we do this, we miss the critical learning and growth involved. At the end of every decision to make a commitment the agony of responsibility for that decisions is ours alone. The willingness to think, pray, and meditate about our commitments require that we value ourselves enough to do so.

BARRIERS TO COMMITMENT

In light of the fact that freedom without commitment is not possible, I find it necessary to mention three previously discussed factors that I believe are the absolute greatest barrier to commitment. They are maturity issues, relational issues, and compulsive/addictive issues that are inherent in the arrested development. Sometimes in the name of truth and love you have to tell people what they need to hear without redefining it or candy coating it so it's easier to swallow.

If no one ever tells us what we most need to hear, we will never get to where we need to go in our personal development. These issues and their profoundly destructive nature upon our lives have left most of us like children or adolescents at best in our thinking and emotional lives. Since the world sees us as adults simply because of our age, we also believe that the freedom and power that comes with adulthood should be ours. Yet the true revelation of our condition is revealed in that we have had little desire for the discipline, responsibility, and commitment adulthood demands of us. As much as we might feel rejected by society and oppressed as prisoners of the state, there is no authority above ourselves to blame for our conditions. The courage we have gained in the previous stage means facing the very things we have fought with all our energy to avoid facing our entire adult lives.

Most of us have wanted the luxuries of adulthood without having to grow up and make a commitment to the things that secure those luxuries. Many are likely to lose their entire lives trying to make it happen, but it never does. Then of course we are faced with the challenge that our maturing process is further arrested by the very nature of a primarily commitment free and responsibility free prison environment. We are removed from the experiences of the natural world that can nudge us toward the maturing process. The result is that aspects of growth slow dramatically or stop completely. Knowing and understanding this is invaluable; facing it is absolutely critical.

Do not be children immature in your thinking... but in your minds be mature men
1 CORINTHIANS 14:20

In the prison environment our lives center on our favorite television shows, recreation, board games and mealtimes. Then once we are released, commitment to the things that really matter – and the problem solving involved in it – creates intense confusion, anxiety, and fear. We become paralyzed by it and see it as an experience of intolerable pain. The result is we retreat into our familiar dysfunction and addictions. At least they represent something familiar in a world that seems to ask too much of us.

Commitment is to rise to a position of maturity and power where we no longer blame anyone for our sad states of affairs and begin to live out the love we have learned in a commitment to the things that secure our freedom. We cannot claim genuine commitment until it is united with the action of consistency. One cannot exist without the other. The final stage we must enter on a consciously chosen path to freedom is consistency.

Take a few moments to consider how important your commitment to a lifestyle of freedom will be upon release.

- What commitments can you begin to make now to secure your freedom?
- Consider what role the previous stages of communication and courage will play in your ability to make and keep this commitment.
- What type of things have you been indifferent to in the past? Has this helped or harmed you?
- What type of things have you been committed to in the past? Has this helped or harmed you?

As we read about the final stage in this progression, keep in mind how important consistency will be to your commitment to a lifestyle of freedom.

CHAPTER TWELVE

Psycho-Social Stages of Reentry (Part Six)

—◈—

COMMUNICATION > COURAGE > COMMITMENT > CONSISTENCY

We cannot remain consistent with the world,
save by growing inconsistent with our past selves.
— HAVELOCK ELLIS —

T he heart behind our commitment to freedom is revealed in the pulse of our consistency toward change and growth. The very basis of our successful reintegration into society is rooted in our willingness to change and grow. If our integrity is defined by our willingness to change and grow, and truth is keeping it real, consistency is converting that integrity and truth into action. Consistency is, in essence, the clear-cut manifestation of our integrity in action.

May integrity and honesty protect me
PSALM 25:21

Webster's Dictionary defines consistency this way: "Compatibility among successive acts, agreement among the parts." This definition will help to provide two important distinctions in the application of consistency. The first is consistency in our personal lives (agreement among successive acts). The second is consistency in our interpersonal lives in society (agreement among the parts.) These two aspects of consistency are closely related to each other. The abundance or lack of consistency we practice in our personal lives will be carried into and revealed in our social lives. We will look at both aspects of consistency in this chapter and how they apply to the goal of reintegration.

Preparing for reentry and working toward successful reintegration once we are released is a constant process of navigating our personal and interpersonal consistency. Organizing and structuring our lives through personal and interpersonal commitments helps to make life manageable. We hold that organization and structure in place through the action of consistency. It also involves problem-solving the things that would attempt to interrupt our consistency.

Inconsistency will rob us of our resolve and prevent our progress, which will remove any sense of control we have over our lives. Consistency exercised in meaningful commitments builds the confidence necessary for reclaiming our lives no matter what challenges we face.

CONSISTENCY AND PREPARING FOR REENTRY

Prison is an environment where we are likely to feel the least amount of control over our lives that we will ever experience. It's part of the design of detention and part of the punishment of corrections. Preparing for reentry throughout our entire incarceration can foster a sense of control over our lives that incarceration has cost us. To gain this sense of control will require that we make meaningful commitments here and now, and practice the action of consistency in those commitments. Here are a few examples of how we can begin.

We have already learned several things we can do in an institutional setting to regain the highest possible sense of control for reclaiming lives. We can make a commitment to developing our life management by design and practice consistency toward growing in all six potential powers we learned about. We can make a commitment to practice the six disciplines that are our tools for acclimating into society, and then add consistency to that commitment to create impressive results. There will be many programs within the institution you can use to support your growth in these areas. Ask to meet with your case manager to discuss your options.

Intelligent people are always ready to learn. Their ears are open for knowledge
PROVERBS 18:15

We can begin to make contact with the network of relationships that are part of the foundation stage of communication. The goal is to make a commitment to these relationships that can help to hold us accountable to this new lifestyle. If we will accept their guidance and consistently apply their wisdom, we will experience a greater sense of control over some areas of our lives than we ever had before, even behind the razor wire.

CONSISTENCY AND REENTRY

Consistency can empower us with a sense of control and help us reclaim our lives upon reentry. We can begin by working to transplant our life management by design in our new community and make connections with people, groups, and organizations that will support it. For example, we can locate a church and fellowship group to support our spiritual empowerment. It can be helpful to involve your family in some of these activities also. This will provide important structures to our daily lives when we are committed and consistent in this transplant process.

Those who work hard will prosper
PROVERBS 13:4

There will be some things during our reentry journey that we will be at the mercy of, and with little or no control of our own. Most of them fall into one of three categories: uncontrollable circumstances (layoffs, unexpected expenses, illness) unchangeable people, (The foreman at work, parole supervisor, relatives), unexplainable problems (when life seems unfair). These things can rob us of our peace. Consistency in the areas we can control will provide the balance we need to ensure that we are not being swept away by the things we cannot control. The result of a consistent life is more courage and greater strength to accept larger challenges and more responsibility for our lives. Through the action of consistency, we are adapting to handle our freedom, while our honor and inner confidence as men becomes greater than our emotions and challenges.

THE CONSISTENT PERSONAL LIFE
(Agreement among successive acts)
The call in our hearts to a life of freedom is, in reality, a call to a life of effort-driven consistency. Regardless of the challenges on our journey toward reintegration, the goal is consistent and unconditional faithfulness to our freedom. The help of family, housing, employment, and relationships will most assuredly provide a very important and predictable degree of support to our freedom. However, we can never afford to allow these potentially inconsistent variables to be the determining factors of a crime free lifestyle.

Our consistent and unconditional faithfulness to a crime-free life is the only factor within our personal control that can guarantee our freedom. If we begin reentry homeless and in a shelter, jobless with no family, or end up that way somewhere down the road, the only way to overcome those disadvantages is to remain free. With four prison numbers I can assure you – if I haven't used the excuses, I have heard them from others. When the dust settles, the only reason we lost our freedom was a lack of consistency to the unconditional faithfulness of a crime-free lifestyle.

He who walks uprightly walks securely,
but he who takes a crooked way shall be found out and punished
PROVERBS 10:9

No matter how challenging our struggles toward reintegration become, if we will resist the urge to commit a crime and instead reach out to others, life transforming growth will take place. We will eventually leave behind the feeling that we cannot cope with a merciless and overwhelming world. From victory to victory, we will discover that we have the ability to overcome the obstacles before us. Our successful reintegration will not be determined by the challenges we face. Our victory is determined by our desire to change and grow.

THE DESIRE TO CHANGE AND GROW

Among the recognized factors of disadvantage upon release, such a perspective fails to take into account something less tangible called, "The desire to change and grow." It is possible for an individual to be extremely disadvantaged and at the same time possess a strong desire to change and grow. In this case, freedom is achieved in spite of personal challenges. On the other hand, a person who is mildly disadvantaged but lacks the desire to change and grow will not be moved an inch from their handicaps, and as a result, will not remain free.

The thing a wicked man fears shall come upon him,
but the desire of the [uncompromisingly] righteous shall be granted
PROVERBS 10:24

There is no doubt that an ex-prisoner's desire to change and grow, not advantage or disadvantage, is the most crucial determinant of success in reintegration. The outcome of success or failure can, for the most part, be traced back to and observed in the prison setting. Some men are highly resistant to change and growth while others openly pursue it. There are those who go through all the motions yet still remain highly resistant to change. They dabble in a little religion, get a little education, and fill their file with program certificates. Some will do these things to appease their conscience; some for other ulterior motives. Unfortunately, they avoid the work of maturity at all costs. The idea that we still have more maturing and growth to do seems almost intolerable for their conscience to accept. However, hidden behind its painful acceptance is the key to our freedom.

The genuine desire to change and grow is revealed in a lifestyle of relentless consistency in all the tools this book provides. There may be resting places, but no stopping points. Most of the consistent actions you take will be done when no one is watching. This makes the desire to change and grow something that is not only hard to measure, but not well understood or even recognized by experts who seek to understand success rates. Many of us know exactly where we stand in our desire to change and grow. For those who do not, you need only take two measurements to find out. The first is a willingness to go to any length required to mature and grow. The second is the measure of our consistency in pursuing it.

GENUINE LOVE AND MATURITY

I will show you a still more excellent way,
[one that is better by far and highest of them all – love]
1 CORINTHIANS 12:31

The desire to change and grow is made of the same form and substance as love. People who consistently walk in the powerful qualities described in genuine love are, by definition, growing and maturing people. Such a concept should not be harshly criticized. They either misunderstand its potential or see it as a weakness. Many people in here believe the people who were supposed to love them betrayed them. False or true, they have a disdain for "love is the answer."

The problem is not in the power and potential of such an idea, but rather in the understanding of the qualities of genuine love and the actions of genuinely loving people. Below are fifteen qualities of genuinely loving people and the actions of genuinely loving people.

QUALITIES OF LOVE - SEEDS OF MATURITY

1. Patient
2. Kind
3. Not jealous
4. Not boastful
5. Not proud
6. Not rude
7. Not demand its own way
8. Not irritable
9. Keeps no record of wrong
10. Not entertained by injustice
11. Never gives up
12. Never loses faith
13. Is always hopeful
14. Endures all things
15. Abides and lasts

These seeds lie dormant as part of the spiritual life we have received until activated. When they are mirrored and modeled to us in an environment of mentorship from competent and caring men of maturity, they become activated. We can see this in practical application using a few examples from the list of qualities we just reviewed.

When we experience a willingness from others to offer their time, attention, and direction, and do so with (1) patience, (2) kindness, (3) without keeping a record of past mistakes, (13) who are always hopeful for us, (11) and never give up on us, something profound takes place. We not only begin to experience our own value, but a desire to change and grow as a result of understanding our own value. When these qualities of love are expressed to us with consistency over time, we begin to practice them in our own lives, and as a result mature and grow. Below are some examples of the fruit of maturity expressed by the actions of genuinely loving people.

FRUITS OF MATURITY - ACTIONS OF LOVE

Galatians 5:22-23		Colossians 3:12-17	
1. Charity	5. Goodness	9. Mercy	13. Forgiveness
2. Joy	6. Faithfulness	10. Kindness	14. Thankfulness
3. Peace	7. Gentleness	11. Humility	15. Harmony
4. Patience	8. Self-control	12. Tolerance	

You will recognize them by their fruits. Every healthy (sound) tree bears good fruit [worthy of admiration], but the sickly (decaying, worthless) tree bears bad (worthless) fruit
MATTHEW 7:16-17

The qualities of our character determine the fruit of our actions; favorable or unfavorable circumstances merely reveal them to us. Circumstances do not make the man – they simply reveal the fruit of his character to him. Every circumstance is an opportunity to discover the fruit we bear in our character. The problem is, we are often more focused on the conditions of things than the man responding to them. Below are some of the qualities found in a character driven by fear. They are seeds of immaturity – that if carried into adulthood will produce the fruit of immaturity and the actions of fear that lead to anti-social behavior and crime.

QUALITIES OF FEAR - SEEDS OF IMMATURITY

1. Impatience	6. Rudeness	11. Always giving up
2. Mean-spirited	7. Self-obsession	12. No faith
3. Jealousy	8. Ill-tempered	13. No hope
4. Braggart	9. Resentful	14. Run from problem-solving
5. False pride	10. Violate rights of others	15. Inability to understand love

These seeds do not lie dormant within us. They are part of our fallen nature and begin to appear in most children by the age of three. Even worse, when they are mirrored to us in our environment, they grow like wild weeds. We can see this in practical application as well, using a few examples from the list of qualities we just reviewed. When we come from an environment where it was normal to express (1) impatience, (6) with rudeness, (2) that are mean-spirited, (10) always violating the rights of others, (15) we will suffer from an inability to understand love, and something very destructive will take place. We will not understand or experience our own value. When these qualities are expressed to us over time, we begin to believe they are a normal way of responding to the world, and as a result we fail to mature and grow. Below are some of the fruits of immaturity expressed by the actions of fear that are directly related to our incarceration.

191

FRUIT OF IMMATURITY - ACTIONS OF FEAR

1. Hostility (Gal. 5:20)	7. Sorcery-drugs (Gal. 5:20)	13. Cheating (1 Cor. 6:8)
2. Quarreling (Gal. 5:20)	8. Arrogance (2 Cor. 12:20)	14. Adultery (1 Cor. 6:9, 10)
3. Jealousy (Gal. 5:20)	9. Envy (Gal. 5:21)	15. Greed (Eph. 5:5)
4. Anger (Gal. 5:20)	10. Murder (Rev. 22:12-16)	16. Stealing (1 Cor. 6:9, 10)
5. Selfish ambition (Gal. 5:20)	11. Robbery (Is. 61:8)	17. Lying (Rev. 22:12-16)
6. Dissension (Gal. 5:20)	12. Drunkenness (Gal. 5:21)	18. Lust (Col. 3:5)

You will fully know them by their fruits
MATTHEW 7:20

What gives this list such credibility is that we can all find ourselves in more than one place on it. I have learned it is never too late to grow up. Growing up is not only about making the right decisions – it's about how we deal with the decisions we have made. There are only two ways to respond: love or fear. In every single instance, nothing or no one has the power to determine our choice. We alone determine if we will choose the actions of love or the actions of fear.

If we choose the actions of love it is not an easy transformation. It requires that we sit at the feet of the wise and the loving while being mentored. However, lame or soft as it sounds, it's the toughest thing you'll ever do. It means following directions that we are not always familiar or comfortable with. Genuine love expressed by others is not always a painless process. Change and growth toward greater levels of maturity can often be very painful. But never as painful as the life of one who refuses to grow up.

People often flee when they experience the vulnerability of being examined and challenged by others. This is one of the principles of acclimation we have learned about. They are tools of discipline our mentor will require us to practice with relentless consistency to change the forceful momentum of our actions of fear to the actions of love. Just because something doesn't fit in our comfort zone doesn't mean that we must escape or avoid it.

CONFIRMATION

Eagerly pursue and seek to acquire [this] love [make it your aim, your great quest]
I CORINTHIANS 14:1

There is good reason to believe that mentorship in the qualities of love and the principles of acclimation can provide the corrective experience needed to produce loving, caring people.

The word of God reveals these principles as the theme of human relationships and the standard for producing healthy people. I received further confirmation while writing this chapter. A local PBS station aired a show that revealed a dramatic potential for this corrective experience and confirmed the impact and power of the qualities of love and the principles of acclimation.

The show began with a middle-aged man describing his earlier years as he drives us past the place of his twenty-fourth and last arrest. While we ride along with him, he explains what changed his direction and salvaged his life. He landed a job as an assistant to a furniture delivery driver. It was only part-time. This was the only job he could get back then. He had no driver's license and was unable to read, write, or do any type of math.

During one delivery he met an elderly man, a doctor who he stumbled into a conversation with. Right away the doctor took an interest in the young man and offered him his phone number. The young man looked at that phone number several times before he summoned the courage to make that call, which led to meetings in the doctor's living room every Saturday.

One of the most important lessons the young man would learn was that the evidence about his own value and potential could be aligned to point in more than one direction. The young man was challenged by his new mentor to look at things in ways he had never before considered. He asked about things he had never questioned. He was moved to ask himself if his own collection of perceptions of his value and potential really had been thorough, and which explanation best fit the totality of the facts?

One reason the evidence originally looked so convincing to him was because it fit his experience at that time. He was an obvious troublemaker and a failure to that point in his life. He was a high school dropout, mostly unemployed, and the product of a broken family. Looking at himself from that perspective, all the evidence seemed to fit concerning his value and potential. Like many of us, he took the existing evidence at face value and never looked much further.

Through the guidance of his mentor, he was able to change that perception of himself and see his life in a whole new light. He had new evidence that led him to a larger truth, regardless of whether it fit his original perceptions of himself. The new evidence was in the value mirrored to him through his new mentor.

The willingness of the mentor to offer his valuable time, attention, and direction was, in fact, the act of loving. The young man went from worthless to valued and affirmed. Experiencing (1) patience, (2) with kindness, (3) without keeping a record of past mistakes, (4) always hopeful for the young man, (5) never giving up on him helped the man mature and become himself a loving, caring person.

Strip yourselves of your former nature [put off and discard your old unrenewed self]
which characterized your previous manner of life
EPHESIANS 4:22

More than twenty years have passed. Many more lessons were yet to come. The young man was never arrested again as a result of that mentoring relationship. He not only no longer created victims, he saved countless lives as a heart surgeon. The young troublemaker who couldn't read or write traveled through a profound transformation into manhood and maturity. He now has a beautiful family and home, and he is one of the country's leading doctors in his field of heart surgery. What does this story confirm for us? If we are willing and have a strong desire to change and grow, our present circumstances do not even remotely resemble the fullness of our future.

'I know the plans I have for you,' says the Lord. 'They are plans for good not for disaster,
to give you a future and a hope'
JEREMIAH 29:11

Was it an easy transformation? Hardly. It required that the young man muster the courage to see the value in himself the doctor had seen in him. It demanded that he accept some hard truths and accept responsibility for the work of maturity. He would have to work toward honest and objective self-examination. He would have to be committed to the challenge of replacing his old behaviors with a whole set of new ones and consistently practice them until they felt as comfortable as the old ones. At the same time, it required that he remain committed to the examination and challenge of the doctor at all times. He used every acclimation principle I provided in part two. If this young man had only his mentor and hard work, how much better are your chances when you have a map prepared for you?

There were high levels of consistent action toward change in order for the young man's life to become a success story. To begin with, the young man had to consistently show up to be guided and mentored. He had to spend a lot of time reflecting and meditating on the doctor's wisdom and consistently practice those new principles in all of his affairs. The young man had to consistently turn away from old crowds, places, and things, or he would have ended up in prison sharing his sad state of affairs with other inmates, long before he would have ever become a doctor. Without relentless consistency, his old ways would have flooded back in before he could effectively replace them with new ones.

What can we attribute such a transformation to? It was certainly not advantages, the young man couldn't even read or write. The doctor didn't pave the young man's way financially, although he easily could have. That might have diminished the young man's learning experience and altered the purpose of the mentor's relationship to the young man. He only provided guidance in an atmosphere saturated in the qualities of love. The doctor provided the atmosphere for the corrective experience. The young man provided the desire to change and grow. The call in the young man's heart to change and grow was a call to freedom, a call to a life of effort-filled consistency.

CONSISTENCY AND FREEDOM

The action of consistency is the basis for effectiveness in our lives upon reentry. The ability to build a positive habit, break a bad one, demolish a destructive lifestyle, or create a positive one, lies in the action and power of consistency. The goal for us is lasting freedom, not a temporary release. Consistency is the substance that shapes, molds and makes that freedom possible. The powerful qualities of love, and the fruit it produces in our lives, is the glue that holds it all together.

For you... were [indeed] called to freedom; only [do not let your] freedom be an incentive to your flesh and an opportunity or excuse [for selfishness], but through love you should serve one another
GALATIANS 5:13

Webster's Dictionary defines freedom this way: "At liberty; not imprisoned or enslaved." We could say that this is FREEDOM TO (at liberty), and FREEDOM FROM (not imprisoned or enslaved). There are probably as many personal definitions of freedom as there are personalities. Whatever our personal definition of freedom may be, it falls under the only two types of freedom that exist, FREEDOM TO and FREEDOM FROM.

We all want FREEDOM TO: choose, have, become, relate, and achieve. What is often not so obvious to us is what we need FREEDOM FROM. We all need FREEDOM FROM: immaturity, impulsive behavior, compulsive/addictive behavior, self obsession, fear, and falsehoods. What we need FREEDOM FROM is directly opposed to our liberty of FREEDOM TO. This awareness is absolutely essential to our success.

I will walk at liberty and at ease, for I have sought and inquired for [and desperately required] your precepts
PSALM 119:45

Consistency in navigation between what we need to break away from and what we need to work toward is adapting to survive our freedom. The problem is, that while humans have an amazing ability to adapt, we only adapt when we believe we have to. This is one reason why a person can spend a decade in prison and survive it well and fail miserably when they are released.

We do not always see the same necessity of adapting to the rules and expectations of society as we do in the prison environment. For example, if the prison social system says we must work in order to prevent being isolated from the rest of population, then we adapt and work in order to experience the benefits of being in population. We take better care of ourselves physically by exercising, eating regularly, and having structured sleeping habits. We discover and develop artistic talents and take programs to learn something that interests us. We can do all these things in society and far more but we often do not, and we fail miserably by returning to the things we needed FREEDOM FROM.

There has befallen them the thing spoken of in the true proverb,
the dog turns back to its own vomit
2 PETER 2:22

This is like the story of the man who had a dog that had a terrible lust for legs. The dog was always drooling for legs – always watching and waiting. Finally, his day came, and he bit both the mailman's leg and the neighbor's leg in the same day. The only obvious alternative for the person who had authority over the dog was to chain the dog up. This only increased the dog's lust for legs; at least before he was chained he could let some of it out. The dog desperately wanted free from his chain. However, the dog lacked the ability to see that the only way he could remain off of his chain was to behave the same way when he was free as he did when he was chained. Unlike many other dogs, he failed to adapt to handle his freedom.

You see, a "chained dog" is not a "changed dog." This is what it is like for the prisoner who lacks the inner controls of self control, such as discipline, morals, and boundaries that help us adapt to handle our freedom. We fail to see the need to adapt without being chained to the outer controls of the prison social system. The principles of commitment and consistency lead to success only when applied to both environments (prison and society) and both freedoms (FREEDOM TO and FREEDOM FROM). Unlike the stubborn dog who refused to learn, we can become active observers of our own participation. Reintegration is a never-ending process of learning and adapting. Consistency in our personal lives expands our learning through increasing degrees of self awareness that adapting requires.

*Before we go any further, take a few moments to reflect on your personal life. What did your actions consistency reflect – love or fear? How would you feel about your life becoming a success story like the young man who was mentored by the caring doctor? What do you consistently need to work toward

FREEDOM FROM? What does FREEDOM TO choose, have, become, relate, and achieve represent to you? With the answers to these questions in mind, let's look at how a consistent interpersonal life can protect our freedom.

THE CONSISTENT INTERPERSONAL LIFE
(Agreement among the parts)

The moment we are released from prison we become like everyone else – interdependent upon human consistency in society. We are stepping into a community that is interacting and functioning as a single unit. Once we enter our community our interactions affect its stability. We help or harm it in a number of ways: Its safety, freedoms, needs, values, goals, financial services, and even its harmony. The goal of this section is to expand our awareness beyond the limits of our own desires, needs, and goals, and include others for our success as PARTNERS in society.

What partnership have right living…with…lawlessness?
2 CORINTHIANS 6:14)

INTERdependence (people combining their efforts for the greatest possible success) is what makes society possible. It is a "high trust" principle that relies on relentless consistency between the people in society. Consistent cooperation between people in society provides a structure that is defined by order and predictability. The concept of society only works because the people are consistently cooperating with each other. They cooperate because of similar interests, and because they need each other to accomplish those things which are beneficial to all, but that none could accomplish alone. Let's look at some examples of this by observing the most common interests people in society share with one another.

COMMON NEEDS
Once we are released, we will share common needs with people in society. No person or group is entirely self-sufficient. This lack of total self sufficiency unites people to create their community. For example, the store clerk, the gas station attendant, and the bank clerk are all highly interdependent on the services each of them provides. Likewise, we don't make our own clothes or harvest our own food. We don't supply our own water or electricity. People are united in society in part because of their common interdependence on those needs and many more.

We become part of our community by consistently supporting and working to supply its needs. For example, when we secure long term employment we work a job that offers a service and supplies a need for the rest of the community. We spend the money we earn in our community to acquire our needs, and in turn, support the financial needs of the other people and services in our community. On the other hand, the more (any) type of crime is committed within a community it prevents that community from meeting the needs of the people while creating chaos and disorder.

One moment we are behaving like a Good Samaritan in our community, and the next moment we are violating the laws of our community, hoping not to get caught. The pain we inflict is much broader than those who are close to us or the consequences we suffer. It affects the safety, needs, goals, and values of everyone in that community. In reality, it is a gross violation of everything society stands for in one selfish act.

You shall love your neighbor as yourself…
LEVITICUS 19:18

Alternating between public Good Samaritan and private criminal is not only extremely inconsistent, but unstable, unreliable, and immature. What makes us part of society is not that we reside in it, but that we work to support the social framework that is in place. This helps to maximize the benefits it offers to all parties in our community. For this to occur there must be an expectation and obligation for each person to function with high levels of consistency in regard to the needs of others.

COMMON GOALS
Once we are released we will share common goals with people in society. Once we move beyond our basic needs, we still require others to reach our goals. They are our visions and dreams to reach beyond what we are. We become part of our community by uniting with others to reach our goals. Our goals may involve specialized education, a skilled trade, financial mobility, or starting your own business. Great achievers are not limited to their own resources.

They are mentored and influenced by others who could take them further than they could have ever reached alone. This is why there is no truth to the myth of "the self made man." The troubled young man who become one of the nation's leading heart surgeons is a good example of this.

You shall love your neighbor as [you do] yourself
MATTHEW 19:19

COMMON VALUES

Once we are released, we will share common values with people in society. Diverse groups of people in society have unity because they hold certain basic values in common – for example, their families, freedoms, and safety. We become part of our community by focusing on those common and basic values rather than focusing on our differences. We can reintegrate into society only by respecting those common values. It's no wonder the qualities of love are so important for success.

You shall love your neighbor as [you do] yourself
ROMANS 13:9

There are several important characteristics that support the needs, goals, and values of the community we are returning to integrate into:

- Cohesion - Mutual interest that holds the parts together
- Consensus - General agreement concerning beliefs, rules, needs
- Cooperation - Working together toward the common purpose of a better life
- Reciprocity - Exchange of favors – trading agreement
- Stability - Dependable and permanent structure
- Predictability - Standards and boundaries of behavior
  = Consistent harmony/conflict and isolation prevention

SECURING COMMON INTERESTS

The high degree of harmony is made possible through a society being integrated by the same rules. Both written laws and unwritten rules govern relationships in local communities, usually leading to harmony rather than conflict and isolation. Laws set important standards and boundaries that are designed to hold this social harmony in place. They are considered sacred for the survival of the many and more important than any one individual.

Uprightness and right standing with God
(moral and spiritual rectitude in every area and relation) elevate a nation
PROVERBS 14:34

SOCIAL REWARDS AND SOCIAL SANCTIONS

Regardless of the level of sanctions or post release control we are given upon release, the moment we walk back into society we're once again granted a certain degree of trust. Over time, greater levels of trust are granted to those who adhere to the needs, goals, and values of their community. When we are released from prison we hope to benefit from the services, opportunities, and privileges

199

within our community. The price society expects us to pay for these benefits is simply for us to live as though we are part of it and not violate it in any regard.

Live in complete harmony with one another
ROMANS 15:5

This harmony is not just refraining from committing minor or major criminal offenses. It involves written and unwritten rules governing: relationships, employment, housing, business agreements, traffic laws, public and private property, credit, parole contracts, and other areas that support social unity. If we violate society's laws or continually disregard its rules, we become a threat to the stability of that social system. We create conflict between us and society when we threaten the well-being of its needs, goals, and values. This conflict leads to social sanction that, when severe enough, means isolation from society for its protection. The isolation and separation is usually satisfied through incarceration.

When we are isolated from society for its protection we are (not) "Victims of the system." Every human life experiences hardship and struggle. Life is hard and not always fair. There are never any "quick fix solutions" to our problems where anti-social behavior and crime can offer a good short cut. Whatever our problems may be, violating the needs, goals, and values of the community we live in is never the answer. Sooner or later it just creates another conflict between us and the trust we violate with our community. At that point we leave society no choice but to isolate us for their protection. Your community wants you as their PARTNER; it will not tolerate you as a PREDATOR and PARASITE.

Let each one of us make it a practice to please (make happy)
his neighbor for his good and for his true welfare
ROMANS 15:2

FINAL THOUGHTS ON THE STAGES
The goal is to prevent ourselves from entering the unconscious progression of recidivism I have repeated on multiple releases from prison. This was outlined in part one of the psycho-social stages of reentry. Several other repeat offenders have reviewed these stages and were heavily impacted by how they could finally make sense of their experiences. I have outlined an alternative set of stages that are potent principles for freedom. These stages were described in parts 3-6. When combined with the principles of acclimation outlined in part two, they become the most powerful principles that exist for successful reintegration into society. How do I know this? Because they are the most common

principles in the designer's handbook. They come directly from the Bible, the bestselling book of all time.

I call them psycho-social stages because if we successfully deal with each personal and interpersonal challenge each stage represents, it will equip us for the next stage. As we successfully negotiate each stage, it will greatly contribute to the mental, emotional, and relational issues that are specific to each of us individually. If we do not successfully reignite our areas of frozen development, social and personality problems will persist upon release. Our relational issues, maturity issues, and compulsive/addictive behaviors will continue to thrive. We will naturally gravitate back towards anti-social behaviors and crime as a result of trying to relate in an adult world through our specific areas of developmental immaturity.

Let me ask you, has any of this worked for you yet? The truth is it never will. The blueprint of human design is that happiness, success, and freedom can only come through a principle centered life. These principles represent the law of the spirit of life. If life is what we want, it is time to admit that we cannot break this law of design; we only break ourselves against it.

Science has spent billions of dollars and endless hours of research looking for answers that the Word of God has been able to provide all along. It takes a competent and caring person to teach another person how to become a competent and caring person. It takes principle centered men of maturity to teach other males how to become principle centered men of maturity. This is the simple and effective way we were designed, and there is no other way to get there. It's about growing and being transformed by these principles through these relationships. All else I have said was merely to describe it.

On the next page is the complete diagram from part one through part six.

Let's take a few moments to reflect on what we have learned.
- This diagram represents a lot of information we have covered. Can you identify each stage?
- This diagram represents two potential paths once we enter the Return to Reality stage. Both paths represent a lot of potential challenges. One path is traveling alone. The other involves support. Are you willing to use the support of others to help secure your freedom? Why or why not?

With the answer to this question in mind, let's look at the most important factors for reentry preparation in the next chapter.

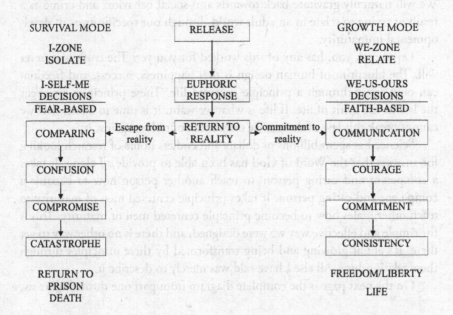

SURVIVAL MODE

I-ZONE
ISOLATE

I-SELF-ME
DECISIONS
FEAR-BASED

RELEASE

EUPHORIC
RESPONSE

GROWTH MODE

WE-ZONE
RELATE

WE-US-OURS
DECISIONS
FAITH-BASED

COMPARING ← Escape from reality — RETURN TO REALITY — Commitment to reality → COMMUNICATION

CONFUSION → COURAGE

COMPROMISE → COMMITMENT

CATASTROPHE → CONSISTENCY

RETURN TO
PRISON
DEATH

FREEDOM/LIBERTY
LIFE

CHAPTER THIRTEEN

Reentry Preparation

—~~—

When men become incarcerated they enter the prison system carrying a tremen-
dous amount of mental and emotional baggage. No one is exempt from this.
We come in with the issues that led to our crimes and the new layers related to
our incarceration. It is unquestionably a time of deep grief and profound doubt.
The traumatic and often dramatic loss of everything that represented our lives,
and the immense deprivation of daily prison life takes its toll on us mentally and
emotionally.

One of the major mistakes we make is only identifying with the drama and not
connecting to the trauma. When the drama passes there is an illusion of healing;
time may allow the drama to fade but it does nothing for the trauma. Wounds
of this kind do not begin to heal unless we get real and begin to deal with them.
This takes courage because the only way past the pain is through the pain.

— THE AUTHOR —

The long and complicated process of reintegration back into the social
systems of family and society are best started at the beginning of our
sentence. The sooner we begin to prepare, the more time we have to
prepare and the better our chances of success. Likewise, how we prepare for
our release will be a major factor in the outcome. The potential outcome of
any circumstance is most heavily influenced by the character we take into it.
To illustrate this point I would like to begin with "The Parable of the Wise Old
Convict."

And He told them many things in parables (stories by way of illustration and comparison)
MATTHEW 13:3

THE PARABLE OF THE WISE OLD CONVICT

There once was a wise old convict who worked in the prison R&D where mail,
packages, and even prisoners were received and shipped out with their property. One day the wise old convict was helping with a group of inmates who had
just been transferred in from another prison. One of the transfers asked, "Sir,
seeing you are a resident here at this prison, can you tell me what it is like here.
Is it a good place to do time?"

The wise old convict began his answer with another question. He understood the old adage, half the answer to any question is best given by asking another question. "What was it like in the prison from which you came?" The newly transferred inmate responded, "It was a terrible place. It was dirty and too full of drama for me. I had a lot of problems there with both inmates and staff. The food was bad and there was nothing to do. I hated it there, so I stayed in trouble."

"I am sorry to tell you young man, the prison to which you have come is much the same thing," answered the wise old convict. He said, "It is everything you did not like in the prison you left behind." The wise old convict continued his days working in the R&D until one day he was helping with the pack-up of another inmate being transferred out to another prison. The young man being transferred asked, "Sir, you look like you have been around a while and done some time. Can you tell what it is like in the prison to which I am being transferred?"

The wise old convict responded, "Can you first tell me young man, how was your experience here?" The young man replied, "Oh, I was fortunate to have come here. Actually, I was treated better than I deserved. I got along well with everyone. I had a lot of good opportunities and experiences." The wise old convict smiled and replied, "I've got some good news for you. I am happy to tell you young man that the prison to which you are headed is much the same as your experience here. I am confident you will do fine."

What's the moral of the story? The wise old convict learned an important principle from his many years of experience. What people are ultimately determines what they will find in any environment. This makes character building the most important method of reentry preparation. There is another important relational principle going on in this parable that is not as obvious. It is through a continual process of deciding how we will respond to people and circumstance that we establish who and what we are. Over time we become a particular type of person. The world comes to know us as that person. This makes community the most important factor in shaping our character and our relational maturity. All of this leads to one important conclusion. We need to experience a healthy and mature community before we can hope to successfully integrate into one.

We pray you will become mature
2 CORINTHIANS 13:9

NICK'S STORY
I would like to illustrate the importance of experiencing a healthy and mature environment by sharing with you about a long-time friend I will call Nick, who just returned to prison for his fourth time. Nick just finished fourteen years on his third number when he was released last time. Fifteen months later

he was back in prison again at the age of forty-five.

Nick was not entirely non-productive while incarcerated. He attended college, worked as a program aide, took some vocational classes, and worked on a minimum security farm.

However, Nick was not much for reforming his character or being part of any type of community group that involved accountability or opening up to reveal what type of help he needed. In reality, he was pretty resistant to change. There were ways of behaving and things he had done since he was a teenager that he was not ready to let go of.

Nick was intelligent and had learned a number of useful skills that helped him to survive in prison. He wasn't maturing in ways that would help him adapt and change to handle his freedom. I already knew these things about Nick. After all, I was the one who encouraged him to take some college classes when he was twenty years old. I have known Nick a long time. I was not in any way judging Nick. I was heartbroken for him. I was at a point on my own journey where his return was, to me, an absolute tragic loss of life. Until we can all see it that way, at least in part, I don't believe we can stay free.

I asked Nick what brought him back to prison again. I was fairly confident at this point in my own journey that I knew the answer. What I wanted to hear was how he saw things. Nick's explanation for returning to prison was as follows:

"Staying at my dad's house I had everything I needed. I just got around these guys I grew up with, drinking and getting high and I messed up." I question further. I asked if he'd found a job. Nick responded, "I probably could have but I didn't do much of anything once I started hanging around those guys and a couple girls I knew. They just used me because I had a ride and my dad was giving me money. They didn't change a bit since they were younger, only maybe a little bit worse. They were grown men acting like they were still teenagers."

I am still deeply heartbroken for Nick. He didn't even give himself a chance. To my way of thinking, he was describing himself when he said, "They were grown men acting like they were still teenagers." Like our parable, what people are ultimately determines what they will find. Nick has absolutely no ability to see that the circumstances of his release were most influenced by the character he took into it. Like the first young man in the "Parable of the Wise Old Convict," he explained everything completely by his circumstances and not by his character.

Let us go on instead and become mature in our understanding.
Surely we don't need to start again
HEBREWS 6:1

Nick did not have the character and relational maturity to reach beyond those he found himself drawn to. He wanted so much more for himself. I know because I talked with him right before he was released the last time. We must come to an understanding that there are powerful principles of design at work in our lives. One of those principles is that we don't attract what we want but what we are. You must first become the thing you want, then you will attract it into your life.

Cast your bread upon the waters, for you will find it after many days
ECCLESIASTES 11:1

REINTEGRATION IS DEFINED BY RELATIONSHIP

The journey from isolation to intimacy and community is "the" major challenge of our reintegration. Failure to form healthy, mature intimate and community partnerships will isolate us from the strong support and accountability necessary for success. It will also alienate us from anything that bonds us to the rest of society. The stronger those bonds and accountability are, the greater our chances of success will be.

The journey from prison to successful reintegration is much the same process as growing up. But instead, reentry reveals whether or not we have grown up. It necessarily begins in the stage of dependence, where everyone initially needs help after release to get their needs met. It is an unspoken expectation that this help is not because we lack the character or relational maturity to succeed. Since we are adults it is reasonably assumed the help from others will lead to the self-support of independence.

Half of all who are re-arrested within the first three years never make it out of the dependency stage. Those who do reach the self supportive stage of independence drastically lower their chances of returning to prison. Those who reach the highest level of living, interdependence (combining character and relational maturity for the best possible good), are the lowest for returning to prison.

If reintegration is fully completed and secured, it will be defined by the interdependent (self supported/other connected) relationships we share with other independent adults in society. There are twelve components that define complete reintegration. I mention them because they are tied to our relationships. We will look at these in a later chapter.

The terms dependence, independence, and interdependence have been discussed in some detail in the chapter "The Path to Adult Maturity." They are vitally important for us to understand for the following reasons: These terms are measuring points on a scale that not only define our level of reintegration, but our ability to function in an adult society. They actually describe levels of freedom in ways few terms can. They are relational terms that describe what levels we function at in intimacy and community. The designer's handbook for life (the Bible) is about interdependent relationships from cover to cover. Science cannot discover something without it somehow being interdependent on something else. If we are going to be successful at reintegration, it is going to happen in the environment of relationship. Why not start now?

TEN WAYS TO RETURN TO PRISON (THE POWER OF HABIT)

1. Pretend prison is a playground rather than a battleground for transformation.
2. Worry more about the strength of your biceps than the strength of your character.
3. Measure yourself by the knowledge in your head and not the purity of your heart.
4. Refuse to be involved in groups working toward change or only go for certificates.
5. Spend as much time as you can watching television.
6. Fill your days with fun and food and avoid self-examination at all costs.
7. Pretend you are the real victim and blame the world.
8. Live for comfort and convenience rather than principle and conviction.
9. Live by your own definition of manhood.
10. Pretend you need no significant change and refuse reentry preparation.

We have spent many years developing specific patterns of living, in and out of prison, that are not always easily modified. Our character as well as our lifestyle are made up of various routines and patterns called habits. The power of habit, character, and lifestyle are rooted in the deepest recesses of our mind and emotions. These things can make change a real challenge.

However, trying to abandon a criminal lifestyle without abandoning the comfortable routines that support it is just not going to happen. We are in desperate need of a coach and a team.

Pitchers on professional baseball teams often develop bad habits. This is why they recruit pitching coaches. Pitchers are able to see only the effects and consequences of their bad habits. What they are doing feels normal and comfortable to them which often makes it hard for them to determine the problem. The pitching coach is recruited because, as another set of eyes, he can see the cause of the problem. As the result of having a coach, the pitcher is able to modify his behavior and then practice the new action in a team setting. The rest of this chapter will reveal how this is the same process we experience in the community of a mentor (coach) and a fellowship (team setting).

Deeply appreciate and thoroughly know and fully recognize such men
1 CORINTHIANS 16:18

Cultivating community through a mentor and fellowship in the prison setting allows us to develop a working relationship with the psycho-social stages of reentry we just learned about in the last four chapters. Community is a type of team setting where fellowship is centered on the principles of acclimation we need to reintegrate into society. The goal is to be able to apply them with at least some degree of skill before we are released.

The Psycho-Social Stages of Reentry:
1. Communication
2. Courage
3. Commitment
4. Consistency

Applied Acclimation Principle:
1. Commitment to truth
2. Commitment to healthy relationships
3. Commitment to personal responsibility
4. Commitment to self-examination
5. Commitment to challenge
6. Commitment to examination and challenge of others

DEFINING COMMUNITY

Real community is defined as a group of men who share a common aim or goal. Community operates through the dynamics of communicating, sharing, and participating as they work toward their common goal. There are many types of groups we can choose from. You may want to be involved in more than one. The church may provide a fellowship or discipleship group. You may want to add a long-term reentry support group that uses the tools in this book.

There are usually other groups available both in and out of prison that aim at various types of recovery from addictions and share other important life skills. No matter what their specialized interest is, they all share a common goal. They aim at personal growth through spiritual disciplines. The result is a strong character and relational maturity.

As each part does its own special work, it helps the other parts to grow
EPHESIANS 4:16

We already share many common characteristics with all the men in these groups before we even enter them. It is only our denial or pride that would tell us we don't fit in with them or have nothing in common with them. We share the same shortcomings and defects with the men in these groups as we do with our old community of friends. Like us, they have defects in their character that have caused them suffering and have handicapped their lives. In these groups it's not only okay to have character and relational issues, it's a requirement.

The real difference between our old group of friends and this new community of fellowship is that these men in the fellowship reveal to heal instead of hide for pride. These men openly share their problems in an effort to resolve them. Real community is a place safe enough to share who we really are and be honored and respected for it without being judged.

Confess to one another therefore your faults (your slips, your false steps, your offenses…)
JAMES 5:16

COMMUNITY CULTIVATES INTIMACY

Learning how to live, relate, and love requires intimacy. This helps to make it one of the most meaningful experiences of our lives. We come to learn that love and intimacy is much deeper and broader than our own physical impulses and desires. There is genuine kindness and warmth in the fellowship of community, balanced with firmness and rigorous honesty. It is a network of men sharing their experience, strength, and hope with each other to solve common human problems through spiritual principles. There is a sense of social equality and mutual respect. You are accepted just for being you, not because of reputation, wealth, titles, or abilities.

Self-discovery is not always serious business. Sometimes it's just casual conversation, food, and fun. It becomes a respected place where people genuinely care about each other. The main focus of fellowship is genuine heart-to-heart, gut-level sharing. It's not like other prison conversations where you tell some fantastic made-for-TV story – and then I tell you one to try and top it. The healing type of heart-to-heart sharing happens when people feel safe enough to get honest about what has happened and is happening in their lives. The difference between the mentor and the group is the level of intimacy or the details we share. These are special relationships where we can share our hurts, reveal our feelings, confess our failures, disclose our doubts, admit our fears, and acknowledge our weaknesses in order to move beyond them.

COMMUNITY CULTIVATES IDENTITY

When we cultivate community with a mentor and fellowship, one of the most important elements of transformation begins to take place. We begin to adopt a new and whole self-image. Our evolving self-image is a critical component to the change process. When our self image is interwoven with the identity God has given us as His ultimate creation, and we are among competent and caring men who affirm it, we are never the same again. People who understand their inherent value and gain a sense of belonging, slowly over time, stop behaving in self destructive ways.

But as many as did receive and welcome Him, He gave the authority
(power, privilege, right) to become the children of God...
JOHN 1:12

Only when we understand the value God places on us are we able to extend that value to others. A mature relationship with God, loving and trusting Him as our Father and Creator, allows us to open up to others while loving and trusting them. God is our source and potential for relationship in all its fullness. We need others to show us how to relate to God. Without this spiritual mentoring, we may be inclined to approach a relationship with God from a selfish, self- centered position. While no one but God is the final authority on our identity and value, our mentor and community are where we learn how to cultivate the character to express it.

COMMUNITY CULTIVATES TRUTH
Our mentor and fellowship group represent advocates of communicating and practicing truth. They can advocate the need for us to clearly see where we are in our personal development. Keeping ourselves in a false sense of who we are, where we are, and what we are about will only keep us buried under a burden of bondage to our defects and shortcomings. This can leave us believing we are able to handle our freedom when we are not. The mentor and the group use truth to gently lead us into reality about ourselves.

It often takes many months of patient work to help us see we are not who we thought we were – and there is a lot of work to be done in our lives. We begin to care what they know when we begin to know that they care. This competent and caring environment of community is the only place our hardened hearts can begin to soften, and we finally begin to see the need to make some changes before we are released.

Today when you hear his voice, don't harden your hearts
HEBREWS 3:8

The purpose of this community is to provide a setting where our issues can emerge naturally through relating and communicating. This allows the experience of community to become a discovery process where we can see ourselves behaving inside these relationships much the same way we do in everyday life. For example, we may act distrustful, control our feelings, and only reveal carefully chosen parts of ourselves. We can discover over time that these behaviors reflect consistent patterns of behavior. The mentor and group exist as a safe and nurturing environment for them to challenge these patterns and point out alternative behaviors. How well we take advantage of this kind of opportunity will depend on our commitment to truth.

To many who were blind He gave [a free, gracious, joy-giving gift of] sight
LUKE 7:21

COMMUNITY CULTIVATES AUTHENTICITY

Cultivating community leads us on a journey of authenticity. What is authenticity? It means being genuine and keeping it real. We discover our authentic self for the first time in our lives by being authentic with others. One price we pay without it is a lack of genuine intimacy in our lives. When someone is wearing a mask and playing a role we are not aware of, we may be props and stage hands in the play, but we are not intimately involved. Intimacy absolutely requires authenticity. When the mask comes off and the guard is dropped, we will find the real person inside of us. Without exception, people like the real self they discover much more than the mask that was laid aside. It is much more comfortable, because it is natural and not artificial.

Be entirely trustworthy and good
TITUS 2:10

COMMUNITY CULTIVATES CARING CONFRONTATION

Character building and relational maturity sometimes involves confrontation. The process of growing and maturing is largely a process of separating fantasy from reality and falsehood from truth. Sometimes it is a matter of us not knowing one from the other. Sometimes it is a matter of clinging to fantasy and falsehood out of security and comfort. Cultivating community is a step we take out of a conviction to change and grow, and not the comfort and convenience of having our defects supported. There are times it's going to be difficult. Confrontation is supposed to be difficult to jolt us out of our comfort zones. We cannot afford to withdraw at the first sign of being confronted. The price of further incarcerations is too big of a price to pay.

Character building and relational maturity are a slow process. We must be patient and persistent and refuse to give up. Confrontation can cause us to entertain thoughts of giving up. It is usually accompanied by a strong desire to return to old behaviors. Whenever we try to avoid or escape the pain of change we short circuit our maturing process. The result is that we end up with a worse and fruitless type of pain that pays no reward, but exacts high penalties like incarceration. To quit is to give up. To stay is to grow up.

Remaining silent when someone is harming themselves is probably one of the most uncaring things we can do. Avoiding confrontation and protecting our comfort zones at all costs means we may yet lack the necessary courage to change. When confrontation is handled correctly both parties are encouraged. We are instilled with new levels of courage each time we are able to face ourselves and grow closer to others in the process. Courage allows us to view confrontation as beneficial, rather than an attack that needs to be defended.

If any person is overtaken in misconduct…of any sort, you who are spiritual [who are responsive to and controlled by the Spirit] should set him right and restore and reinstate him, without any sense of superiority and with all gentleness
GALATIANS 6:1

COMMUNITY CULTIVATES HEALING

It is so important for us to come into the realization of our need for new levels of growth and maturity and understand that there are people who truly care to help us. If we believe we are in fairly good shape other than being locked up, we won't see our need for help. When men become incarcerated, they enter the prison system carrying a tremendous amount of mental and emotional baggage. No one is exempt from this. We come in with the issues that led to our crimes and the new layers related to our incarceration. It is unquestionably a time of deep grief and profound doubt. The traumatic and often dramatic loss of everything that represented our lives, and the immense deprivation of daily prison life, take their toll on us mentally and emotionally.

One of the major mistakes we make is only identifying with the drama and not connecting to the trauma. When the drama passes there is an illusion of healing; time may allow the drama to fade, but it does nothing for the trauma. Wounds of this kind do not begin to heal unless we get real and begin to deal with them. This takes courage, because the only way past the pain is through the pain.

It takes courage like nothing else because getting past our baggage requires that we admit it, accept it, and openly expose it. Mistaking cowardice for courage may have brought us to prison, but only courage will determine how well we prepare for release and if we remain free.

The cheap substitutes found in the prison environment are not real courage. The truth is, courage is an uncommon virtue in prison. There are many falsehoods and myths about courage. It is likely to mean changing the way we define it, because mistaking cowardice for courage will sabotage our maturity and freedom. To get through our prison experience doesn't necessarily require courage; to grow through it does.

MISTAKING COWARDICE FOR COURAGE

Cultivating community will not only introduce us to genuine courage expressed by other men, but also support us in developing it. One thing may be important to express in this section. Courage doesn't mean not being afraid of anything. Sometimes it means being afraid of the right things. Just look at how ridiculously we misunderstood it.

We are willing to fight another man over nothing, but lack an ounce of courage to stand up to ourselves and fight our lives' worst enemies within. We will stick a drug in our system with no knowledge of what's in it, but we wouldn't dare share with someone that we are confused and have no real answers. We will walk out of a night club with someone who has a disease history we know nothing about, but we are afraid to be seen walking up the hallway with a Bible or into a chapel.

It is as sport to a [self-confident] fool to do wickedness, but to have skillful and godly wisdom is pleasure and relaxation to a man of understanding
PROVERBS 10:23

We will steal a car, burglarize a house, or risk blowing ourselves up cooking meth, but we wouldn't dare be caught on our knees crying out to God. We feel less vulnerable condemned to incarceration in a courtroom full of people than we do opening up and sharing in a group of caring people. I could go on of course, but really, isn't there something just a little bit wrong with all of this?

Cultivating community helps us meet a basic need for healing and that is the courage to openly communicate. When we experience other men who openly communicate and share their flaws, faults, fears, hurts, past failures, and even laugh at themselves, we may be surprised that we find part of ourselves admiring their candor and courage. We begin to discover a sense of belonging as we are shocked by how much we can relate to what they share in common with our lives. Belonging leads to a new sense of security when we realize self-exposure will not mean judgment and rejection.

THE RETURN EQUALS THE INVESTMENT

Our new courage allows us to begin testing the waters and share our own lives. We notice that we feel a little better each time we do. We begin to find closure and emotional healing for the past and solutions for our present and future when we open up. Sharing our flaws, faults, fears, hurts, and past failures opens the door to self-examination. Verbalizing them allows us to hear them for the first time. We begin to see our need to take personal responsibility for healing and change. In every way that we invest in our mentor and group we receive large returns.

When we invest in listening and relating, the return is a sense of belonging. When we invest in sharing, the return is a sense of acceptance. There are profound differences between the belonging and acceptance in our old circles and our new community of fellowship. The sense of belonging and acceptance in our new community of fellowship is genuine. The type we experienced in our old circles belong to the image we projected and the mask we wore. It had nothing do with who we really are.

We proclaim to you what we ourselves have actually seen and heard so that you may have
fellowship with us
1 JOHN 1:3

A real sense of belonging and acceptance unite together to form the conviction of personal value. When we connect with that value we can finally begin to face that we "are where we are," and if we are ever going to be ready for reentry we must stop fooling ourselves. We have to stop denying that we have a lot of growth to do and we must get down to the business of doing it.

COMMUNITY CULTIVATES EMPATHY AND SYMPATHY
Cultivating community dries up self pity and fearful self preoccupation. Self obsession is a major trait that led to our incarceration. Without the experience of community, prison only heightens this obsession. Community allows us to experience getting past ourselves for once and enter into another's pain and suffering. We learn to understand what others in our fellowship have gone through. This helps us to better understand how our actions have hurt others. These types of relating and carrying one another's burden are called empathy and sympathy. They are critical components of learning how to live, relate, and love.

Bear (endure, carry) one another's burdens and troublesome moral faults
GALATIANS 6:2

RECOGNIZING THE SEASONS OF OUR LIVES
Character development and relational maturity are just like nature's process of growing healthy and ripened fruit. It requires a full season to plant, cultivate, and harvest. The same is true when it comes to learning how to live, relate, and love. It not only requires a full season, but it must be done in the right season.

This is our season. The question is, will we recognize it, or will the field of our life remain barren as a result of our self obsession?

For everything there is a season, a time for every activity under heaven. A time to plant and a time to harvest
ECCLESIASTES 3:1-2

Our inability to rightly relate to God and others has led to the severe penalty of incarceration. Our tendency is to pull away from the only things that can heal our brokenness – the right relationships. At the very deepest level we avoid God and exposure to others, because we are not ready to face the reality of what we've done, what we've been like, and what we've become. To remain free, we must be ready.

There are no words to adequately describe the hellish living of self obsession we have suffered. It is a meaningless and repetitious life where we strive with all our hearts to meet the demands of self, while each experience is empty and unsatisfying – yet demanding of another. It means to drive ourselves with the whip of selfishness that cause us to trample over others and hurt those who truly love us over and over again. A life of self obsession is a life full of misery and sorrow with brief intermittent moments of pleasure. It leads to part of our mind becoming darkened and evil, with moments of complete insanity that end in incarceration. We can only harvest what we plant.

Those who plant injustice will harvest disaster
PROVERBS 22:8

Anyone who has ever lived this kind life knows more about hell than many preachers.

Self-obsession is a living hell. The more we feed the self-obsessed beast within, the more ravenous it becomes. Which one will grow the strongest during your incarceration, the ravenous beast or the principle-centered man of maturity? You know the answer; the one you feed the most before you are released.

So let us not get tired of doing what is good.
At just the right time we will reap a harvest of blessing if we don't give up
GALATIANS 6:9

It is simply immature thinking to believe that we are here without issues – just as it is to believe that we can avoid them, or that we can change our own deep rooted lifelong handicaps alone. Cultivating community is the only counter force strong enough to retrain our mind, reshape our habits, develop a new lifestyle, and transform our character. This makes cultivating community the most powerful force for reentry preparation. I am absolutely convinced God is right about all of this. The solution for us is relationally based not rationally based.

Listen (consent and submit) to the words of the wise…
I have made known these things to you today, even to you
PROVERBS 22:17, 19

THE FRUIT OF CULTIVATING COMMUNITY

1. Conviction of value	9. Reliable
2. Emotional healing	10. Honesty
3. Self-awareness	11. Dependable
4. Validation	12. Unselfish
5. Discipline	13. Responsible
6. Authentic	14. Trustworthy
7. Accountable	15. Patient
8. Humility	16. Sympathetic

It's time once again to reflect on what we've learned.

- Which person best describes you in the Parable of the Wise Old Convict, the first or the second man? Do you think Nick's story could ever be your story? Why or why not?
- In our list of 10 ways to return to prison, which ones do you show the least discipline? Which ones do you show the most discipline?
- What most attracts you about cultivating community? What most bothers you about it? Do you see how cultivating community can better prepare your character and relational maturity to reenter your family and society?

With the answers to these questions in mind, let's learn about family reintegration in the next chapter.

CHAPTER FOURTEEN

Family Reintegration (Part One)
—⁓—

*I had crossed de line of which I had so long been dreaming. I was free; but dere
was no one to welcome me to the land of freedom. I was a stranger in a strange
land, and my home after all was down in de old cabin quarters, wid de ole folks,
and my brudders and sisters. But dis solemn resolution I came: I was free.*

*Oh, how I prayed den, lying all alone on de cold, damp ground;
'Oh, dear Lord,' I said, 'I haint got no friend but you.
Come to my help, for I'm in trouble.'*

*Twant me, twas the Lord. I always told Him, "I trust You. I don't know where
to go or what to do, but I expect You to lead me," and He always did.*
— HARRIET TUBMAN[1] (1820-1913) —

Reentry for many men will represent visions of returning home to their
families. There will be some who are returning home to their family of
origin and others to families of their own. Whatever the case may be,
returning home to family is likely to represent the beginning of your quest for
a new and fruitful life of freedom and liberty.

Family is the first and most basic institution of society; it offers us refuge
from, as well as connection to, the larger social system of society during reentry. This makes family an important agent of adjustment and encouragement
during our reintegration process. They can offer us a healthy balance of support and accountability. This is especially important during early reentry when
we feel most vulnerable and decision making is most critical.

A person who strays from home is like a bird that strays from its nest
PROVERBS 27:8

---

1 Harriet Tubman was an escaped slave. She repeatedly risked her life to free other slaves.
During the Civil War she worked as a Union spy, and after the war she helped set up schools
for freed slaves. You can be free and not know it, and thereby still act like a prisoner. You can be
free and know it. Harriet Tubman knew she was free and her life reflected it in both her words
and actions. Her words speak to all of us who face the struggles and challenges of remaining
free after prison.

It's no wonder that the idea of returning home brings forth such powerful emotions as love, joy, and hopeful anticipation. Family is where we live out the most powerful of all human experiences. It is the source of life's greatest human convictions of value, such as acceptance, belonging, and security. Family is a survival and growth unit for our reintegration into society – a major resource in our re-socialization process. A healthy family matrix provides the social soil in which we can plant ourselves as we begin the journey from isolation to intimacy and community as we discussed in the previous chapter.

NO HOME TO RETURN TO
A growing number of men being released from prison will return to society with no family to return to. This should not be viewed as a barrier to successful reintegration, but rather a goal to work toward and look forward to. If you are without a family and returning to society keep in mind that you are returning to rebuild your life. You are likely to have a family in the future if you remain free.

God places the solitary in families and gives the desolate a home in which to dwell;
He leads the prisoners out to prosperity
PSALM 68:6

Regardless of your situation upon release, family reintegration still has a major significance in your life. It will help you to better understand your family of origin and prepare you for the family you will create. Until you have a family of your own, your mentor, church fellowship, support group, and other competent, caring people can act as a temporary substitute for family. Embrace them, love them, and practice the principles in this book with them as you prepare for success in a family of your own.

NOT RETURNING HOME
Returning home is not a safe choice for everyone. It is possible that what you once called home represents an environment that is not supportive to your stability and freedom. This may be true whether it is your family of origin or the family you created as an adult. If this is the case, the choice not to return home can be one of the most difficult decisions concerning reentry. There is little doubt it will take tremendous courage. The best possible choices that involve protecting our freedom will often be the hardest to make.

Be careful that no one misleads you [deceiving you and leading you into error]
MATTHEW 24:4

For example, there may be alcohol and drug issues at home. It may be that home represents crime and gang activity. Home may be an atmosphere of violence and severe emotional abuse. On the other hand, it may be that the neighborhood your home is in represents all of these risks. These are only a few examples of a home environment that is potentially not supportive to your stability and freedom upon release. There may be a possibility of other risks and dangers you must consider. Each case is unique. Hard decisions such as these are best made with the input of others, like your mentor.

Your reentry mentor can see past the powerful emotions that may distort your perceptions and provide encouragement for the best possible choice. You will need to be totally committed to truth in order to make the best possible choices for your life. Your reentry mentor can only point; you must be the one who chooses which direction you will go. Conviction of truth over comfort and convenience is the narrow path that leads to freedom and liberty.

We cannot oppose the truth, but must always stand for the truth
2 CORINTHIANS 13:8

The moral support of a mentor strengthens the resolve of newly formed convictions. He may be the only safety net we have that keeps us from turning toward the path of least resistance and into danger. Not returning home after release doesn't mean it has to be permanent or that you cannot return to visit. On the other hand, it may mean not returning home at all. It's your freedom. Place it first. Use the principles and disciplines in this book and always use the insight of other people. If you do these things, the right decisions will come and so will the courage to carry them out.

THE PROCESS OF SOCIAL SYSTEM REINTEGRATION

The final product of reintegration into the family and society is, in reality, a lengthy growth process that requires a specific series of stages. These stages are designed to lead us into the delicate balance between our need of individuality and our need for conformity with the family and society we are integrating in to. These four stages are listed below:

The social system reintegration process:
1. Reentry preparation
2. Reentry
3. Acclimation
4. Reintegration

We cannot integrate what we do not have or own. This is significant since part three of the Human Design Model revealed that we can only offer our family and society the health and wholeness we take into it. We can use the analogy of a human organ transplant process to better help us understand the reintegration process. In the following analogy, the organ will represent the person. The body the organ is being transplanted in to will represent the family and society.

REINTEGRATION IS A TRANSPLANT PROCESS
1. Reentry preparation.
The first stage in the organ transplant is the work of preparation. The prep work is a critical stage in the organ transplant process. If anything is left out, the transplant efforts may fail. The transplant is a process of integrating needs and functions. Both the organ with its own needs and functions and the body with its larger and complex needs and functions must be totally prepared. Once the preparation work is complete, it's time to move into the second stage.

2. Reentry.
The second stage of the transplant process is to put the organ into the body in the right location and carefully make the right connections. The fact that the organ has been placed in the body does not actually make it part of the larger system. However, if the organ is healthy and functions properly – and is put in the right place with the right connections – it will have a fighting chance.

3. Acclimation.
The organ is not functioning as part of the larger body until it goes through an acclimation process. This often requires a significant amount of time. The acclimation process is where the organ (the person) becomes accustomed to the new system and conditions, and the system (family/society) recognizes the organ as supporting it.

4. Reintegration.
If the critical adjustment period of acclimation is successful, the organ that was one a foreign body trying to adapt is now fully integrated into the larger system. The organ has become part of the larger system by supporting its needs and functions, while the larger body supports the needs and functions of the individual organ. The organ is aiding and being aided through the life supporting interaction. There exists connecting relationships to the larger body while maintaining its own unique individuality and purpose within the larger system.

The health and wholeness of the organ is determined by the life-giving interaction it experiences while in the body. The harmony between the individual parts equates into balance throughout the system and order is established. There is complete integration defined by the life support factors of wholeness, relationship, balance, and order. If you want to be successful at genuine reintegration once you are released, you cannot avoid these stages. Let's take a closer look at each stage.

1. FAMILY REENTRY PREPARATION

TO MAKE READY TO ENTER A SOCIAL SYSTEM BY A SPECIAL PROCESS

The first and most important step of preparation toward family reintegration is our quest for greater levels of maturity in our manhood. Day by day, each action we take toward wholeness in our design of authentic manhood is security and stability for the future of our family upon our reentry. In this way, we become the organ in our transplant analogy that is healthy and functioning properly. We know we have fully grasped this concept when who we are upon release is more important than when we are released.

Wisdom and success are often falsely assumed to belong to the man who has all the answers. The problem is, no one ever really does. Wisdom and success usually belong to the man who remains open-minded and asks the right questions. Likewise, it will benefit us to consider the following questions. Is it possible that successful reintegration into your family may require more than just returning home? What will this four-stage transplant process require of me? What might family reentry preparation look like?

Through skillful and godly wisdom is a house (a life, a home, and family) built, and by understanding it is established [on a sound and good foundation]
PROVERBS 24:3

More often than not, everyone in the family is "caught up" in surviving the crisis of incarceration and focused on the goal of being reunited. There is little or no thought put into what type of complications long-term separation might create. It is easy to overlook what changes need to be made to secure a stronger family foundation, or even what potential problems might arise as we attempt to reassert our role in the family. Likewise, it is easy to overlook what type of healing work you and your family need right now.

It is important not to pretend that the family hasn't suffered devastation and profound grief as a result of your incarceration. Denying it won't make it go away. Once the initial drama of incarceration passes, a sort of family trance begins in the form of mental defenses that kick in to bury the trauma of the crisis. We go on communicating and visiting with the family while pretending this is just another phase or complication of life that will pass after release. The family defenses act as a survival method for the family while at the same time robbing the emotional life and freedom of each individual within the family.

FAMILY DEFENSES

The family defenses can be summarized as a set of unhealthy responses that are triggered by the crisis of incarceration. This does not mean these defenses were not part of the family prior to incarceration. It only means that now the crisis is the focus of their application. These defenses operate as acts of desperation to preserve the family at all costs. Let's look at a few of the most common family defenses:

1. THE NO TALK RULE. Don't talk openly about any thoughts, feelings, or experiences that focus on the pain and loneliness related to the family dysfunction or crisis of incarceration.

2. DISHONESTY AND PRETENDING. We are not to notice what is happening to the family and the price everyone is paying for incarceration. We are to pretend it is not happening. Rather than directly express what we think or feel, we are to pretend. We are to smile when we feel sad or laugh instead of express grief or worry.

3. DENY INDIVIDUAL FREEDOM. There is extreme self-monitoring by everyone in the family. It is a measurement being imposed that avoids the potential drama that would reignite the trauma. We must act as though we are not afraid and always in control. Anyone rocking the boat would upset the status quo.

4. MYTH MAKING. Always look at the bright side. Reframe the hurt, pain, and distress in such a way as to preserve the family. Myth making rationalizes what good may come as a result of incarceration while denying the penalties everyone pays.

5. INCOMPLETION. Don't complete transactions or resolve issues. Keep the same fights and disagreements going that have been going on for years to distract from the trauma of the crisis. This involves chronic conflict and fighting over petty issues without resolution. Incompletion may also mean the exact opposite. This is where the family agrees to never disagree. There is either conflict or confluence, but never healing and closure.

6. ILLUSION AND FANTASY. Never allow yourself to see yourself, the family, and circumstances as they really are. See the crisis as a unique circumstance or situation that is never likely to occur again. Like a bad dream, everything will be okay after incarceration. Forget that everything was not okay before the crisis, and expect change without anyone making any changes.

The shared secrets and the shared denial of the defenses do not protect or save the family.

They only leave it vulnerable to repeat and repetition of crisis because the defenses prevent healing and closure. Each family member agrees to share a certain unspoken focus and denial. "Everything will be all right after the crisis; there is nothing wrong with our family."

It's about continually denying the obvious in spite of the facts. It is about expecting the same behaviors to have different outcomes. Each member of the family falsely assumes that if the real problems are confronted it would be unbearably painful and would break up the family.

THE NEED FOR HEALING AND CLOSURE

The work of healing and closure is no doubt painful. Most of us understand this at least instinctively. This causes just about everyone to ask two universal questions. "Why go back to the past? Why relive any of that pain again?" The fact is, we never went through the pain and so we buried it. Everyone missed expressing those feelings when they occurred. The drama produced by the crisis distracted from the traumatic feelings that incarceration created. It's as if there was no time or even enough energy to deal with both the drama and the trauma. We opted to focus on the most obvious and threatening to family survival, the drama of the crisis.

I will never forget this awful time, as I grieve over my loss
LAMENTATIONS 3:20

THE NEED FOR GRIEF WORK

Grief work, as experts such as Kübler-Ross have shown us, is the process of healing. According to new research, grieving is not a completely fixed or predictable process. Each of us are likely to experience it a little differently. However, common experiences of grief for arrest and incarceration involve and often begin in shock and denial. It can move to a type of bargaining and then on through anger, guilt, remorse, sadness, and finally acceptance. Healing begins when we openly confess our pain.

My heart is filled with bitter sorrow and unending grief
ROMANS 9:2

Most of us, including our families, have been stuck in the grief process since the onset of the crisis of incarceration. We have been stuck in a stage of denial. Being stuck does not mean we are denying the event of incarceration, but rather the trauma of the event and the underlying dysfunctions that led to incarceration. This denial is expressed in the defenses we just reviewed.

Grieving any kind of major loss can take a long time. The emotional attachment to the loss determines the intensity and length of the grieving. Incarceration of a family member (us) is a tremendous loss in the lives of our family members. It creates a major void in their lives and profound grief, even if no one expresses it outwardly as a result of our defenses. It is a form of social and civil death for our family and us. This death of the old will require the birth of the new, and family life will never again be exactly like it was. While family life can be better than it was with the right action, it still doesn't free us from the grief process we all must encounter. As men and leaders in our family there are things we can do to help.

MOVING FROM DEVASTATION TO RECONSTRUCTION

When it comes to the healing experience of grief work there are several ways to go about this process. You can encourage and guide your family toward some form of therapeutic healing. While I don't believe everyone needs to be in formal therapy, many people do. Nevertheless, everyone can benefit from some type of informal group therapy. These groups provide the kind of support and encouragement that are most needed to guide the grieving toward healing. These groups can help family members identify what they are truly feeling and help them develop a language for those feelings that can be communicated to you for healing and closure.

The best kind of groups and programs provide a spiritual foundation that addresses both cognitive and feeling work. Our family's grief resulted from, and ended in, unhealthy relationships. Informal therapy groups and other programs can provide healthy interactive relationships; they are a healing phenomenon in themselves. A loving relationship of any kind is tremendously healing. Love is God's design for the ultimate form of therapy.

Above all things have intense and unfailing love for one another
1 PETER 4:8

Healing work for you and your family is most effective when done both separate and together. Individual therapeutic healing helps provide a foundation for each of you separately. Then when you come together each of you can share ideas, feelings, and communicate effectively with each other as part of the resolution process. This combination, along with family workshops, is most effective.

When you are heavily invested in your own healing and growth process, it is much easier to encourage your partner and family to seek out a support group in their area that can help.

Local churches help a multitude of families, including incarcerated partners, in a number of ways. They are in the business of restoration. The church may provide individual child and gender counseling or a family support group. If the church does not provide them directly, they may be able to direct the family to other groups that are being held right on the church premises. You will be encouraging your family to grow with you spiritually, seek out healthy supportive relationships, and identify themselves as an over-comer rather than a broken person or a victim.

You will grieve, but your grief will suddenly turn to wonderful joy
JOHN 16:20

There are also a growing number of family programs becoming available within the institutions that focus on reuniting you with your family. Contact a staff member in your institution and find out all the ways they are able to help you build healthy connections with your family while you're incarcerated. Your willingness to take these actions will begin to help reestablish you as a positive role model and mature male leader within your family. It is proof of love in action and evidence of your commitment to a better life.

While it certainly is conceivable that this grief work between you and your family could be done without informal therapy support, it is highly improbable. It is easier to begin processing our grief outside of emotionally charged relationships first. Once trust and confidence is established, we will be better equipped to open up with those who are connected to our grief. On the other hand, family workshops and programs without the grief work is a tempting path of least resistance. The problem is, it represents half-hearted attempts that do more to conceal the grief than to reveal it. After the program ends, the unresolved grief remains, leaving the family all the more confused about their healing and feelings.

Even in laughter the heart is sorrowful, and…is heaviness and grief
PROVERBS 14:13

Having a healthy family is a major responsibility. There is so much that can be done and it won't happen by accident. If you are fortunate enough to have your family come and visit you, open and honest communication during these times can be great opportunities for healing and closure. You can share a copy of this book with them to better help them understand you and support you in walking it out. Do not make these times all about you.

Encourage your family to express how your incarceration has affected them and the struggles they currently face as a result of it. You may need to reframe the way you view their expressions of these matters. You can choose not to look at them as personal attacks, but rather the need for them to process their thoughts and feelings for healing and closure. It can also help if you take ownership of this crisis.

In the end, people appreciate frankness more than flattery
PROVERBS 26:23

You may need to say something like this to your family: "Your suffering in this circumstance is the result of my selfish behavior. I want you to know I acknowledge that. I am taking full responsibility for my actions and seriously working toward change while I am here. Help me to understand how this has affected you and how I can help you." When I said these words to my mother in the visiting room, I could visibly see some of the tension leave her face.

MY OWN GRIEF WORK EXPERIENCE
I was divorced when my mother visited me for seven years in prison. I had spent a lot of time over those years in formal therapy and informal group therapy. These experiences proved invaluable for me to learn how to open up to my mother and encourage her to open up to me. For the first time in our lives we were having the kind of discussions where we learned who each was as a person. For the first time in my life, I was able to see her as a woman, rather than only my mother.

I was able to express to her things about my childhood experiences that I had always wanted her to know. For example, I was able to express to her how being home alone all the time while she worked and without a father left me feeling lonely and isolated all my life. She was able to express to me how she struggled as a single mother trying to raise two boys. I learned things about my mother as a person I would have never known. This grief work was extremely healing for us. The incarcerated and everyone who identifies themselves with loving an incarcerated family member will have to grow through their grief if they want to be free emotionally.

My plea to you is, don't waste your visits focusing on vending machine food, being self-absorbed, or only aimless conversation. Your family needs and deserves more than that. The quality of the connection you have with your family when you return home depends on your commitments today. It's also critical that you allow your family to heal at their own pace; it's the only way they can. If you set up expectations, you set yourself up for disappointment and deny them their own unique timetables for healing.

For everything there is a season, a time for every activity under heaven.
A time to laugh and a time to grieve
ECCLESIASTES 3:1, 4

THE THREE HEADED BEAST – I, SELF, ME

Don't make your incarceration all about your needs and wants. That mentality is how we ended up incarcerated in the first place. Don't pretend your struggles are worse than that of your family. I can assure you, they are not. Our families have at least been secondary victims of our crimes. It means we have abandoned them, leaving them to pick up the pieces and fill the void. Let me tell you, there has never been a book written on how to do that. Along with all of this, they suffer the pain of our incarceration right along with us.

DON'T BECOME A FINANCIAL BURDEN

Be self-responsible and don't become a financial burden on your family. For families who are struggling, every dollar you take from them is a dollar you have taken from them.

Likewise, phone calls, commissary, and gifts from approved vendors are nice prison comforts, but not necessary in most instances when the family is struggling. Remember, your family is trying to survive while you are being taken care of by the state.

KEEP COMMUNICATION OPEN

Take time to write home regularly. If you call it's likely their dollar – their investment. If you write, you invest your time and attention. Letters arriving in the mail can mean a lot, especially when they are supportive, caring, and express words of healing. Letters help people slow down and communicate their thoughts better than phone calls. Remember all birthdays and holidays. Send a card if you can, or at least a letter. See that your children receive presents through the Angel Tree Project at Christmas if they meet the criteria.

If you are doing all of these things and not getting responses, just be consistent and give them time. If they ask you to stop writing or calling, respect their request and keep it in prayer. Our family's grief resulted from unhealthy relationships that require healing. I have seen dramatic changes as a result of committed and consistent prayer. It will also provide you with inner peace while you hope and wait.

NEVER – NEVER GIVE UP!

Don't give up on yourself, even if your family gives up on you. Life goes on. However cold or unfeeling that may sound, that is not my intention. Keep in mind that you may not fully comprehend how painful your incarceration has been for them. The loss of family while incarcerated can be absolutely devastating. I know. I lost my mother while incarcerated.

However, I can promise you this. Once you get past the initial grief and do the work in this book that you can do, life will have meaning and be worth living once again. No matter what challenge you face, there will always be many new beginnings greater than you could have hoped for if you just never give up on yourself.

One thing I do [it is my own aspiration]:
forgetting what lies behind and straining forward to what lies ahead
PHILIPPIANS 3:13

The journey from devastation to reconstruction will be a long one. When I say a long one, I mean years. It begins in reentry preparation and continues into reentry. After the initial reentry preparation with the family there will need to be a process of reestablishing the foundation of a healthy, vibrant, and productive family. One of the most important ways we can do this is by identifying and reestablishing the beliefs, rules, and needs that will govern, guide, and guard the family.

The beliefs, rules, and needs that you and your family agree upon become the substance and quality of your family's relational imprint. The process of redefining the family relational imprint can actually begin after the initial grief work of healing and during your family reentry preparation. The real work in this area will take place after reentry and in the acclimation process. This is the time where your family will begin to put these new beliefs, rules, and needs into practice. Our next order of priority is reentry – the vital importance of understanding what it actually means to reenter the family social system.

It is time to pause again and consider what we have learned.

- Take a moment to consider what returning home represents to you.
- Have you done your preparation work to make your transplant process successful?
- Consider what defenses we have reviewed. Are any of them at work in your family now? What steps can you take to begin the grief work your family needs to experience?

With the answers to these questions in mind, let's look at what reentering the family represents.

2. FAMILY REENTRY

ENTERING AGAIN OR RETURNING TO A SOCIAL SYSTEM

The family is like the larger society; it is a dynamic social system. This means it is an energy or force in motion made up of different personalities with various beliefs, rules, and needs. Successful reintegration into either of these social systems is no easy task. This is made painfully obvious by the greater than 50% divorce rate in America, and the roughly two-thirds of released prisoners who return to U.S. prisons. To be brutally honest, the odds are not in our favor. However, if we have some general knowledge of our family as a dynamic social system and the relational impact that governs it, we can have a better chance of determining which side of these statistics we stand on.

Desire without knowledge is not good
PROVERBS 19:2

THE FAMILY AS A DYNAMIC SOCIAL SYSTEM

The chapters on the Human Design Model revealed that our own individual life management can be challenging enough. Integrating that management into the dynamic social systems of family and society takes the complexity and skill set to a whole new level of challenge. Let's take a look at some of the reasons why.

Reentering the family is going to have a huge impact on it. Within our own unique individuality each of us carries a set of beliefs, rules, and needs that govern our lives. The social systems of family and society function in many ways like the individual, and they carry their own set of beliefs, rules, and needs. Each are what the individual, as well as the larger social system, has determined are beneficial and necessary for survival. This is where things can get challenging.

The legitimate need to be a unique individual with our own set of beliefs, rules, and needs can clash with the need to conform to the beliefs, rules, and needs of the family and society for the sake of the many. There exists a polar tension between individuality and conformity of the people for the greater good of the larger social system as a whole. The ability to find the right balance in this polar tension is largely what reintegration means.

He must love what is good. He must live wisely and just
TITUS 1:8

We are social beings by design and not by choice. This makes belonging an essential need of our design that we cannot disentangle ourselves from. We seek a balance between our individuality and conformity because it aligns us with the fulfillment of our essential needs as social beings. We want to be part of family and society and reap the many benefits and needs both of them meet. The balance between healthy individuality (maturity/identity) and belonging is our place on a scale. We are all somewhere on this scale – and all in need of becoming more individually mature with our own identity and more in need of belonging (relating) and achieving as we leave prison.

Our well-defined individuality that comes from a strong sense of maturity and identity is always rooted in our belonging. Part of our identity comes from the social context of our lives. We cannot have maturity and identity without belonging. This is why belonging is such an essential need of our social nature. This is the reason I have united family and social aspects of our lives into the Human Design Model. They are part of our individuality, wholeness, and identity. The ultimate goal was to create a model that best portrayed the masterful design called humanity. The process of becoming a unique individual unites our needs of relating to others and achieving through our need of belonging. Like our organ transplant analogy, we become part of a social body.

We are many parts of one body, and we all belong to each other
ROMANS 12:5

The polar tension between our own individuality and our conformity to family and society is where people fail at reentry. Crime of any sort is always a violation of the beliefs, rules, and needs of both family and society. It is the area we most struggle with as we cross that line from conformity to crime. This is why I have gone in to such detail of mapping out both processes of reintegration into family and society. It involves adapting to, and then adopting the relational imprint or the beliefs, rules, and needs of the social system we are entering. The beliefs, rules, and needs of any social system form the social reality for that system. It is simply how any social system relates. Whether it is family or society, this relational imprint is the consensus reality of that social system. The consensus reality is what everyone agrees upon for the sake of integration into the benefits of their family and society.

You shall not oppress and wrong one another
LEVITICUS 25:17

From a social-system viewpoint, reintegration is just like our organ transplant analogy.

The main function of family and society is two-fold. They act to preserve unity and protect its wholeness, relationship, balance, and order, while meeting the needs of the individual. Crime, immorality, anything that violates the beliefs, rules, and needs of either of these social systems creates (like the human body) a systemic response to preserve itself. We cannot succeed if we act like a virus that preys on the system it inhabits as it tries to escape detection. It will mean refusing the offer of these social systems to be integrated into them.

The model of the transplant analogy helps us understand the need for a well-defined method of integrating ourselves into these social systems. It helps us meet our need for seeing reintegration from a larger perspective than ourselves – a design perspective of method with purpose and intention. We can begin to understand that success is determined by the relatedness of all the parts, or in this case, the people. All life exists as a result of relationship. To a larger extent, our reintegration is determined by the outcome of our relationships.

TRANSPLANT COMPLICATIONS

If we can recall our organ transplant analogy again for a moment, one thing becomes clear. The more thorough the preparation (ourselves and family), the less likely transplant complications will occur. Nevertheless, transplant complications are still common during reentry. Preparation means having the skills and tools ready when they do arise. This requires that the first order of preparation is the changes we need to make in our own lives. We change or we make the family pay for all our suffering we experienced before reentry. The transplant requires a healthy and well-functioning person to be put into the family body. We will be returning to the family to contribute or contaminate it.

My personal plea to you is that you do not allow yourself to contaminate your family with your unresolved pain. Their love for you will only allow them to hope and believe in the best for you. To my own horror and dismay, I have personally had the experience of making my family pay for my suffering and pain. I wasn't as bad as before I was incarcerated. I had gone through so much now that it was far worse than before. They no longer knew who I was and neither did I anymore. Your current sincerity won't protect you from it, and the only qualification you need to make that lifelong regret come true is to keep playing god in your own life.

I will behave myself wisely and give heed to the blameless way…
I will walk within my house in integrity and with a blameless heart
PSALM 101:2

It's important to keep in mind that the structure and dynamics of your family will be different at home than they are in the visiting room. This is because all the relationships have changed in response to the change in your role in the family. The inactive partner/parent role is a much different relationship than the active partner/parent role that operates in the midst of the daily dynamics of the family. Visiting you as an inactive partner/parent is a much different relationship than living with you in the full capacity of that role.

Once you return home, the structure and dynamics are likely to be resistant to sudden change. This is because the roles have adjusted to the needs of the family in your absence. For example, your partner's independence, authority, and responsibilities have adapted to your absence and to the needs of your family. Their personal interests, habits, hobbies, and lifestyle may have changed in your absence. The children have become accustomed to a single authority figure instead of two and a female instead of a male.

This can be confusing when trying to understand what your role in the family is upon release. It may appear (at least on the surface) that your place in the family as it was before you left is being rejected. This may be true initially, but not completely. Both the wife and children may be resistant to only parts of your role – how the rules operate, needs are determined and met, as well as daily activities.

Start slowly and just be there for your family. Allow them their own time-tables to adjust and to extend their boundaries and accept your role, whatever that role might be. If you force your role it may take longer than it would have otherwise or even be rejected. Your role in the family may never again look exactly like it did before you left. Be flexible and without preconceived notions of how things are supposed to be. It will take mature observation, patience, and skill to rediscover and fulfill your role in your family.

It has taken your family time to adjust to your absence, and it will take them time to adjust to your presence. They have traveled through both time and character and are no longer the exact same people you left behind. You may need to rediscover who they are and rebuild fresh new relationships with each of them. Think from the perspective of character and not from authority when you present to them who you are now.

Wherever your treasure is, there the desire of your heart will also be
MATTHEW 6:21

Let's take a few moments to consider what we have discussed in this chapter.

- Consider your family circumstances before your incarceration. How can you use the tools in this chapter to make returning home an even better environment than it was before?
- Has this chapter changed your view of family reentry? In what ways?
- What beliefs, rules, and needs govern your family?

With these questions in mind, let's take a look at part two of Family Reintegration and discover just how important the family relational imprint is.

CHAPTER FIFTEEN

Family Reintegration (Part Two)

—⚏—

The family has always been the cornerstone of American society. Our families nurture, preserve, and pass on to each Succeeding generation the values we share and cherish, values that are the foundation for our freedoms. In the family, we learn our first lessons of god and man, love and discipline, rights and responsibilities, human dignity, and human frailty.

Our families give us daily examples of these lessons being put into practice. In raising and instructing our children, in providing personal and compassionate care for the elderly, in maintaining the spiritual strength of religious commitment among our people. In these and other ways, America's families make immeasurable contributions to America's well-being.

Today more than ever, it is essential that these contributions not be taken for granted and that each of us remember that the strength of our families is vital to the strength of our nation.

— PRESIDENT RONALD REAGAN —

I t is important to keep in mind that even the most thorough preparation for family reentry can still leave us with unrealistic expectations. For example, minimal family conflict while incarcerated, mixed with moderate levels of self-discipline in a controlled prison environment can leave us with visions of coming home "large and in charge." The more we can learn about the family as a dynamic social system, the more we will understand how the "large and in charge" idea is not practical or realistic. It fails to take into account that becoming part of the family once again is a process that takes place over a long period of time. We need to look at returning to the family as a period of adjustment for everyone. Like our transplant analogy, the acclimation stage is a process of adjustment after the transplant, of finding our God-given position in the design of the family.

Not domineering [as arrogant, dictatorial, and overbearing persons] over those in your charge, but being examples (patterns and models of Christian living)
1 PETER 5:3

3. ACCLIMATION

THE PROCESS OF BECOMING ACCUSTOMED TO A NEW CLIMATE, SURROUNDINGS, OR CONDITIONS OF A SOCIAL SYSTEM

As I pointed out in part one, family systems have components, principles, and structural dynamics. The components are the individual family members. The principles are the beliefs, rules, and needs that make up the family's relational imprint and determine its social reality. The structural dynamics are the individual roles each person has within the family and how those roles affect each other.

The Family System
- Components: The family members
- Principles: Relational imprint-Consensus reality
- Structural dynamics: Individual roles=Father-Mother-Children

Family systems fail to thrive according to their potential when the family is operating from a faulty and grossly inadequate relational imprint. This happens when the beliefs, rules, and needs of the family originate somewhat randomly and by default rather than by design. If the family relational imprint is not designed from enduring spiritual principles, it becomes a mixed bag of conflicting ideas and concepts that no one is sure where they came from, or even why they were adopted.

After being in the prison subculture for a substantial period of time, there is also the danger of taking that relational imprint into your family upon re-entry. This is not what your family needs. Nevertheless, that is exactly what we will do, along with returning to the old family relational imprint, unless we take steps to prevent it. Family survival will require that we make a quality decision to redefine our family relational imprint. The key to this redefining process is found in our belief system and the spiritual principles we build the foundation of our beliefs upon.

Choose for yourselves this day whom you will serve, whether the gods which your fathers served...but as for me and my house, we shall serve the Lord
JOSHUA 24:15

The family beliefs are what determine the family rules, as well as what the family needs are, and if those needs are being met. The family belief system determines everything. Therefore, transforming the family relational imprint comes through new belief systems. When the family belief system is governed by design rather than default, it will provide a secure foundation for everyone in the family to exercise their need to BECOME, RELATE, and ACHIEVE. Family systems are people producing systems. Our individuality comes from the social context of our lives.

THE FAMILY RELATIONAL IMPRINT	CREATES	INDIVIDUALITY/IDENTITY
1. Beliefs		1. Becoming
2. Rules		2. Relating
3. Needs		3. Achieving

1. BELIEF AND BECOMING

For whoever would come near to God must [necessarily] believe that God exists and that He is the rewarder of those who earnestly and diligently seek Him [out]

HEBREWS 11:6

The foundation of the entire family belief system comes from the value placed on what it means to be a human being. Every other belief the family holds will reflect that fundamental belief. It is the most sacred of all beliefs and is legitimized within the family by the rules and needs expressed within the family.

The importance of this fundamental belief in human value leads us to what families need more than anything else, a personal revelation of God's love for us as individuals. This revelation is the foundation for all healthy and wholesome human relationships. Outside of our narrow and self-serving opinions, the only way to see the true value of another human being is to look up to God before we look around at others.

Since God is our Creator, Father, Provider, and Sustainer, no one else has the capacity to express our precious unrepeatable uniqueness like He can. Let's take a moment to look up and see why. Here is an authentic letter from God to you personally. It is authentic because everything it says comes directly from what He says about you in His word. These words will change your life if you let them.

A LETTER FROM YOUR FATHER

My dear son,

You are my special child (Deuteronomy 7:6). I chose you when I planned creation (Ephesians 1:11-12). I knew you before the foundations of the world (Ephesians 1:4). You were not a mistake, for I knit you together in your mother's womb (Isaiah 44:2), and you are my offspring (Acts 17:28). Before I formed you in your mother's womb I knew and approved of you (Jeremiah

1:5). You are fearfully and wonderfully made (Psalm 139:14). You are precious in my sight and honored (Isaiah 43:4), for you were made in my image (Genesis 1:26). I have tattooed your name on the palm of my hand (Isaiah 49:16). How precious are my thoughts of you, they number more than the sands on the seashore (Psalm 139:17-18). My dear child, you are the apple of my eye (Psalm 17:8).

I know everything about you (Psalm 139:1). I know when you sit down and when you rise up (Psalm 139:2). I am familiar with all your ways (Psalm 139:3). For in me you live and move and have your being (Acts 17:28). All the days of your life are written in my book (Psalm 139:16). I have numbered every hair on your precious head (Matthew 10:30). As a shepherd carries a lamb, I carry you close to my heart (Isaiah 40:11). I love you with an everlasting love (Jeremiah 31:3). You are my treasure (Exodus 19:5), and I rejoice over you with singing (Zephaniah 3:17).

I have been misrepresented by those who don't know me (John 8:41-44). I am not distant and angry, but am the complete expression of love (1 John 4:16), and it is my desire to lavish my love upon you (1 John 1:3). If you seek me with all your heart you will find me (Deuteronomy 4:29). I am the Father that comforts you in all your troubles (2 Corinthians 1:3-4). When you are broken hearted I am close to you (Psalm 34:18). I have put every tear you have ever shed in my bottle (Psalm 56:8), and one day I will wipe away every tear from your eyes (Revelation 12:3-4). I will take away all the pain you have suffered on earth (Revelation 21:4).

I offer you so much more than your earthly father ever could (Matthew 7:11). Every good gift comes from my hand (James 1:17), and I will meet every need you will ever have (1 Timothy 6:17). I will do more for you than you could ever possibly imagine (Ephesians 3:20).

Delight in me and I will give you the desires of your heart (Psalm 37:4). It is I who will put those desires in your heart (Philippians 2:13).

I will never stop doing good for you (Jeremiah 32:40). I will establish and strengthen you (1 Peter 5:10). My plan for your future has always been filled with hope (Jeremiah 29:11). I want to show you great and marvelous things (Jeremiah 33:3). In my word the depth of my love is revealed (John 3:16). I have given all I love to gain your love (Romans 8:31-32). Nothing can ever separate you from my love (Romans 8:39). Come home and I will throw the biggest party ever seen (Luke 15:7). I have always been Father, and will always be Father (Ephesians 3:14- 15). My question is, will you be my child (John 1:12-13)? I am waiting for you (Luke 15:20)!

Love, your Dad
Almighty God

A MOMENT OF REFLECTION

What could we have possibly become with this kind of belief about ourselves? How much differently would we have been able to relate to others? What kind of impact would such a belief have on what we were able to achieve in our lives? If we had a deep abiding conviction in our hearts that these words were actually the deepest truths about ourselves, how much differently would our lives be today than they are? Finally, if everybody in your family shared this deep conviction, how would that affect the relational imprint and quality of your family life? Think carefully – think long, it determines everything.

RESPONSIBILITY OF THE HIGHEST HONOR

The concept of family is not a human design, nor some random biological accident of procreation as some might have us believe. God wanted a family – someone to give His love to – so He created us to experience the highest possible honor of being His sons and daughters. God is the author and designer of the human family, and His design has always been that the fabric of humanity would be woven by the strong fiber of each individual family. Not only would the family create the individual, but the society as well. From this perspective, family is the highest responsibility God could bestow on us.

Whether it is the curse of our self-absorbed fallen nature or our lack of understanding super intelligent design, we rarely take into account the intricate and masterful design of the family. God made us in His own image (Genesis 1:26). He then placed him in families (Psalm 68:6) that are designed to be people producing systems (Proverbs 22:6), which create societies (Psalm 12:1), and ultimately determine the conditions of humanity (1 Peter 2:9). We can safely conclude that the quality of human life is determined by relationship and family.

THE FIRST ORDER OF RELATIONSHIP

All love and relationship is possible only because it already exists and is ever present within God (1 John 5:7). God is love (1 John 4:16) and love, like God, has never existed outside of relationship (John 1:1-3). God used love and family relationship to bring life out of death (John 3:16), freedom out of brokenness (Isaiah 61:1), and to turn darkness into light (Acts 26:18). God's intention was never just man, but relationship and family; man was merely His first step. God designed every human being so that their purpose and potential is forever linked in relationship.

The first order of relationship begins in a relationship with God. This determines our relationship to ourselves (identity/value), which determines the quality of our relationship with others. Knowing God loves us and created us for relationship with Him gives us confidence in realizing that we are unique beings of special value. When our relationship with God provides this deep conviction of special value in our hearts, we spend our lives seeing that value in others and expressing it to them.

Unfortunately, I am confident that many people reading this book do not have a healthy relationship with themselves. If this is true for you personally, how are you supposed to have a quality relationship with your family upon release? When our relationships fail we blame others, never truly understanding why they failed. The truth is, many of us do not actually comprehend the love that God has for us. If we really knew deep down inside how much God loves and values us, we would relate to others much differently than we do most of the time. This is not some form of theology or religion, but an observable fact in others who do comprehend God's love.

RELATIONSHIP DETERMINES BELIEF

The foundation of the family belief system begins with the husband's relationship to God as Father and his resulting relationship to himself. This sets the foundation for his relationship to his wife. Likewise, and just as important, is the wife's relationship to God as Father and her resulting relationship with herself. This sets the foundation for her relationship with her husband. What we see are two whole and complete human beings rooted in a deep conviction of identity and special value.

All of you should be of one and the same mind [united in spirit], sympathizing [with one another], loving [each other] as... [of one household], compassionate and courteous (tenderhearted and humble)
1 PETER 3:8

The quality of these relationships determine the quality of the family and govern the family system. If the marriage foundation is healthy relationally, the children will have a chance to function as whole and healthy human beings. If the marriage foundation is not built upon both parents living out their lives according to their individual design, the marriage will suffer from varying degrees of dysfunction. The result will be that all the family members will live out their lives as incomplete human experiences.

BELIEFS DETERMINE PARENTAL MODELING

If the foundation of the parental belief system is established in a relationship to God as Father, the parental relationship will be secure and the roles will be healthy. The parents will be able to fulfill their role as model, exhibiting "THE WAY TO" in the lives of their children. For the parental role to be a healthy model requires that there be love expressed through discipline.

PARENTS MODEL "THE WAY TO" EXPRESSED IN DISCIPLINE

The Way to:	Discipline expressed:
1. Serve God as His child	1. Commitment to truth
2. Function as human beings	2. Commitment to others who are committed to truth
3. Be a man or woman	3. Commitment to personal responsibility
4. Be a husband or wife	4. Commitment to challenge
5. Be a father or mother	5. Commitment to self-examination
6. Be in a relationship	6. Commitment to examination and challenge of others

Being the right kind of model for your family is the most noble calling on earth. When parents model "THE WAY TO" in the lives of their children, they will have chosen to impart life's most important lessons in identity and discipline, shown in the previous chart. Modeling identity and discipline offers learning that shapes the mind and molds the character toward correct behavior.

Each man must love his wife as he loves himself, and the wife must respect her husband... Children, obey your parents because you belong to the Lord, for this is the right thing to do
EPHESIANS 5:33; 6:1

To be this kind of model to your children means to love them enough to guide them into a state of order where they can function as God intended. It is a choice that will affect future generations of your family. In contrast, if parents do not fulfill their role as model, the children will learn their lessons of life from peers, gangs, the media, and other sources that are not credible.

2. FAMILY RULES AND RELATING IN ACTION

Teach me good judgment, wise and right discernment, and knowledge, for I have believed (trusted, relied on, and clung to) your commandments
PSALM 119:66

Families have a wide range of rules that govern them. These rules exist in all family systems, consciously or unconsciously, spoken or unspoken. Following are the ten most common areas where these rules exist.

1. Communication	6. Sexual
2. Emotional	7. Sickness and health
3. Behavioral	8. Financial
4. Social	9. Educational/Vocation
5. Household	10. Celebrational

239

When the rules that govern the family in each of these ten areas express our Creator's purpose and intention, they will promote two critical values that promote individuality. First, each person is precious and unique. Second, everyone is accountable. This requires that the beliefs, rules, and needs of the family involve consistently high levels of communication. The rules will be clear and specific, yet not rigid and inflexible in every circumstance. Mistakes and broken rules will be viewed as learning experiences and accountability as occasions for growth. Family rules that promote these standards produce high levels of awareness about self and others.

Not combative but gentle and considerate, not quarrelsome but forbearing and peaceable...He must know how to rule his own household well, keeping his children under control, with true dignity, commanding their respect in every way (not demanding it) and keeping them respectful

1 TIMOTHY 3:3,4

Family rules should promote unity and intimacy while fulfilling the ultimate goal of promoting healthy individuality. Everyone in the family is constantly developing the skills of relating as they negotiate the family rules. A phenomenon of healthy families is that as individuality increases, togetherness grows. As people discover their individual uniqueness and move toward becoming whole and complete human beings, real intimacy becomes possible.

Individuality produces personal boundaries unique to each person – which we can then choose to extend toward others. When we choose to extend those boundaries as we are choosing various levels of intimacy, to each degree we do we then extend those boundaries.

The goal of family is not the loss of individuality for the sake of unity. When this happens genuine intimacy is no longer possible. A good example of this is seen in the family defenses outlined in the previous chapter. They clearly show a family sacrificing individuality and intimacy for the sake of unity. When the family rules are vague or conflicting it leads to poor communication. It also means accountability will be lacking or extreme in its consequences. This self-sacrifice is believed to preserve the family when it is the very thing that is likely to destroy it. It is forsaking individual freedom to preserve the family and, in the end, everyone loses.

If a house is divided (split into factions and rebelling) against itself, that house will not be able to last

MARK 3:25

Family rules that promote the sacred belief of the value of the individual while promoting intimacy can be summed up as follows:

WHEN FAMILY RULES ARE HEALTHY

1. Parents do what they say, practice what they preach, and are healthy role models.
2. Communication is open and direct and behavioral specific.
3. Problems are openly acknowledged and resolved.
4. Parents don't play God – each person is of equal value.
5. Family members can be different.
6. The rules require accountability.
7. Mistakes are viewed as learning tools.
8. Rules are clear and specific, yet flexible.
9. The family exists for creating healthy individuals.
10. Personal boundaries are respected.
11. The rules promote freedom of expression in thought and feeling.
12. The atmosphere is fun and spontaneous.

CONFLICT RESOLUTION

Working out a compromise between two family relational imprints (his and hers) is a major task in marriage. In a mature and committed marriage, the couple will be willing to enter the process of working out their differences. This requires that differences be acknowledged and accepted. Each partner will be working toward compromised solutions. This does not mean there will never be conflict. In fact, the capacity for (healthy/productive) conflict is a mark of genuine intimacy, a type of contact that has the potential to begin negotiation.

Since both partners are unique individuals and each comes from a family relational imprint that was different, conflict is inevitable. A difference in family rules is an emotionally charged area that lends itself to conflict. This is true even when spiritual principles are the mediator and final authority. Their interpretation alone can be difficult to negotiate. For example, rules on how to raise children, right methods of discipline, and how to handle money, are all potential areas of negotiating family rules. It is always much easier to find compromise when we remember we are not negotiating "my rules" or "your rules" but God's rules concerning such matters.

Peace and mercy be upon all who walk by this rule
[who discipline themselves and regulate their lives by this principle]
GALATIANS 6:16

241

In healthy conflict, it doesn't turn into destructive forms of fighting. Conflict can actually be constructive when both partners strive for contact and compromise, instead of striving to be "the one" who is right and in control. We have already determined that incarceration is a byproduct of a self-centered life. This may be an area that requires special effort on our part.

Conflict can bring two people closer together if the goal is mutually satisfactory solutions. Mature and committed couples do not withdraw, nor do they cop out and agree to disagree. Healthy couples have conflict, and they learn how to fight fair. How we choose to deal with family conflict will either erode our relationships with each encounter or create deeper levels of genuine intimacy. Let's take a look at some fair fighting rules that promote intimacy and resolve conflict.

FAIR FIGHTING RULES

1. **Prepare for a constructive engagement.** Plan ahead to avoid counterproductive tactics such as mockery, name calling, insults, and sarcasm. Write a letter or list of points for your own clarification. Be sure you are ready and calm.
2. **Carefully choose a time and place.** Wrong time and wrong place means wrong outcome. Choose a time and place you both agree upon.
3. **Be an active listener.** Listen calmly. Listen carefully without interrupting verbally or with body language (shoulder shrugs, eye rolling). Do not begin to formulate your response before the other person is finished talking. Really listen.
4. **Give feedback.** Restate what the other person has told you for accuracy. Get their agreement on what you heard before responding.
5. **Practice rigorous honesty.** Level with your partner about your feelings. Say what you really think. Be candid but not hurtful.
6. **Avoid judgment.** Don't attack the person verbally. Focus on concrete behavioral details and not their character. Use "I" statements rather than "you" statements. "I" statements show an effort to communicate feelings in a self-responsible and nonjudgmental way.
7. **Focus on the present.** Avoid score keeping. Don't relive the past. Don't dredge up a long list of grievances and overwhelm the other person. Don't overstate frequency.
8. **Don't assign blame.** Don't create scapegoats for every grievance against you. Don't blame other people or circumstances for your behavior. Take responsibility for your actions.
9. **Focus on solutions.** Suggest specific, relevant changes to solve a problem. Choose solutions that involve both points of view. Proposed solutions need to be reasonable.

10. **Be open to compromise.** Real negotiations involve both parties giving in a little. Find a middle ground without backing either partner into a corner.
11. **Think win-win (not) winner, loser.** Don't make the conflict a competition. Think of each other as allies attacking a mutual (family) problem.
12. **Stay in there.** Unless you are being abused, hang in there. This is very important. Go for a solution. Never leave issues permanently unresolved.

3. FAMILY NEEDS AND ACHIEVING

You know that these hands of mine have worked to supply my own needs
and even the needs of those who were with me.
And I have been a constant example of how you can help those in need
ACTS 20:34

First and foremost, the family needs a marriage. Without a marriage (absent partner or present but unavailable) there is a loss of wholeness in the family. The loss of wholeness is absolutely devastating. The family as a system of interacting people will lack vital relationships, be out of balance, and suffer a loss of order. The loss of these four life-support factors threatens the survival of the family remnant that is left. In order for the remnant to survive, each person in the family will be required to give up their natural role to adapt to the loss of the missing partner.

We are pressed on every side by troubles, but we are not crushed.
We are perplexed, but not driven to despair…never abandoned by God
2 CORINTHIANS 4:8, 9

The loss of our natural role in the family is the loss of selfhood, in order to keep the rest of the family together. It is the loss of selfhood because everyone must sacrifice their own path toward completion and wholeness to fill the vacuum created by the missing partner/parent. The focus of the family as a growth unit of BECOMING, RELATING, and ACHIEVING will necessarily be sacrificed for the focus of survival. The loss of security is in reality the loss of freedom. It is the loss of self-discovery and the pursuit of unique individuality and identity, which the four life support factors provide in a family that functions according to its intended design.

For example, the remaining parent will give up their natural role to become a hybrid of both parental roles. The elder child will give up their childhood to help out as an adult parent to younger siblings. A least to some extent, every child becomes an adult child in order to survive and fend for themselves. For everyone it means a loss of vital growth integrationally, and developmentally as we looked at in part three of the Human Design Model. It means the abandonment of the path to adult maturity we looked at in chapters five and six. The loss of a partner/parent is terribly destructive to the rest of the family. It is estimated that 85% of those incarcerated have experienced this devastation and that's why each of these chapters were carefully chosen for this book.

MY FAMILY EXPERIENCE

My mother sacrificed her life, her freedom and growth, as a result of becoming a single parent raising two boys. She worked, cooked, cleaned, and looked after our needs, most often sacrificing her own needs. The vacuum created by my absent father left my mother no room to be Violet Lenora Thompson, only mom and the single parent. My brother and I had to forsake the lessons a father would have taught us, and surrender major aspects of our childhood. In the end, no one had their needs adequately met, but we survived.

A COMMON TRAGEDY

My family circumstance was not unique. In America today, two parents seem to be viewed as an optional luxury, though it was first designed to be a standard feature. Marriage and family are no small responsibility. That's why it requires a man of maturity and not just a male. Incarceration is a form of family abandonment. Most of us abandoned our families long before we committed our crimes. The act of abandonment is just a symptom of incompletion. It's about adult males with an arrested development making their own families, while seeking to meet our own unmet developmental needs through illegitimate sources. Far too often the final product of unmet developmental needs in adults is underachievers. No one is able to achieve their unique potential in a state of incompletion and unmet needs.

Live joyfully with the wife whom you love all the days of your vain life, which He has given you under the sun....For that is your portion in this life
ECCLESIASTES 9:9

OUR MOST BASIC HUMAN NEEDS

Let's return to our transplant analogy once again. The process of acclimation is complete when the transplanted person becomes accustomed to the new social system and conditions, and the family recognizes the person as supporting to it. A good indicator of this is when everyone in the family has their most basic human needs met.

(FAMILY SYSTEM VIEWPOINT) To protect the wholeness, relationship, balance, and order of the family while meeting the needs of the individual. Below are our most basic human needs.

The Need for:

1. Physical security
2. Spiritual grounding
3. Belonging
4. Relatedness
5. Intimacy
6. Self-worth
7. Responsibility
8. Productivity
9. Structure
10. Affirmation
11. Challenge
12. Stimulation

Basic Needs within Our Human Design Model

The more the four life support factors of wholeness, relationship, balance, and order are expressed in the design of family, the more they can be expressed in the lives of each individual within the family. Families are people producing systems, and when the four life support factors are fully expressed within a family, it creates the potential for every need to be met. When needs are being met in a person's life, it frees them to turn their focus onto a journey of self-discovery through BECOMING, RELATING, and ACHIEVING.

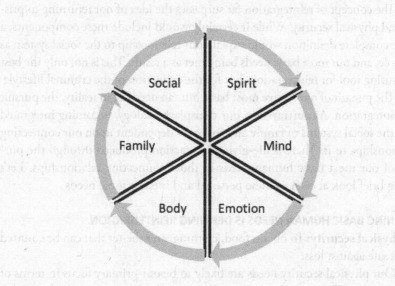

THE DESIGN OF FAMILY

1. **Wholeness**: All the people that signify the purpose and intention of family are present. The family is not merely a result of its numbers and proximity. The family is a result of the vital interaction between the people.
2. **Relationship**: Each person retains their own individuality, as well as carrying the relational imprint (beliefs, rules, needs) of the whole family.
3. **Balance**: Families are thriving social systems where every individual is affected by every other individual, as well as the environment as a whole. When one person's life is out of balance it creates imbalance throughout the other parts of the family social system.
4. **Order**: The order of the family hierarchy allows the social system to function at its maximum efficiency and potential of creating godly offspring (Acts 17:28).

4. REINTEGRATION

RETURN TO BEING IDENTIFIED AS PART OF THE WHOLE SOCIAL SYSTEM

For decades, the goal of ex-felons leaving prison has been reintegration. What's important is that we have a definition for it and a clear picture of what it should look like. Otherwise, how are we supposed to understand the need to pursue it, and how can we actually tell when we get there? This applies to the family as well as the larger social system of society.

The concept of reintegration far surpasses the idea of not returning to prison and physical security. While it certainly would include these components, a more complete definition would explain our relationship to the social system as a whole, and our most basic needs being met as a result. This is not only the best measuring tool for reintegration, but for the extinction of the criminal lifestyle.

The pursuit of our twelve most basic human needs is, in reality, the pursuit of reintegration. As portrayed in our transplant analogy, becoming integrated into the social systems of family and society is dependent upon our connecting relationships to it. There is life-giving interaction produced through the pursuit of our most basic human needs in those connecting relationships. Let's take a brief look at each of these personal and interpersonal needs.

DEFINING BASIC HUMAN NEEDS IS DEFINING REINTEGRATION

1. Physical security: To obtain food, clothing, and shelter that can be counted on as safe against loss.

Our physical security needs are likely to be our primary focus in terms of reintegration. They are most basic to our survival. However, we are shortsighted if we stop there. In many ways, these twelve most basic human needs are all interdependent. They rely on each other for fulfillment. For example, in order for our physical security to be safe against loss, it will depend on our needs of productivity, responsibility, and structure being met through employment. When our physical security is stable and can be counted on, it provides an overall sense of personal security to pursue and refine our other needs.

2. Spiritual grounding: To establish a foundation in the first principles and disciplines of the spiritual life.

This most basic human need has a far-reaching impact on every other basic human need. We have already concluded that the physical life and the spiritual life are not separate; it is the source of wholeness in manhood. The spiritual path is a journey toward higher levels of maturity, and provides the principles and disciplines that produce a successful life. It is the source of faith, hope, and love, which are critical to reintegration. We will walk in greater peace during challenge and struggle and be able to make better choices. Statistics provide convincing evidence that those who pursue the spiritual life have the lowest rates of recidivism. Those statistics are a result of the impact the spiritual life has on every other basic human need.

3. Belonging: To be part of a social system and have our own special place in it.

Every single person leaving prison has a place in a family and society where they belong. Some already know this place and have it waiting for them. Those who do not simply need to discover it. On the other hand, where we think we belong may be incorrect. There is only one determining factor for where we truly belong, and that is where we are aiding and being aided in meeting our most basic human needs. Nothing else can so fully meet our need for belonging. If we are getting these basic needs nurtured in our lives, and we are able to help nurture others in meeting their needs, we can be sure we belong there. Conversely, if we are in a place that is unwilling or unable to nurture our needs or allow us to nurture theirs, we can be sure we do not belong there.

4. Relatedness: To be connected in thought and meaning to other people.

Being connected to others by family ties of blood and marriage is surely a comforting source of relatedness. However, it is far from enough to fulfill this most basic human need. This need has a wide range of potential. It is only limited by the ways we can share a connection to the needs of other people. The wider the range of these connections of relatedness, the more we meet this need and experience a sense of fulfillment. Anything we can do that builds close associations to others is relatedness, such as spiritual grounding, productivity, challenge, stimulation, and so on.

5. Intimacy: To be familiar with someone, close to them, and personally well-known. An inner regard and affection that allows us to fully open up and reveal ourselves.

Our many intimate connections with other people are like the many cuts on a beautiful diamond. They are all of the same gem, but each reflects the light of the gem in a different way. Intimacy reaches far beyond the limits of romance. It must if we are to adequately meet this most basic human need. Intimacy is special time with your children. It is telling God, your partner, and close friends your joys, struggles, hopes, and fears. Intimate communication is the only solid ground for mental health. Withholding intimate communication is fertile ground for mental illness.

6. Self-worth: To be useful, deserving of merit, and having importance in the lives of others.

This basic human need is commonly misunderstood. Self-worth is not determined so much by what we are capable of or what we can do for ourselves. The word "self" means it belongs to you and you receive it. The word "worth" comes from the value God has placed on us, and in how we nurture the needs of others. It has nothing to do with wealth, popularity, physical powers, talents, or abilities. It is how we use "self" to enhance the lives of others.

7. Responsibility: To be trustworthy and reliable in our obligations, duties, and areas of life we are accountable for.

Rarely do we realize that responsibility is not just a powerful acclimation principle; it is a basic human need. We have a basic vital need to be responsible "for" ourselves and responsible "to" others as social beings. For example, it is a punishment for me to be taken care of by the state correctional system. I have a strong desire to experience the value of being responsible for myself, because it is a basic human need for purpose and fulfillment. I also have a need to be responsible "to" others by respecting the beliefs, rules, and needs of family and society. These two types of responsibilities allow us to thrive, excel, and set self-protecting limits on our lives. Any quality of life we desire above merely existing will directly correspond to our level of responsibility.

8. Productivity: To work hard to create and bring into existence that which is needed and valuable to enhance life.

Probably more than any other, we can see how this basic human need relates to all the others. If we want physical security we are going to be productive. Even relatedness and intimacy require a certain degree of hard work to bring them into existence. Anything we acquire in life that has quality and lasting value will require hard work. The harder we work for anything the more we value it, and this includes staying free. Statistics show that a lack of productivity is a major cause of recidivism. Productivity also provides a sense of well-being and accomplishment that you can't put a price on. This is especially true when our productivity enhances the lives of our family and society.

9. Structure: To have an ordered and organized arrangement of the parts of life.

The more structure we have in our lives, the more manageable our lives become. The structured times we sleep, eat, work, socialize, and even play, are how we manage and balance our lives. The less structure we have in our lives, the less manageable our lives become. Every person that functions well, and is successful, does so as a result of structure. It takes a high degree of responsibility and has a powerful affect on our productivity. Structure is a powerful tool for the extinction of criminal activity. It requires that we think hard enough to organize our lives. Structure means setting priorities and putting our values in order.

10. Affirmation: To confirm and declare positive statements and actions toward self and others.

Yes, we can affirm ourselves both in word and in deed. We can change all the statements of "I can't" and "I won't" into "I can" and "I will" statements. Positive affirmations are powerful tools for success. We can speak God's promises over our life instead of repeating the words of the world. Likewise, positive steps toward meeting our basic reintegration needs is action of affirmation that we value ourselves enough to put forth the effort. This alone is not enough to fulfill this need. Everyone has a need to be affirmed by others. If we are always looking for opportunities to help meet these twelve basic needs in the lives of others, we will soon find we are being affirmed by others in both word and deed.

11. Stimulation: To be stirred to action, ambition, and excitement that is life-enhancing.

Constant stimulation and lack of stimulation in our lives are both destructive. Consistent, yet intermittent and brief periods of stimulation in a wide variety of ways can help make us better at everything we do. It is essential to keeping life refreshing and fun. We have a need for stimulation in all six areas of our Human Design Model. If artificial stimulation through alcohol and drugs have been a problem in your life, healthy and natural forms of stimulation like sports, hobbies, and recreation can reduce these cravings.

12. Challenge: To call or command to interest, feeling, and effort.

When we welcome challenge, we welcome life. Life is full of learning experiences and problems that require solving. When we are actively involved in challenge, we welcome the experiences that make us larger as a result of overcoming them. Without challenge we cannot grow into a larger state of being than we already are. Sometimes challenges are welcomed; sometimes they are not. Nevertheless, both have a rewarding sense of accomplishment and competency when properly managed. The challenges of life offer us the opportunity to fulfill a basic need to become more than we already are.

LOVE - THE FOUNDATION FOR MEETING FAMILY NEEDS
It's hardly possible to discuss family and meeting basic human needs without addressing the environment that will allow those needs to be met. When I prayed and meditated on writing this section I could think of no greater importance than that of us connecting at the level of disciplined love. All that I understand of God's purpose and intention of family is that it has its highest meaning in love. The secret of family success is found in one simple command, that we love each other as He first loved us (John 15:12, 17). The intention of such a masterful design was that it would be simple enough that anyone could do it.

God's love has been poured out in our hearts
hrough the Holy Spirit who has been given to us
ROMANS 5:5B

Love is one of the most profound responsibilities God could have given humanity. He must have had a lot of belief and faith in His creation to trust us with it. It begins with our choice to turn on the light of disciplined love inside of us, and then shine it into the lives of others. We can't turn their light on. It must be their decision to do it. When you return home, remember it is our shining that helps them to trust the decision.

Its light can be seen by all who enter the house
LUKE 11:33

As we have already discovered, real love has its sources through a relationship with God; it is spiritual and therefore disciplined. For needs to be met through an environment of disciplined love requires entering the relationship mature and whole as a result of a spiritual life.

A healthy relationship requires two people who have already embraced responsibility for their own mature individuality and happiness in life before they come together. Each clearly understands the other cannot make them whole and complete. These are qualities brought into the relationship to nurture the basic needs of the other, needs that even whole and complete human beings have.

Now I passed by you again and looked upon you; behold,
you were maturing and at the time for love
Ezekiel 16:8a

Both partners recognize that the other is in a life-long process of maturing and spiritual growth toward self-completion. Each partner is willing and able to enhance the other's journey toward fulfillment of their self-completion. They understand that while they are accountable to each other in this way, they are not responsible for that growth. When two people are committed to each other they are able to add to the quality of that personal responsibility through helping to meet their twelve most basic human needs.

A strong sense of mature commitment to the work of nurturing our own needs and the needs of another is a state of union in which each partner is providing the other with the opportunity of self completion. Each person grows from the disciplined love of the other, which by expression, nurtures our own basic human needs. This makes disciplined love in a relationship a circular process of an absolutely masterful design. Let's see why.

The choice to extend ourselves in the action of expressing the qualities of disciplined love is a choice to extend the limits of our own discipline, and therefore it grows into a larger state of being as a result. The act of nurturing the needs of another through expressing the qualities of disciplined love is an act of self evolution according to God's intended design. This is true even when the purpose of the act is someone else's growth. I meet some of my own basic needs by meeting yours. I become more because I have deliberately chosen to express disciplined love in the life of another.

Love (affection and goodwill and benevolence) edifies and builds up
and encourages one to grow [to his full stature]
1 Corinthians 8:1

LOVE IS CHOICES NOT FEELINGS

The conscious choice to extend disciplined love for the purpose of nurturing another's basic human needs involves our heads as well as our hearts. Disciplined love can only be an exercise of deliberate choice. Real love, by its nurturing nature, is not effortless. Love is as love does, not as love feels. This can be seen in the fifteen qualities of love we reviewed in the chapter on consistency. For an example, let's use patience, the first quality in this list. Every single need

LARRY DEAN THOMPSON

we nurture in another requires patience. However, I don't always "feel" patient. In fact, I often feel impatient. Nevertheless, I can feel impatient and still choose the "action" of disciplined love by extending myself and expressing the action of patience. When I do this I become more mature and less impatient.

Every conscious and deliberate choice I make to express disciplined love is literally a choice to nurture my most basic human needs and enhance my own well-being. "It is not good that man should be alone…"(Genesis 2:18) is God's way of saying, "If man has someone to love he will be more like Me than he ever would have been." When love is disciplined and genuinely nurturing, it is a self-enlarging experience for us as well as others.

NEEDINESS IS NOT THE SAME AS BASIC NEEDS
There is a profound difference between having basic human needs and the neediness of immaturity and incompletion. Disciplined love is spiritually mature. It is not "starving" and "craving" like the emptiness of immature and undisciplined love. People who lack wholeness are obsessed with connecting to some person or experience that will make them whole. It never does. Neediness, as we have discovered in the chapter on "The Path to Adult Maturity," results from spiritual bankruptcy and unresolved developmental conflicts.

God is love, and he who dwells and continues in love dwells and continues in God.
In this [union and communion with Him] love is brought to completion and
attains perfection with us. There is no fear in love [dread does not exist],
but full-grown (complete, perfect) love turns fear out
1 JOHN 4:17,18

Trying to meet the needs of someone else who is in a state of neediness and incompletion is simply impossible. Absent a relationship with God, nothing can fill the emptiness and too much help is never going to be enough. If the immaturity of incompletion will prevent us from getting our needs adequately met, it will prevent our reintegration.

WHEN LOVE IS FEELING BASED
The neediness of undisciplined love is feeling based and self-referential. This is why when love is undisciplined, it is capable of experiencing the extremely powerful feelings associated with love, and yet still act in all manner of unloving and destructive ways. This is a strong warning to us returning home. These undisciplined feelings, absent the maturity to expressed disciplined love, is what allows human beings to commit all manner of horrific crimes, all in the name of love.

252

We see a good example of this in the story about the Santa Claus Killer, back in part two of the Human Design Model. We also noted that the prisons are full of stories like this. Stories like this are proof positive that we can't truly love without a moral foundation. The weaker the moral foundation, the weaker the love. While disciplined love inspires emotions that enhance our well-being, these emotions are not in themselves love, and they are, in this case, undisciplined and morally deficient.

Woe to those who call evil good and good evil, who put darkness for light and light for darkness, who put bitter for sweet and sweet for bitter!
ISAIAH 5:20

The desire and intention of undisciplined love is to posses and control another human being, although they are not capable of realizing or admitting it. Like our Santa Claus Killer, what undisciplined love cannot control and posses, it will often try to destroy, all in the name of love. It is a highly refined (non-spiritual) form of self-interest and self-seeking where no one ever gets their needs met.

People who enter relationships to fill their inner emptiness end up more empty and unsatisfied than when they were alone. People who enter relationships without adequate levels of maturity and discipline end up less mature and less disciplined than when they were alone.

People who enter relationships for self-completion end up less complete than when they were alone. Get the picture?

People who enter relationships while still lacking maturity and wholeness devour each other in an attempt to experience completion through another human being instead of God. This helps to explain a major aspect of broken families that statistics report. Such people bond as a result of their common lack of wholeness and remain bound by their neediness, sometimes to the point of self destruction. An attempt to reintegrate into society through a family environment like this is going to fail miserably and possibly tragically.

CHILDREN AND HEALTHY PARENTS

If you are leaving prison and returning home to children of your own, this leaves you with a profound responsibility in your role as model and teacher. Your parenting style will have a lifelong and deep-rooted impact on your children as they naturally fulfill their role as learners.

Children are naturally curious, their needs are unending and require constant time, attention, and direction. Every moment you are teaching them something as they constantly observe and absorb.

Fathers, do not irritate and provoke your children to anger [do not exasperate them to resentment], but rear them [tenderly] in the training and discipline and the counsel and admonition of the Lord
EPHESIANS 6:4

When two people in a relationship are mature and self-responsible human beings, they can model self-discipline and unconditional love to their children through this relationship. They become examples of how to get your needs met and properly nurture the needs of another. This provides an atmosphere where children have the security and freedom to grow integrationally and developmentally. Enormous power results from this kind of security and freedom.

The father shall make known to the children your faithfulness and your truth
ISAIAH 38:19

Integrational development means all the child's personal powers we learned about (spiritual, mental, emotional, physical) are available to them. They are free to flow outwardly to resolve their own natural developmental conflicts. The more stable and secure the environment of the parental relationship, the more proactive the children will be in accessing their natural powers for their own development.

Children are a gift from the Lord; they are a reward from him
PSALM 127:3

The more parents love and accept themselves and have resolved their own conflicts, the more they will be able to accept and nurture each other. Then they will be able to help their children discover their precious uniqueness as God's special creation. When a family relates from the strong sense of personal development and wholeness of each parent, everyone is able to get their needs met. They do the work that nurturing love demands because they are disciplined models. From this standpoint, there can be no better solace from and connection to the larger system of society for our reintegration.

Let's take a few minutes to consider what we have learned.

- Does this last paragraph describe the context from which you enjoyed your childhood? If it was, you are indeed fortunate and blessed. For many of us, it would have been had our parents known what to do differently. What will you do differently?
- What beliefs will govern your family, the world's or the one who created it?
- How will you be a good model? Let's see what one is in the next chapter on "The Reentry Mentor."

CHAPTER SIXTEEN

The Reentry Mentor

—w—

Governments can hand out money,
but governments cannot put love in a person's heart,
or a sense of purpose in a person's life.
The truth of the matter is that comes when a loving citizen puts their arm
around a brother or sister in need and says,
"I love you, god loves you, and together we can perform miracles."
America is the land of the second chance, and when the gates of prison open,
the path ahead should lead to a better life.

— PRESIDENT GEORGE W. BUSH —

1. WHO NEEDS A REENTRY MENTOR?

Everyone returning to society after a period of incarceration, regardless of the length of their time of imprisonment, is in need of a Reentry Mentor. Incarceration is the single factor in our qualifying for this need. Determining this need is not based on education, what you have accomplished while incarcerated, or what you have waiting for you upon release. Your removal from society for its protection, along with any period of absence from functioning in the normal operations of daily life, are the two primary factors of this single qualification.

THE NEED FOR ACCURATE SELF APPRAISAL

Choosing a Reentry Mentor is taking back charge of your life. It represents your first step toward expressing one of the most important principles of going home to stay: "YOU ALONE CAN DO IT, BUT YOU CAN'T DO IT ALONE." Ex-offenders seeking to permanently reintegrate into society cannot afford to view choosing a Reentry Mentor like some optional feature of reentry. Your Reentry Mentor is a vital standard feature to developing every principle and discipline that you will need to meet the qualifications of genuine reintegration outlined in this book.

If you are struggling with the concept of needing a Reentry Mentor, and believe you came to prison as a result of some unfortunate circumstance, you are suffering from an inaccurate self appraisal. Our incarceration is the result of issues serious enough to cause us to be removed from society. We need assistance. It takes more than isolating yourself with a Bible and prayer or goodwill intentions to remain free once we are released. We need a guide and a community of support. If you are honest with yourself, you don't know how you will respond to the many challenges of reentry. Every release is new territory. We don't even know what those challenges, obstacles, and disappointments will be.

I warn everyone among you not to estimate and think of himself more highly than he ought [not to have an exaggerated opinion of his own importance], but to rate his ability with sober judgment
ROMANS 12:3

THE EMOTIONAL PAIN OF PROBLEM SOLVING

The early challenges of reentry are often painful emotionally. There is no substitute for this pain if you intend to grow, mature, and remain free. There may be bouts of anger, self-pity, depression, and fear. Much of this may be directed toward yourself. These feelings can exist for years without being released and triggered by reentry. We cannot afford to deny, mask, or medicate them. The cost is just too high. Our only alternative is to allow ourselves to move through these feelings as this energy runs its cycle.

Reentry represents hard questions that often come with hard answers to face. Early reentry is often a time of trial and error. Intense emotions that arise can trigger our preoccupation with our self-obsession, which only leads to comparing and then the confusion that follows it.

There can also be emotional withdrawal without recognizing it. To believe you can handle all these challenges and problems you will face on your own would be downright foolish and stubborn. It is vitally important that you have a Reentry Mentor. He is a man who is modeling the qualities of manhood you desire and is a model for successful living.

Plans succeed through good counsel
PROVERBS 20:18

The transition from a structured prison environment to the many uncertainties of society can cause us to go from feeling stable, adequate, and in control, to feeling inadequate in a free world upon release. These are normal experiences in the process of major life changes. It is certainly not something anyone should face alone. There is the danger of these feelings leaving us prone to isolating ourselves after incarceration. The reentry transition can cause you to feel awkward and as if you don't fit in or belong. This is a result of the missing social history in your life that so strongly connects us to others. The less one feels they belong, the more one's sense of self-worth diminishes, and the more one's choices and decision-making skills diminish. It slowly erodes our freedom.

Learning how to live is a life-long process and reintegration can take one to five years. You will need as much supportive interaction as you can get. Likewise, we must let go of the willfulness of trying to control outcomes or expecting that "grand experience" – a visitation from God that fixes everything. An obsessive desire to control things or expecting specific outcomes can cause us to lose contact with reality. The Reentry Mentor helps to remind us to surrender our desire to control and to avoid looking for that illusive grand experience.

When defenses such as control and fantasy are erected we are not likely to see them, but the Reentry Mentor can. He is the dependable in the unpredictable. Without the caring eyes of a Mentor it's so easy to slip into a number of dangerous frames of mind without us even realizing it. All of them have one destination – self-destructive behaviors that lead to incarceration.

THE PEOPLE GAP

Reentry creates a people gap in your life. Prior to release you may feel like you can't wait to get away from the people congestion of an overcrowded prison environment. However, we have become accustomed to the familiarity of being surrounded by people. To the astonishment of the recently released ex-prisoner, it often has a major affect on him. This can be a time of dangerous vulnerability for choosing wrong associations.

Many will say they are loyal friends, but who can find one who is truly reliable?
PROVERBS 20:6

When a Reentry Mentor and other supportive fellowship helps to fill the people gap, the old people, places, and things are not as likely to seem so attractive. You will desire relationship. We must be aware that there is a major difference between being "up for grabs" and "up for offers" of friendship. The Reentry Mentor is a mature and responsible choice. He can connect you to a community of other competent, caring, mature men for you to surround yourself with.

As men are removed from society, one area of their lives that has particularly suffered is the area of healthy relationships. Reentry is likely to mean a journey of discovery into what healthy relationships are. It is one of the most powerful forces to make successful men in the world. Our vital need for healthy relationships makes our Reentry Mentor so much more than just another method of informal social control. He will not only help us to stay out of prison, but guide us toward solid plans for successful living.

COMPETENT AND CARING GUIDANCE

Guidance is an important beginning to a life of freedom after incarceration. It is the transforming power of caring. Dr. Martin Luther King, Jr., once spoke an all-important truth when he said, "To change someone you must first love them and they must know you love them." The mentor relationship allows you to see yourself as acceptable and accepted in the eyes of at least one other human being besides family upon release. He is someone who can help you believe in yourself through his genuine investment in your success.

Having a Reentry Mentor offers us the advantage of helping us negotiate the healthy psycho-social stages outlined in this book, and avoid the stages that lead to recidivism. Our path to success begins with the foundation stage of communication. Without a mentor these stages are all but impossible, and we will avoid the painful work of psycho-social maturity that we so desperately need at all costs. The darker side of self with its hidden chambers of secret obsessions will remain unaddressed. Hidden behind this accountability is the key to our freedom.

We have learned some important lessons about relationships in the previous chapters.

First, the principles that will lead to freedom can only be developed through the environment of relationship. Second, these principles cannot be developed in isolation, books, or classrooms.

Principles like trust, truth, integrity, and honesty can only be developed in relationships. Self-honesty alone is not enough, although it is an important beginning. We need to be accountable to at least one other person. It is only through honest and open communication that we can discover who we really are, and recover our self-respect.

A Reentry Mentor relationship assures the ex-prisoner that there is at least one person who understands his situation and fully cares. He is the one person to turn to without embarrassment when questions, doubts, and problems linked with reentry arise. Mentorship gives the ex-prisoner an understanding and sympathetic friend when one is needed most.

There are 'friends' who destroy each other, but a real friend sticks closer than a brother
PROVERBS 18:24

LEARNING IS THEORY – EXPERIENCE IS KNOWING

You may have acquired many pro-social tools, self-management skills, and facts about the challenges of reentry while incarcerated. This will prove to be a great benefit upon release. However, learning about these things in an institutional setting is one thing, applying them in a challenging adult society is quite another. They are not even in the same league.

Learning about the principle centered life is not at all the same as living it. The Reentry Mentor's success and personal experience trumps all head knowledge and theory. He can offer essential guidance in applying these principles in everyday life. Being able to see the principle centered life lived out in someone else's life and the results it creates will prove to be a very important experience for remaining free. The rewarding two-way street called mentorship means "sticking with the winners" upon release.

2. WHO DO I CHOOSE AS A REENTRY MENTOR?

The process of matching an ex-offender with a Reentry Mentor is largely an informal one. There are no specific rules, except for maybe one. The one rule is that the Reentry Mentor be of the same sex. The rest of the suggestions are guidelines that have been proven through countless lives and experiences involving mentoring. The reason for this one rule is that no matter how committed we are to the principles of mentoring, we remain thoroughly and remarkably human. We are subject to emotions that might divert us from our primary purpose of successful reintegration through principle centered maturity. The potential for the relationship lines becoming blurred and changing the relationship into something else can prove to be destructive for both parties.

FOCUS ON CHARACTER, NOT PERSONALITY

When seeking a Reentry Mentor, there is a tendency to look for someone who is "your type" of person or friend. This can prove to be a problem if our intention is finding an easier, softer way of being held accountable. He is a Reentry Mentor, guide, and model, not your buddy or your pal. He is a genuinely caring friend to grow with and learn how to live life on life's terms. Nevertheless, released ex-offenders often feel most at ease with a mentor of similar interests and background – another person who was down and out and rose above. Others prefer someone close to their age or of the same race and ethnic background.

However, many have been greatly helped by mentors totally unlike themselves. This is because their attention is focused on the most important things any mentor and ex-offender have in common. That is the desire to become, relate, and achieve through principles of successful living. Therefore, age, race, background, and other external factors are not as important as what the mentor can impart to you. For some, it is best to choose a mentor who is totally unlike yourself outwardly, someone tough who keeps you on your toes, someone who has seen you in your worst moments and who you cannot manipulate.

They are to give good counsel and be teachers of what is right and noble. For we also were once thoughtless and senseless, obstinate and disobedient, deluded and misled; [we too were once] slaves to all sorts of cravings and pleasures, wasting our days in malice and jealousy and envy, hateful (hated, detestable) and hating one another

TITUS 2:3, 3:3

Anti-social behavior and crime are primarily relational issues. It requires a relationship with a noble character of unconditional love in our lives to confront and resolve these issues. The Reentry Mentor is not someone who is an expert with inmates or reentry. He does not have to be someone who has been incarcerated. He does not have to be someone who has walked a mile in your shoes or experienced your exact forms of suffering. Your relationship with a Reentry Mentor is based on common solutions and not common problems. The goal of the relationship is to impart, support, and nurture you in the disciplines and truths of principle centered maturity.

The Reentry Mentor can lead only in so far as he has traveled on the path of principle centered maturity. He must be someone who is mature, who can guide and encourage, as well as lovingly confront you when necessary. Equally important is the mentor's capacity for patience, understanding, and willingness to devote time and effort to you. He must be someone who is willing to become an example, representative, and model of principle centered maturity, enjoying a quality level of peace in his own life. Although the specialized training to become a Reentry Mentor can prove to be extremely beneficial for both parties, any competent, caring, and committed adult can help an ex-offender learn how to cope with life without self-destructing and resorting to crime.

A pattern and model of good deeds and works, teaching what is unadulterated, showing gravity [having the strictest regard for truth and purity of motive], with dignity and seriousness

TITUS 2:7

YOUR FATE IS IN HOW YOU RELATE

The secret to our success or failure upon release is hidden in our relationships. The Reentry Mentor is someone who listens and supports you, but also calls you to action and will accept nothing less than change and growth from you. One sure way to lose your mentor is to not follow through with action. He will not accept lip service, nor stay involved if you refuse to grow and keep messing up. The Reentry Mentor is someone we can expect to be constantly confronting us with the truth. You can expect to experience firsthand, someone who is walking in the qualities of genuine manhood and maturity and willing to confront you when you are not. It is not always going to be a comfortable relationship but you can expect it to be effective.

That he may be able both to give stimulating instruction and encouragement in sound
(wholesome) doctrine and to refute and convict those who contradict and oppose it
[showing the wayward their error]
TITUS 1:9

The mentoring relationship is based on a clear understanding and constant communication of the goals of no new arrests and complete reintegration. All the information Reentry Realities contains will provide invaluable goal-oriented communication with your Reentry Mentor, as a survival guide and map for successful reintegration. His experience and insights are likely to make the principles and disciplines in this book come to life.

YOU ALONE CAN DO IT – BUT YOU CAN'T DO IT ALONE

Your Reentry Mentor is not going to make you do anything. He wouldn't if he could because that's not how it works. He can only point you in the right direction and make suggestions. You alone must make the right choices, but you should not make those choices alone. You alone are responsible for the thoughts and emotions you experience, but you should not handle them alone. You can listen to 98% of what your Reentry Mentor tells you, and I promise you, it will be that hard to accept the 2% that leads you back to prison.

It is common for an ex-offender to start off reentry highly motivated and excited about having a Reentry Mentor. Then work starts, life begins to get better, and you lose enthusiasm for the importance of the relationship with your Reentry Mentor. It is easy to believe that once life starts working well the Reentry Mentor has fulfilled his purpose. If you allow this to happen, none of the reasons you give will add up to logic and sound reasoning in the eyes of your Reentry Mentor in light of what's at stake. It makes no sense to quit what has been working. This can only sabotage your freedom. The real truth will be that there is a maturity issue involved in your commitment and consistency.

Put first things first
PROVERBS 24:27

3. WHAT SHOULD I EXPECT FROM A REENTRY MENTOR?

Don't expect him to swallow any of your excuses. He won't because he genuinely cares about your success. A lack of commitment and antisocial behavior are not part of maturity in manhood and is not excused by unfavorable circumstances and environments. If your freedom does not mean any more to you than your next desire or impulse, you might as well resign yourself to a life of incarceration because you are never going to change that way.

Our Reentry Mentor will require a level of commitment to action that pulls us out of repeated attempts to slide back into our extreme self-centered desires. The more committed to the mentoring process we become, the less self-centered we become, and the less important those destructive desires and habits become. Our "want to" desire is our familiar sanctuary from the pain of reality. Reintegration into society means embracing reality with the support of a Reentry Mentor, not escaping it. The mentoring relationship empowers us with the ability to deny ourselves our own destructive indulgences, where at times, nothing else can.

ACCESS TO YOUR MENTOR

One of the main factors of concern when choosing a Reentry Mentor should be his location and accessibility to him. Your Reentry Mentor should be someone in your area or community who can meet with you on a regular basis, and on short notice when there is a crisis. Support and accountability requires someone who can look us in the eye, examine us, and challenge us with the truth. Phone contacts alone can never create this kind of impact. We need to feel supported and accountable. The only way this will happen is with someone who is within close physical proximity to us. On the other hand, if you are having trouble locating someone in your area, you can use someone who is further away as a temporary support. Any support is better than no support until you can locate someone in your area.

WHEN YOU HAVE SPECIAL NEEDS

Alcohol and drugs are major culprits in antisocial behavior and crime. Statistics show that 80% of those incarcerated were involved in alcohol and drugs prior to incarceration. Many experts consider it the single most important factor of recidivism. If this is true of your own history, your Reentry Mentor will expect you to seek out support and fellowship for this problem as a method of prevention. He can help you search the Internet or other information sources for this need and other special needs.

The Reentry Mentor does not provide any such services as those offered by licensed counselors or social workers. He is simply a model and guide to successful living, who helps the ex-offender solve one problem: how to live a life of principle-centered maturity without re-offending. This is accomplished through encouragement and accountability in the real work of "applying" the principles of acclimation, the psycho-social stages of reentry, and the other tools in this book. It is not highly specialized training that enables the Reentry Mentor to give effective help, but rather simple observation and experience. He will expect you to expose your known triggers for trouble, such as handling excessive amounts of money, ATM cards, people, places, and other things. He is likely to point out some potential triggers of concern and hold you accountable to a trigger prevention plan.

PRINCIPLES OVER PERSONALITIES

In all the work with the ex-offender, the mentor underscores the fact it is Biblical principles, and not the mentor's personality or position that is important. This way the ex-offender learns to lean on the moral principles and not the personality of the Reentry Mentor. Personalities fall short, principles do not. The most effective Reentry Mentors recognize and convey to the ex-offender that the goal is for them to eventually stand on their own two feet and make their own decisions. He will know the difference and maintain solid boundaries between helping you learn to stand and holding you up.

In the first few weeks and months of early reentry, an ex-offender is sometimes so bewildered or indecisive that he needs extra attention and perhaps extra help in making personal decisions. He is likely to want you to call him daily for the first ninety days and meet with him one to two times weekly. Calling your Reentry Mentor and meeting with him will be your number one priority as long as your freedom is. However, such utter dependence on a Reentry Mentor, when carried past the early period of release, often becomes damaging to both parties.

And having done all, to stand, stand
EPHESIANS 6:13, 14

MENTORSHIP MEANS COMMUNITY CONNECTIONS

Mentorship also provides the bridge which enables an ex-offender to meet other safe people in the community through fellowship groups, organizations, and churches. It is networking to build a whole new community of support that strengthens our grasp on freedom. It is not the sole responsibility of the individual mentor to support us. He is only one man and cannot possibly always be available. Networking enables us to have many resources when we are unable to contact our Reentry Mentor. You can telephone and meet with other contacts to sort out the best possible solutions for almost any problem troubling you at that moment.

The Reentry Mentor will want to see us meet many other competent and mature men as soon as possible. The ex-offender with more than one contact shares in a wide range of experience. We can hear a wide variety of ways to view the principles and disciplines we are learning to live by. Having several contacts also works as a means of better averting the many forms of crisis that can arise in reentry. For example, it is unlikely that five of our five contacts would be unavailable at the same time during a crisis.

THE ISSUE OF OVER-DEPENDENCE

If the ex-offender persists in showing a pattern of over-dependence after the early stage of reentry, the Mentor will continue to point out that our reliance is on principle centered maturity, and not on any one individual personality. If we are unable to grasp this, our chances are not very good. Another way the Reentry Mentor may try to resolve such an issue is to redouble his efforts to see that we are socializing with several others in our support network. If these efforts fail, he is likely to try a more direct approach of confronting us with specific instances of over-dependence and the great potential cost of continuing it.

Let our own [people really] learn to apply themselves to good deeds (to honest labor and honorable employment) so that they may be able to meet necessary demands whenever the occasion may require and not be living idle and…unfruitful lives
TITUS 3:14

THE ISSUE OF A LACK OF DEPENDENCE

There are likely to be those who are unwilling to depend on and work with their Reentry Mentor. If we reject his help, there is little our Reentry Mentor can do except assure us of his willingness to help when and if needed. Mentoring is a flexible venture and mentors themselves are flexible in working with others. He will not thrust unwanted help upon an ex-offender, nor will the mentor refuse him help when he asks for it. In such a circumstance the mentor may offer to introduce you to a potential mentor you are more willing to work with.

Obey your spiritual leaders and submit to them [continually recognizing their authority over you], for they are constantly keeping watch over your souls and guarding your spiritual welfare . . . [do your part to] let them do this with gladness and not with sighing and groaning for that would not be profitable to you [either]
HEBREWS 13:17

THE MENTOR'S STYLE AND APPROACH

As an ex-offender adjusting to the challenges of reintegration back into society, you are the one who needs help, not him. Do not try to be an advocate for helping your Reentry Mentor understand his job because of your book knowledge, programming history, or opinions. Your job is to trust the process and practice the principles and disciplines in all your affairs. There are times when you may feel your Reentry Mentor is being too firm, to blunt, or unwilling to see your point – or even under-involved. These methods should not always be viewed as unsympathetic and uncaring. He is likely to have his reasons for his approach. The successful adult life is based on tried and tested principles. Firm mentorship emphasizes this and usually works well at convincing an ex-offender he can only disregard those principles at serious cost.

Try to recognize such firmness as an attempt to remain factual and avoid conflicting emotions.

Not all Reentry Mentors will use the same approach to mentoring. A lot will depend on what his past experience and personality suggest. Some Reentry Mentors adopt a "take it or leave it" approach. Others exhibit extreme patience and great personal interest in the people they mentor. Still others are somewhat casual, content to let the ex-offender take the initiative in asking questions or seeking help in special situations. Each approach is sometimes successful and at times fails. The Reentry Mentor will decide the need in each particular case. He recognizes the importance of flexibility in working with ex-offenders. He may not rely on any single approach and may try different approaches according to your needs.

POOR DECISION MAKING

It can be most discouraging for the Reentry Mentor to work with an ex-offender who starts to make progress for a period of time and then descends into a cycle of poor decisions. This can be a delicate time for you and your Reentry Mentor. The mentor will seek to steer a middle ground between harsh confrontation and sympathizing with you. He will not seek to push you away, nor will he enable you. If you do make poor decisions, you may even be more discouraged and may find it extremely difficult to return to your Reentry Mentor and supportive network for a fresh start. Your ability to return will depend, to a large degree, on realizing the full extent of understanding and love the mentor and your support network has for you.

Always be humble and gentle. Be patient with each other, making allowance for each other's faults because of your love. Make every effort to keep yourselves united
EPHESIANS 4:2-3

A poor decision will not exclude you from the help of those whose only desire is to see you succeed. Later, the Reentry Mentor is likely to want to discuss the kind of thinking that led to the poor decision in the first place. The mutual goal would be to turn them into learning experiences. At the same time, the ex-offender should keep in mind that mentorship is a privilege and success depends on your communication, courage, and commitment to the process.

MEETING WITH THE FAMILY

The Reentry Mentor should meet with the ex-offender's family and explain his position.

You should be willing to embrace this, even if you feel somewhat uncomfortable with it. The knowledge of added support often provides a sense of comfort and security to the uncertain family. He will point out that you are more likely to be successful when relatives take an interest in the reintegration process. Becoming familiar with your unique challenges, special needs, and the principles and disciplines you must learn to practice involves your family in your success.

The Reentry Mentor may convey to your family that you need their patience and understanding, especially during the first days and weeks of reentry. This does not entitle you to be pampered simply because you are living responsibly and maturely. In general, the Reentry Mentor can help your family give you every chance to make good on your commitment to a life of principle centered maturity, and not expect too much too soon.

THE REENTRY MENTOR IS NOT A FAMILY COUNSELOR
In some cases, marital and other family relationships have become strained and estranged as a result of the ex-offenders crime and incarceration. The Reentry Mentor cannot be your professional marriage and family relations counselor in such situations. However, he can be supportive in the healing process. He cannot mentor your family, although he may offer helpful guidance and support at times.

Become useful and helpful and kind to one another, tender-hearted (compassionate, understanding, loving-hearted), forgiving one another [readily and freely]
EPHESIANS 4:32

Your family cannot act as a Reentry Mentor. They can support you and share your progress with the Reentry Mentor. The mentor's communication with the family prevents closed information loops that foster problems and secrecy. The family can and should hold you accountable. If you are serious about your freedom, you will welcome your family holding you accountable. You can share this book with them to help them better understand the challenges you will face. Once they are aware, they can be more alert and more helpful. The family's close proximity allows them to be a tremendous help in the area of prevention. While your family's help may feel uncomfortable, it may prove priceless to your freedom.

SHOULD YOUR MENTOR MEET WITH YOUR EMPLOYER?
Whether or not a Reentry Mentor should involve himself with an ex-offender's employer depends upon the individual circumstances of each case. A surprising number of employers who are anxious to have competent employees wel-

come the news that you have turned to moral support to secure your freedom. The employer may feel more confident hiring someone with a criminal history if they know there is someone holding them accountable. The employer may wish to speak with the Reentry Mentor before he makes an employment decision. When it comes to having a poor work history and an offender status, your Reentry Mentor may be what makes the difference. However, you should not assume a position of entitlement just because you are doing the right things.

KEEPING WITH THE MENTOR'S CENTRAL PURPOSE

The Reentry Mentor is not your personal taxi or loan agent. These areas are always a matter of individual judgment as to where to draw the line. Involved in where this line is drawn is the basic fact that the Reentry Mentor has one central purpose, to assist you in learning how to live a life of principle centered maturity. The Reentry Mentor who continually crosses the line does so at the risk of altering the dynamics of the relationship, and thereby running the risk of slowing down the ex-offender's progress.

Transportation and money, or a lack of it, have never been a key factor in an individual's ability to live a crime-free life. This does not mean the Reentry Mentor will not be willing to provide transportation or a small financial gift if it supplies a genuine need and is supportive to long-term success. If the Reentry Mentor is willing and it is applied directly to your ability to stand on your own two feet, so much the better.

In today's world, there are a number of professional agencies who can furnish a wide variety of assistance if it is needed. Most ex-offenders, when living a consistent life of principle centered maturity, can, over time, solve their own domestic, financial, and employment problems. The Reentry Mentor can provide the best support in these areas by guiding you to potential solutions for solving these challenges on your own. He can help you learn bus routes, figure out how to open a savings account, prepare a budget, set financial goals, and pay bills.

4. WHEN SHOULD I GET A REENTRY MENTOR?

Reentry specialists generally believe a Reentry Mentor is necessary as soon as possible to establish a supportive and trusting relationship. This means the time to choose a Reentry Mentor is right now. The reasons for this are further discussed in the chapter on communication. The importance of this cannot be over-stressed. The Reentry Mentor is someone who should be there to meet you at the gate as part of your identified welcome home and support group if possible.

Walking out of prison with them upon release provides a tremendous sense of security and support. It doesn't matter how well prepared you believe you are. Release from prison represents the threshold of a major transition in your life. It begins with a few steps from where all aspects of your life are structured and controlled and continues to where virtually no structure and no control are present in your life.

A prudent person foresees danger and takes precautions
PROVERBS 22:3

You are going to be entering a path of restoration and reconciliation to society and to your local community. Such a process never begins as a result of being turned loose. It begins with the steps toward change you will make and the reinforcements you recruit. The process of restoration and reconciliation begin long before you leave prison and the moment you choose a mentor and begin your journey toward change. It cannot begin too early if you are going to be ready for that transition.

IT'S NEVER TOO LATE
While it is never too early to recruit a Reentry Mentor, it is also never too late. Don't make the mistake of using that excuse on yourself. Getting to know a Reentry Mentor, talking frankly, and listening to his experience can make the whole concept of reentry and the current social trends open up into a broader perspective for us.

For the offender who has been able to achieve only interludes of commitment and consistency to change and turn from the old life, the Reentry Mentor may just make all the difference. Those who have a tendency to associate with people who stay on the fringes of society commonly nourish secret reservations about completely letting go of the old life. For such a person, a firm and caring mentor may be the final weight that tips the scales in the right direction.

Bad company corrupts good character. Think carefully about what is right
1 CORINTHIANS 15:33,34

5. WHERE DO I FIND A REENTRY MENTOR?
The concept of a Reentry Mentor is growing in understanding. Many studies have been done to investigate their effectiveness. The results are positive and impressive. My hope is that staff or inmates, in time, will be able to access a website that can provide information on how to match men returning to society with willing mentors in their community. In recent years, faith-based organizations have shown an increased interest in the responsibility of restoration and reconciliation of the fallen behind the prison razor wire. Faith-based organizations are increasingly involved in many activities in the prison system.

Not counting up and hold against [men] their trespasses [but canceling them], and com-
mitting to us the message of reconciliation (of the restoration to favor)
2 CORINTHIANS 5:19

I would like to see specialized training for those who have the courage and heart to become Reentry Mentors, as well as reentry seminars that make potential matches long before a release date. I could envision a statewide, non-profit organization that recruits, trains, and organizes Reentry Mentors according to community. I would like to see mentoring programs within the institutional settings that prepare and educate incarcerated men on the need for mentorship and how to respond to it. Even if such visions are realized, it will still require us to be self-motivated and take the initiative to reach out and make the contact. No one is going to do it for us or make us do it.

PERSISTENCE OVERCOMES RESISTANCE

Your initiative and creativity is likely to require a little more effort for now. I know you can find a Reentry Mentor if you are serious about remaining free. I have done it myself without much difficulty. It may require that you inves-tigate leads through chapel services in your institution. If alcohol and drugs have been a problem in your life, you can also attend self-help groups such as Alcoholics Anonymous or Narcotics Anonymous in your institution. You can often make outside contacts for mentorship through their central office address. You may have prior contacts in the church or A.A. that you will need to humble yourself and write. It may require that you contact a church in the community you are returning to. There may be a family friend or someone else in your past that is living a responsible life of principle centered maturity that you admire.

Come back to the place of safety all your prisoners who still have hope!
ZECHARIAH 9:12

You can make these contacts and explain to them that you are looking for someone to make yourself accountable to. You can explain that you want to make the right choices and you understand it will be a challenging transition. If they agree but are not sure how they can help, inform them that you have a book that explains your challenges and the principles and disciplines for successful reentry. Ask them if they would be willing to review this book and use it in discussions as a map and a survival guide to successful reintegration.

MY REENTRY MENTOR EXPERIENCES

The first time I used the support of a Reentry Mentor was through guests I had met in the chapel. I had begun to attend church regularly upon release and entered a young man's fellowship group as a result of my mentor's guidance. Life got better because I got better. My life began to work well for me because I worked the principles that made it work well.

I made a foolish mistake by putting the rewards of progress ahead of the principles and support that produced the rewards. I had developed an unrealistic perception that because things were going well, I didn't need the support anymore. In reality, the opposite was true; I needed their support even more to protect the progress I had made. I not only lost the rewards but my freedom as well.

The second time I sought the support of a Reentry Mentor I made contact with people in Alcoholics Anonymous. In the first couple of days of release I was in meetings with them. I made several costly mistakes in this situation. I started off humble and listening. When life began to improve for me, pride and ego reasserted themselves, and it wasn't long until I thought I knew as much as they did. I started making judgments and decisions that were in opposition to their advice. I wanted too much, too fast, too soon. They were trying to save me from myself, and I would not let them.

The wise are glad to be instructed, but babbling fools fall flat on their faces
PROVERBS 10:8

At some point, I thought I should be welcomed as an equal within these social circles and invited in all that they did, before I even proved myself. Life doesn't work that way. I felt they should initiate contact with me. As a result, I chose to see myself as alienated, when in reality I was not. I didn't give time – time. Instead of persisting to be a part of a group of winners, I drifted back into crowds where I could feel important without earning it. In the end, I lost my freedom once again. Finding a mentor and other support was the easy part; it was the maturity to be committed and consistent that I lacked.

6. HOW DO I RELATE TO MY MENTOR?
Relationships require our investment of genuine commitment or we don't stay on very long. The same is true when it comes to your Reentry Mentor and support network. Listening to sermons, leads, and testimonials are not enough. It requires heart-to-heart, gut-level communication. Consistent transparency, through being humble and open, helps to keep our "want to" problem from dominating us. Just knowing that someone is available if and when we need help – exhorting us toward victory – is a tremendous inspiration.

EXPANDED PERSPECTIVE MEANS PROTECTION

The Reentry Mentor relationship is about growing and learning through teamwork, developing unity and cooperation with another human being. It improves and expands our awareness by enlarging our perspective view and potential. It sharpens relationship skills for other relationships as well. The person who is mature enough to function in adult society and reality has the humility to recognize their own limited awareness. They can appreciate the rich resources available through communicating with the hearts and minds of other people.

We are each conditioned to interpret reality differently. Unless we allow ourselves to see the possibilities in alternative views, we will never transcend the limits of our own individual past conditioning that led us to incarceration. The Reentry Mentor relationship is particularly powerful in dealing with the negative forces of hiding and protecting our "want to" problems that come from our limited worldview and work against our freedom. This is a design principle of relationships where combined individual forces are maximized for the ultimate good of both parties.

Walk with the wise and become wise; associate with fools and get into trouble"
PROVERBS 13:20

DISARMING DESTRUCTIVE DECEPTIONS

Crime is not a mere "one simple deed." It must be seen as a series of thinking errors that ends in a series of poor choices. It is an observable process that begins inwardly and then manifests itself outwardly. This is why we need a Reentry Mentor. He may be the only tool that can disarm our "want to" problem. The temptations we face in reentry only seem irresistible because they are laced with deception. They lack the opposition of truth that a mentor can provide. The deception of these temptations ignite faulty logic and errors in thinking, quickly carrying us to a place where we can no longer defend ourselves. Let's take a look at this process and how our mentor can help us abort it.

For we have built a strong refuge made of lies and deception
ISAIAH 28:15

THE FOUR STAGE RELAPSE PROCESS

The process of relapse into alcohol and drugs, antisocial behavior, and crime, has four stages. Stage one begins with a passing thought or a series of passing thoughts. For example, "have a drink" or "commit the crime" – the I "want to" problem. This is the stage where we must act to abort the process. If the thought enters our mind a second time, we simply make a call to our mentor or others in our support network. Major wars are won by victory in the small battles. Don't wait until the battle is too big to resist.

It is critical that you tell your mentor that you are calling to interrupt this line of thinking and explain. This transparency gives your support enough information to help you. They may ask you if you need to meet with them, or you may want to suggest it. Many times, the call and the humble openness are enough to return us to reality. Be realistic with yourself about what you need most at this time. Your support team will not judge you for those thoughts. In fact, they are likely to be highly impressed with your complete honesty.

If you avoid this call and the thoughts continue, you will enter stage two. By the time you have the thought for the third time, the promise of satisfaction becomes attached to it, and you become enticed. As you enter the second stage, the enticement takes control and carries you away to an illusionary world of the hope of fulfillment where you are literally defenseless. You become intoxicated with the fulfillment of the desire (any desire), and the powers of clear discrimination are lost. As this enticement progresses, we become like a dog mesmerized by a piece of meat hanging just out of reach. When we are at this point, the potential of arrest and incarceration don't seem like a real possibility to us. When we think "just once" we are at the point of no return. One bad decision leads to another, and we enter stage three when we commit the act.

After the act, we have no intention of returning to the "old life," and we believe we are still in control. The act is never equal to the plans and expectations. Once the act is completed, we enter stage four. The fourth stage involves the resulting consequences of emptiness and remorse.

There are always consequences that immediately manifest inwardly, and eventually they will manifest outwardly. As this four-stage process begins, we are never able to see all the way through to the fourth stage of consequences. Without honest transparency with at least one other person, it's only a matter of time before the four-stage process begins all over again. It is life on a merry-go-round, over and over again, until we experience our impending catastrophe of re-incarceration.

ACCOUNTABILITY MEANS RESPONSIBLE REINTEGRATION

The importance of Reentry Mentors to released prisoners was clarified by Dr. Byron Johnson in his study of the Texas Prison Fellowship Program, under contract with the state. Dr. Johnson's study found that those in mentoring programs were two and a half times less likely to be re-incarcerated than inmates in a control group. Dr. Johnson emphasized that mentors were "absolutely critical" to the impressive results.

The accountability in the environment of the mentor relationship is our best method of prevention from returning to the old life upon release. The goal of learning to live life on principle centered terms introduces common ground for this adult relationship. This goal provides the common ground for communication and cooperation, as it pushes back the barriers of reentry, transforming them into driving forces for commitment and consistency. Through this relationship we learn to involve ourselves in our problems (instead of avoiding them) and become part of our own solution.

Let's take a few moments to reflect on our need for a Reentry Mentor.

- Do you see the importance of a Reentry Mentor for your reintegration? Why or why not?
- What plan would you use to recruit a Reentry Mentor? Do you posses the courage and humility to ask for this help?

It is time to shift gears and look at employment. We will study the qualities that would make you successful in the business world. Keep in mind how your Reentry Mentor could help you develop these qualities.

273

CHAPTER SEVENTEEN

Powerfully Employed

—⁓—

*There are some books that are absolutely indispensable to the kind of education
that we are contemplating, and to the profession that we are now considering:
and of all of these, the most indispensable, the most useful, the one whose knowledge is most effective, is the bible. There is no book from which more value can
be learned. There is no book whose style is more suggestive and more instructive.
None which you open with such confidence and lay down with such reverence;
there is no book like the bible."*

— CHARLES ANDERSON DANA —

EDITOR-IN-CHIEF, *THE NEW YORK SUN*

Y ou stand before a formidable challenge upon release. You must find
a job and remain employed. You have decided no pleasure or short
cut to financial gain is worth years of your life behind the razor wire
of a state prison. You are committed to proving to yourself that you can
actually succeed through creating legitimate plans. A lack of vision looms as
the worst enemy of your success. A lack of vision and planning always leads
to the wrong character and the wrong people. You got into this challenge by
being a male; you will overcome this challenge by being a man. What will
true manhood look like?

> *Where there is no vision [no redemptive revelation of God], the people perish;
> but he who keeps the law [of God, which includes the law of man]
> blessed (happy, fortunate, and enviable) is he*
> PROVERBS 29:18

You begin with the right decision, and then you stick to it: "That's it! I'm
through with the old life. I'm going to turn away from all the things that could
threaten my freedom and bring me back to prison. I don't care what it takes.
The old life stops here. I mean it, the old life stops here and that's final. I'm
going to find a job and become a productive member of society."

When it comes down to it, the definition of manhood is pretty simple: it
means hearing the Word of God and then doing it. That is God's only definition of manhood – a doer of the word (James 1:22). No doubt, God's definition of manhood is not easy. But the easy life is not a good life, and a good life
is not easy. The good life is based on principles – God's principles – and the
manhood to stick to them. The prayer of true manhood is not that the way be

made easy, but rather to have the courage to live in such a way so as to enjoy the difficult.

It's difficult to live victoriously upon release. There are always specific terms in regards to victory. Choosing victory cannot be done on our terms and agendas. Personal success is like any other invention. You seek out the right principles that will allow it to work, and then you design your plans by the strict guidelines of those principles. We told ourselves repeatedly, "We wanted out and we were not coming back to prison." Words and the intentions behind them mean nothing. Talking isn't the same as doing. They are literally different realms of existence. The words I spoke of wanting to work and rebuild my life were met with the challenge to prove it.

THREE TIME LOSER RELEASED FROM PRISON

I was released for the third time after doing four years and six months in prison. I was alone and on my own. My father died of alcoholism. My mother died of cancer, and a drunk driver killed my brother. I had no family. The only place for me to go was a state certified halfway house. In a matter of a few hours, I went from wearing state blues and sitting on a prison bunk to sitting in this new environment of the halfway house. The sudden and abrupt change was a powerful culture shock after years of incarceration. I remember sitting in the living room of that halfway house with my stomach churning from intense anxiety.

The halfway house appeared to be a positive enough environment, and I was certainly happy to be out of prison. The place was busy and full of life. Some guys were wearing fast food uniforms, factory uniforms, and others were dressed like they were working construction. Some of the guys were between jobs and casually dressed. They all had what I did not – family and strong connections with society.

The positive emotions of release, mixed with the mountain of challenges before me, was a little overwhelming to say the least. To begin with, I was unfamiliar with the city I was in, and I didn't know anyone. The need for a job appeared extremely urgent to me. Once my required stay at the halfway house was complete, I would have nowhere to go. I needed to be able to rent a place to live in and support myself in just a matter of months.

There was a moment when all I could see were the challenges before me and no immediate answers. My circular thinking led me to feel trapped. I felt I couldn't get a job without a car to get there. Yet, I couldn't get a car without a job to buy one. I couldn't get a driver's license without a car to take a test in, yet I couldn't get a car without a job. My head was spinning and my stomach wasn't helping. I went from a reasonably predictable prison life to total uncertainty.

We walk by faith [we regulate our lives and conduct ourselves by our convictions or belief...thus we walk] not by sight or appearance
1 CORINTHIANS 5:7

I just kept telling myself to have faith and stay calm. Let things unfold one day at a time.

This meant not looking at my conditions as a lack of potential provision. I knew a little about faith. We all do actually. We practice it constantly in our daily affairs without even realizing that we do. It's just when we are forced to exercise it that we often get a little weak in the knees.

The more substance there is to what you put faith in, the less faith it actually requires. For example, standing in the middle of a lake on two inches of ice requires a lot more faith than standing in the middle of a lake on four inches of ice. It's all about the depth of what you put your faith in. Faith in God's promises and prayer provided the courage and strength to do what I could and allowed me to trust God for the rest. In order to do my part and be successful at reentry, I knew I would need some strong personal qualities. To begin with, I would have to be bigger on the inside than the challenges of life on the outside. Hope is one of those qualities. It means <u>H</u>olding <u>O</u>n (with) <u>P</u>atient <u>E</u>xpectation.

But hope [the object of] which is seen is not hope. For how can one hope for what he already sees? But if we hope for what is still unseen by us, we wait for it with patience and composure
ROMANS 8:24-25

I was able to purchase a ten-speed bicycle from one of the guys at the halfway house. My goal was to ride around and learn about the city I was in. How strange I thought, here I am in my mid-forties, riding on a ten-speed bicycle in a strange town, and living in a halfway house.

Nothing felt normal about my circumstances, and I was uncomfortable about all of it.

I wanted to be ashamed and discouragement kept wanting to take hold of me. I had a strong desire to succeed, so I kept my eyes focused on the success I was trying to get to, and not what I was going through. I knew I needed a lot of patience and a lot of humility to make it through this transition. I remember that I would laugh at myself, and say to myself out loud, "This is all temporary if I accept the challenges and the unknown as a normal part of the journey of reentry."

After several weeks, I landed a job interview through one of the guys staying at the halfway house. I rode my ten-speed bicycle and followed a hand drawn map to the location of my job interview. I was honest about my circumstances and past. I simply spoke from the heart and communicated my desire to work and rebuild my life.

I was given the job, and this is when the words I spoke of wanting to work and rebuild my life were put to the test. I remember having to get up extra early to ride that ten-speed bicycle all the way to work each morning just to be there on time. It was all uphill. The season was mid-summer, and by 6:30 am I was dripping wet with sweat from the long ride. The work was hard labor and long hours, but I was free and rebuilding my life. I remember a time when my feet were covered with blisters from wearing prison state boots to work. I was in such pain I could barely walk. My success required that I accept the bad and focus on the good, so that's what I did.

I worked every day and every hour my boss would allow, and I began to feel like I was part of the community I was in. I was trusted, counted on, and I continued to stay hopeful and grateful. Having a job gradually began to remove many of the uncertainties from my life. Life started to feel like it was working for me because I was working. It wasn't long and I was finally able to put away that ten-speed bicycle. I was given a truck full of expensive tools to drive back to the halfway house every night. You see, something happened I could have never foreseen in my early days of intense anxiety at the halfway house. My boss allowed me to use his brand-new car to take my driver's test in.

In four months, I was released from the halfway house two months early. Those four months consisted of nothing but work and programming at the halfway house. A vision backed by faith, discipline, and hard work paid off. I had a bank account, a car of my own, and a house I had just rented.

While we were yet with you, we gave you this rule and charge: If anyone will not work,
neither let him eat. We hear that some among you are disorderly [that they are passing
their lives in idleness, neglectful of duty], being busy with other people's affairs instead of
their own and doing no work
2 THESSALONIANS 3:10-11

In two and a half years I had my own trucks and tools and was working for myself. None of my successes were possible without the right vision, the right people, and the right principles in my life. Every kind of success is always about the right vision, the right people in your life, and following the right principles. Conversely, every kind of failure can be traced back to a lack of vision, being involved with the wrong people, and a lack of principle-centered guidance.

THE TRANSFORMING POWER OF REVELATION KNOWLEDGE

Many people find it hard to believe that you can operate under the principles of the Bible and still be successful in what many view as the dog-eat-dog world of business. It is the proclamation of God that life will constantly prove His principles are the surest and safest way to be successful. The principles revealed in the Bible have set the standards for success in the world of business as we know it. No nation ever needed a patent or copyright law until this book of revelation had been given to it. There is not a sphere of human life that has not been greatly impacted by it.

Study this book of instruction continually.
Meditate on it day and night so you will be sure to obey everything written in it.
Only then will you prosper and succeed in all you do
JOSHUA 1:8

Certainly, we must admit, social conditions have an impact on our lives. Nevertheless, I am convinced through personal experience that God has given us the revelation to rise above these powerful influences on success, and our lives become totally different from what anyone could have predicted. This is possible as a result of the powerful principles God's Word reveals to us. It is the theme of this book that every person is responsible for what they become once they are released.

I call heaven and earth to witness this day against you that I have set before you life and
death, the blessings and the curses; therefore choose life
DEUTERONOMY 30:19

The revelation of God's Word is not that He has provided a way for a humanity that cannot succeed, but in fact, that He has provided a way in which you can (Ezekiel 36:26). If our lives have been a failure due to our character being flawed, we no longer have a right to say, "That's just the way I am." Consider this, if the Word of God is revelation from God to man, it was written to solve our human problem not describe it.

APPLIED REVELATION: THE FOUNDATION FOR SUCCESS

The Word of God is a revelation of truth for all people, in all places, in all circumstances, and at all times. It's where we need to discover what traits should be developed for enduring success in the business world, just as it has been where we needed to turn for those personal qualities that make up manhood. In reality, success and manhood are one and the same. When the people asked Jesus (The Master Model of Manhood) what more than anything else constituted success, He responded with the following words:

> *And Jesus replied to him, 'You shall love the Lord your God with all your heart and with all your soul and with all your mind (intellect). This is the great (most important, principle)....And the second is like it: You shall love your neighbor as [you do] yourself'*
>
> MATTHEW 22:37- 39

According to the Son of God, it is love for God and for others that is the foundation for the character that leads to all true success. People who love are happy and successful. It is as simple as that. Loving people enjoy life, enjoy others, enjoy their work, and enjoy themselves.

The theme of the Bible, from cover to cover, is the character of love. However, there is a chapter in the Bible that many call "the love chapter" because it breaks down the character of love. These are qualities or principles that will establish you as a happy and successful person in the world of business.

We have already reviewed these qualities of loving people in the chapter on Consistency.

We learned how people who express them are, by definition, growing and maturing people. These qualities are strengths of character, that if applied to your job search and lived out in the workplace, will establish you as the kind of person who earns the respect of others and is known to walk in the favor of both God and man. These strengths of character (traits of a loving person), more than anything else, will help you succeed in finding a job, securing a job, and moving on to promotion. Just as importantly, they will turn you into the kind of person you can respect.

THE QUALITIES OF SUCCESSFUL PEOPLE

> *Love is patient and kind. Love is not jealous or boastful or proud or rude. It does not demand its own way. It is not irritable, and it keeps no record of being wronged. It does not rejoice about injustice but rejoices whenever the truth wins out. Love never gives up, never loses faith, is always hopeful, and endures through every circumstance....*
> *Love will last forever!*
>
> 1 CORINTHIANS 13:4-8

1. Patient	6. Not rude	11. Never gives up
2. Kind	7. Not demand its own way	12. Never loses faith
3. Not jealous	8. Not irritable	13. Is always hopeful
4. Not boastful	9. Keeps no record of wrongs	14. Endures every circumstance
5. Not proud	10. Not rejoice about injustice	15. Lasts

No matter how we look at these qualities, it's always about relationships. What we are going to do is view them from a fresh new application. Let's do something we have not done and examine each of these qualities and see how they will enable us to excel in our quest for success in business.

1. Love is patient. Like it or not, we all have to wait. The inner strength of patience is more about how we respond to waiting. The attitude we express toward how long it takes for things to unfold in our lives says a lot about our humility or lack of it. If we are impatient and lack humility we are likely to operate from a "sense of entitlement" (a belief that we have a right to something being unfairly delayed or being withheld from us). It is a desire to express some kind of control over life that no one really has. People who lack the humility required for patience are always "clashing" and "crashing" in life. A sense of entitlement is an expression of extreme self-centeredness. The result is that it always alienates us from people, places, and opportunities. Impatience will frustrate your job search and create problems for you once you are employed.

On the other hand, patience is not idleness. Patience says, "What positive and productive things can I do while I am waiting?" Patience operates from a foundation of faith. When we operate from faith, we don't have to see a desired end to know it is on its way. Patience does not move hastily through life, nor does it rush headlong into the unknown.

Patience in dealing with other people on the job is critical to your success. People we are patient or impatient with become joyfully or painfully aware of our attitude toward them.

Impatience expresses an exaggerated and irrational belief that we deserve special treatment. Patience expresses a belief in the equal value of all human beings and, when genuine, moves mountains in the world of employment. No wonder it holds the #1 position on God's list.

2. Love is kind. People who are kind always try to take into account how their words and actions might affect other people. When it comes to our words, it involves being truthful. The truth properly presented is an act of kindness. Being truthful is kind because it expresses the belief that another person is valuable enough to deserve the truth no matter the outcome. Lying is always a form of brutality because it misleads others. When it comes to our actions, successful people always look for opportunities to extend a helping hand in acts of kindness. Such actions express our ability to see our partnership with humanity. When random acts of kindness are performed on the job, they are remembered long after the event has passed. Look for at least one opportunity each day on the job to perform an act of kindness. Your kindness will reward you (Proverbs 11:17).

3. Love is not jealous. To be jealous is to (covet), to crave a position or a possession that belongs to someone else. This craving goes beyond admiring what someone else has. Coveting includes envy – resenting that others have what you do not. Such desires often lead to desperate and destructive actions. Jealousy is a form of greed that leaves people feeling miserable and divided from others as they maneuver for title, position, or recognition on the job. Jealousy is foolish and irrational because it involves comparing one human being with the specific qualities, abilities, and blessings of another unique human being. People who are not jealous are happy when others are recognized or receive a benefit – knowing their unique life will experience its own rewards. The Master Model of Manhood warns us not to measure our lives by how much we own (Luke 12:15).

4. Love is humble. Meekness (humility) is not the same as weakness, even though they sound the same. To see them in action is to see they are worlds apart. Genuine humility does not lessen manhood, personal stature, or the ability to exercise authority. To the contrary, the power of humility establishes these things through its ability to command respect and gain loyalty and the alliance of others. On the other hand, few things are as hard to be around as an over-inflated ego. Most people realize that the smallest package in the world is the person who is all wrapped up in themselves. Humble people are successful in business because they are teachable. They don't claim to have all the answers or think their way is always best. Few qualities can earn the respect of an employer as much as humility. Humble people respect authority and are able to follow directions. Humble people become the best leaders because they were best at following orders. Humble people are a pleasure to work with because they view no person inferior to them. No wonder the Bible says the meek (the humble) will inherit the earth (Matthew 5:5).

5. Love is not boastful. Conceit and arrogance combine to be a communication style that projects to others that we are prideful and self-important. This kind of person gets it wrong nearly every time they open their mouth. Their words are often injurious. The revelation of God's Word has a lot to say about our words. James said, "The tongue is a flame of fire" (James 3:6). You can never hide who you truly are. Your words, especially in times of anger and frustration, will reveal your heart. "For whatever is in your heart determines what you say" (Matthew 12:34). Speech lies at the very center of personality. Stop and think before you speak, both when you are interviewed for a job and once you are employed. The words you speak at the workplace will make a difference, because they will have an impact on those you work with. The arrogant and overbearing are literally intolerable to work with. Instead, choose to be loving and mature. Say something inspiring to someone every day. It may feel awkward to begin with, but in time it will feel like the most normal thing to do.

6. Love is not rude. People who are rude are impolite and often crude. They may not express the pride and self-importance of the arrogant, but rude people often get pleasure out of the shock value of their comments and actions. Rudeness can often hurt people as deeply as physical pain – and be longer lasting. Do you consider others before you speak or act? Loving people are instinctively courteous. The result of being courteous is that it makes other people feel good about themselves and about being around you in the workplace. It often makes others feel valuable and important. Courteousness allows others to feel their boundaries are safe in your presence. Success or failure are often in the tongue (Proverbs 18:6, 7).

7. Love is unselfish. Love does not demand its own way. Loving people never allow themselves to exploit others on the road to success. If we are going to be successful we have to build bridges on our journey, not burn them down. Love's character is not against profits from hard work and sound bargaining. It does not allow us to put selfish interest ahead of the best interests of others. Unselfish people operate from a position of the best outcome for all. To be unselfish is to expand our focus to include others. In the workplace it also means our time, talent, and assistance are directed toward the good of other people without thought of gaining a benefit or reward. The Master Model of Manhood said, "If any of you wants to be my follower, you must turn from your selfish ways" (Matthew 16:24).

8. Love is not irritable. Those who operate from the character of love do not easily lose their temper. They are able to stay calm when things go wrong. People determined to be successful will have nothing to do with the kind of intimidation that losing one's temper is usually aimed at creating. Successful manhood has no desire to see people cow down or to be made afraid. A hot temper can quickly burn like a fire out of control and ruin everything. It divides people in the workplace and pushes us into hasty decisions that end in bitterness, guilt, and poverty. Anger itself is not wrong. Anger can be a legitimate reaction to injustice and evil.

When you feel yourself getting angry in the workplace, look for the cause. Are you responding to an unjust situation, or are you responding selfishly with a prideful desire to control others? The best way to be sure is to be slow to anger (James 1:19).

9. Love keeps no record of wrongs. When anger is unresolved and wrongs are unforgiven, it turns into resentment. The revelation of God tells us there is no weight heavier to carry than resentment (Proverbs 27:3). Resentment can result from a lot of things: broken promises, misunderstandings, false friends, our own illusions, or untruthful words. More often than not, resentment is the result of the failed expectations we have placed on others. If you remain employed long enough people will fail you in the workplace. Sometimes even well-meaning people with the best intentions cannot live up to their words and promises. This is why we need to practice forgiveness. To forgive means to pardon, erase the record, and be merciful to others. We are told to put our faith in God only and not in man (1 Corinthians 2:5).

10. Love does not rejoice about injustice. We live in a world that is often unfair and violates the rights of others. Injustice is no respecter of persons. It can strike anyone at any time. No one is completely free from its potential victimizing power. Not rejoicing about injustice is deciding where we stand as a man. We stand for something, or we become vulnerable to anything. Making a stand for right and truth involves courage and risk. If we want what we never had (security and stability), we must do what we've never done: tolerate only fairness and justice in and around us in the workplace (Proverbs 25:26).

STAYING POWER

Nothing can defeat you! Who wouldn't want to be this kind of person? These last five qualities represent the "staying power" of love that we can have on the inside of us – making us bigger than any situation or circumstance presented by the world around us.

Walking in love's staying power is not a matter of memorizing these fifteen

11. Love never gives up	Bears	"All Things"
12. Love never loses faith	Believes	"All Things"
13. Love is always hopeful	Hopes	"All Things" = "Abiding Faith"
14. Love endures every circumstance	Endures	"All Things"
15. Love is forever	Lasts in	"All Things"

qualities. Like all truths, it's much simpler than that. Abiding in God's revelation allows the law of the spirit of life (Romans 8:2) to transform us into the image of these qualities of love (2 Corinthians 3:18). God's revelation transforms our thoughts and heart into His (1 Corinthians 2:16), so that our ways will be transformed into His ways (1 Corinthians 4:17).

The law of the Lord is perfect, converting the soul
PSALMS 19:7

Refusing to remain in the revelation of God's word is the same as failing to abide. The result is a failure to bring forth the fruit of success that He has planned for your life. Jesus said, "I am the vine; you are the branches. Whoever lives in me and I in him bears much (abundant) fruit. However, apart from me (cut off from a vital union with me) you can do nothing" John 15:5). Abiding alone provides the identity, security, and belonging required to bear, believe, hope, and endure "all things" that come our way.

Without abiding faith, there will be compromise in trial and crisis. In the heat of the crisis, we will surrender to the false promise of the compromise. The very least compromise will mean a detour from the path of success. At the very worst, it will mean we crash and burn. Abiding faith is the result of understanding who God is, and who we are in Him (Romans 10:17). It's time to give up our own shallow schemes for success, and try out the principles that have been proven in the lives of countless people who put their faith in them.

This is the victory that conquers the world, even our faith
1 JOHN 5:4

EMPLOYMENT SUPPORTS YOUR FREEDOM

Suffering no new arrests is our first and highest goal once we are reunited with society. In order for us to reach this goal, we must understand what factors gradually increase our positive social behaviors and reduce our negative social behaviors. Experts who have spent decades studying reentry and recidivism agree: employment is the number one pro-social factor known to reduce the likelihood of returning to prison.

When we have steady employment it will increase our productivity and provide a legitimate avenue for us to care for ourselves and our family. Having a job also helps to develop valuable life skills, such as employment skills, problem-solving skills, and life-management skills. Employment strengthens pro-social community connections and provides a sense of belonging. If we are willing to establish a connection and stake in the welfare of our community through employment, we will be less likely to engage in criminal activity and forfeit our freedom.

SUCCESS IS 90% PREPARATION

Many prisoners are returning home with their educational and vocational needs unmet.

The problem is, our excuses do not go over well with parole officers, families with unmet needs, and employers seeking people who are the most likely to be productive and help produce a profit. For many inmates, there seems to be a sort of magical thinking. The idea of getting out is all that matters – with little or no thought beyond that. If the idea of employment comes to mind, there is little or no vision, planning, or proactive preparation. Skills for employment can only be developed or kept sharp by practicing them.

Those too lazy to plow in the right season will have no food at the harvest
PROVERBS 20:4

Those who fare best at employment upon reentry are those who challenge themselves mentally by constantly learning new information and involve themselves in prison jobs, OPI programs, and vocational trades. These are activities that stimulate the skills and character traits that are most needed in the world of employment. If you can't get in the program you hoped for due to qualifications or waiting lists, choose another. Do not get discouraged and give up. You will find something positive and productive to do if it really matters to you.

POTENTIAL BARRIERS TO EMPLOYMENT

Even for the most prepared, finding employment is a challenge facing ex-felons who are seeking to successfully reintegrate into society. Since the economy has slowed, the job prospects for returning prisoners are even less promising than in times of national economic prosperity.

Not only are low-skilled jobs declining in the United States, but there is also increased competition as a result of increased unemployment of non-offenders. People who have no criminal history are now competing for the same jobs as ex-offenders.

Aside from the social barriers facing us as ex-offenders, there are a number of potential personal barriers to employment. To begin with, studies suggest that prisoners generally have a poor employment history. Many prisoners have low levels of education and a significant lack of previous work experience. There also exists a high rate of substance abuse issues and undiagnosed mental health problems. Residing in poor inner-city neighborhoods can also act as a weak link to connections for stable employment opportunities.

There is often a lack of motivation to work and attitudes of distrust and alienation toward traditional employment. Criminologists have documented that over time unemployed ex-offenders become "embedded in criminality" which gradually weakens bonds to the rest of society. These weak bonds to society can be a lack of commitment to family, traditional employment, education, and other community connections. I have not discussed these barriers to discourage you. If any of this describes your circumstance, be patient and committed to overcoming these challenges. After years of engaging in criminal behavior and incarceration, reestablishing these important bonds can be difficult.

Guard your heart above all else, for it determines the course of your life
PROVERBS 4:23

Prison programs and post-release community-based programs can help significantly in overcoming these potential barriers to employment. Community based programs have increased in recent years to aid us in our efforts to reintegrate into society. However, we need to be motivated to work, and have a desire to be reintegrated into society, before things like job skills, education, and community assistance can make a difference. Our first step is to embrace reintegration as our goal as well as a process that requires multiple levels of assistance.

POTENTIAL BARRIERS TO EMPLOYMENT

1. Felony conviction
2. Economic conditions
3. Employment history
4. Lack of job skills

5. Employment connections
6. Social bonds
7. Neighborhood links
8. Lack of motivation

9. Attitude toward employment
10. Substance abuse issues
11. Mental health problems
12. No release preparation

KEEPING THE RIGHT PERSPECTIVE

There is no question that the handicaps you will face upon reentry will prove to be a challenge. The more than 600,000 other ex-felons that are released the year you get out will face many of the same common challenges you will face. The danger is in believing your challenges are unique. It can be tempting to start the blame game, or begin believing that you are a victim and not being given a fair chance. As an ex-offender just released back into society, it is possible that you will encounter numerous frustrations, disappointments, and rejections along the journey of finding a job. Then again, you may not. What's important is to be ready and willing to face these challenges if necessary. Whatever the case, you cannot afford to forget that you are in these challenges as a result of past choices that led to incarceration.

If your progress is not up to your expectations, you may begin to allow false pride and self-pity to derail your efforts. They may help you forget you are responsible for your own employment fate. False pride and self-pity will never do anything to motivate and inspire you to press on toward success. Discouragement and self-pity will come into play to the degree you operate without a faith-powered vision for your future.

Put your faith into practice.....It is by your own faith that you stand firm
2 CORINTHIANS 1:24

When it comes to facing major transitions and challenges in our lives, motivation, inspiration, and a high energy attitude are essential to success. In our efforts to find a job and then hold on to it, there is only one name for those of you who lack enthusiasm: "UNEMPLOYED." There is only one place you can find success ahead of work, and that is in the dictionary. A positive, high energy attitude is often the number one personal quality employers seek in potential employees. The military works so hard on a soldier's attitude because they believe it is likely the only thing that will keep them alive in the midst of battle. Attitude may be the only thing that allows us to survive our job search.

COUNTING THE COST OF A JOB

Always count the cost. This is the sound advice the Master Model of Manhood wants us to follow before we make a decision. He said, "Don't begin until you count the cost" (Luke 14:28). Counting the cost before choosing a job is extremely important. There are always sacrifices (costs) that come with any type of employment. In whatever job you might be applying for, you must consider if you are up to paying the price that must be paid.

For example, I once took an over-the-road truck driving job shortly after I had a new family. We needed the money, so we didn't think we needed to discuss the sacrifices that were involved. A young woman at home and a child I couldn't be near each day was more than any of us could bear. I quit the job after six weeks, during my first trip home. I was discouraged and disillusioned, but I was home.

Some people craving money have pierced themselves with many sorrows
1 TIMOTHY 6:10

If you have just reentered society from prison, your primary concern about a potential job is, "Will this job take me away from the things that are crucial to my stability?" You cannot afford to let ambition or financial fears after release lead you into a job that isolates you from what matters most. Our Creator is a God of order (1 Corinthians 14:40). Without order, there is only chaos and destruction. The things that are crucial to your stability are those things that nurture a crime-free lifestyle and transform you into God's desire for you.

Let us hold true to what we have already attained and walk and order our lives by that
PHILIPPIANS 3:16

We cannot afford to let all the growth and changes we have made in our lives go down the drain over a job. To prevent this, we must give order to the priorities of the following values: family, church, fellowship, mentoring, drug and alcohol programming, and reentry requirements. We must always ask our-selves, "How will this job impact my reentry?" You are seeking to reestablish yourself in society. Still isolated from society with a pocket full of money can be fatal to your freedom as well.

Family must always be given special consideration when choosing a job (1 Corinthians 7:32-34). When considering a specific line of work the question to ask is, "How will this job impact my spouse and my children?" Some jobs require long shifts, require you to work weekends, or take you away from home for extended periods of time. Your spouse needs a partner and your children need a father. These are tough but necessary questions. Discuss these questions with everyone you confide in or are accountable to. This may in-clude your spouse, your children, mentor, and parole officer.

COMMITMENT TO A BALANCED LIFE

A job that leaves your spiritual life, family life, and social life disconnected from their sources is a job that can destroy you. It is counterproductive and defeats our goal of living happy, joyous, and free. You must be realistic. You cannot afford to let your desire for money become an obsession that leaves the other areas of your life lifeless.

When I was promoted from machine operator to shift supervisor for a steel tubing company, I lost all balance in my life. I became so obsessed with the money I was making that all other areas of my life suffered. I worked six days a week. I went in hours before my shift started and stayed hours after it was completed. The few hours before and after my eight-hour shift dramati-cally increased my income.

All my relationships suffered. I was isolated from the people important to me and important to my very well-being. All life outside of work slowly evap-orated. The lack of balance began to affect my performance, and I made a lot of mistakes. Phyliss, a dear friend of mine, was like a stepmother to me. She pleaded with me to stop living this imbalanced life. Making all the money I could became like an addiction to me, dominating my life and snuffing out ev-erything else important. In the end, I didn't get ahead, instead much was lost.

The Master Model of Manhood asks us, "What do you gain if you fill your life with riches and possessions and lose everything that is really important?" He also said that such a man is not rich in the truest sense (Luke 12:18-22). No matter what a job offers, if it robs your life of balance it's destructive. You must weigh in the consequences of such realities before it costs you more than you are willing to pay. Life management by design in chapters three and four should always be a consideration.

There was a time when I let the false illusions of security that a job and money creates make me think I did not need the feedback of my mentor. I suffered every consequence he said I would. He was a real friend because he spoke the truth in my life – and not what he thought would make me feel better. The Master Model of Manhood thought friends were very important. When Jesus wanted to honor His disciples, He did so by giving them the title of friends (John 15:15).

A friend is always loyal, and a brother is born to help in time of need
PROVERBS 17:17

Friends are important when it comes to the strength and support necessary to remain free and faithful to your vision. If you are to live out the reentry resolution this book will ask you to write in the next chapter, the counsel of real friends is crucial. They are the ones who hold us accountable to all that we need to do to live a crime-free life. Our support network is a form of power in our lives upon reentry. They are the people who love us and care about us, even after they really know us.

THEN THERE IS MONEY
It is important to consider how a job will change your life as far as income is concerned.

There are several factors to be considered. The security and atmosphere a job offers must be weighed in the balance of the wages offered. For example, there are times that an employer may offer less money than you had hoped for, yet because of the long-term security and atmosphere, it is a fair trade off. For you personally, you may find the opposite to be most important. You may find a job offers the money you desire and your current needs override your concern for long- term security or atmosphere.

Trust in your money and down you go! But the godly flourish like leaves in spring
PROVERBS 11:28

Let whatever you choose be a result of the decision process we discovered in the chapter on commitment. If you use this process, you will be more likely to stick to your commitment and not become discouraged when the costs you decided to pay come to collect. There is little question, higher wages create greater freedoms for your life. Higher wages are both freeing and enslaving. To a point, wages are liberating. Beyond the balance we have discussed, wages become enslaving. There are a lot of nice things that money can buy. Then again, there are a lot of priceless things money cannot buy.
1. Money can buy a house; it cannot purchase a home.
2. Money can buy fun; it cannot purchase happiness.

3. Money can buy companions; it cannot purchase true friendship.
4. Money can buy a clock; it cannot buy back the time lost seeking riches.
5. Money can buy real estate; it cannot purchase you a place in heaven.

> *The blessing of the Lord makes a person rich, and He adds no sorrow with it*
> PROVERBS 10:22

POINTS TO PONDER

While seeking a job and filling out applications, don't take anything personally – it's not – it's business. If you take it personally it's going to have a heavy impact on your attitude. You can't afford a negative attitude. Landing a job is just like everything else in life. It's all a numbers game. The more you apply for jobs, the more you raise the percentage in your favor of finding employment. In the beginning, progress towards finding employment may seem slow, and then it can all come together very quickly. Don't obsess, do the groundwork, and allow it to unfold. Look at the first year of release as a series of temporary transitions. This will allow you to be more able to tolerate the impact of all the uncertainties and changes.

It's important to realize most jobs have parts of the work you may not like. There is only one name for that – employment. We don't live in a perfect world. We do what we are required to do, taking the bad with the good. If you happen to get into a position you are not happy with, try to stick it out and develop your work history. If you are let go on a job because you are not suited for that line of work, stay positive and just move on. There are plenty of things we are not all cut out for. It doesn't give us a license to give up. You will find what you can do well.

Success requires that we have enough humility and faith to start at the bottom level of jobs available if necessary – and the bottom positions of those jobs. Consider this: with our history it is a great expression of trust just letting us in the door. If you are truly motivated, like I was, you won't stay at the bottom long.

The kind of people we become is highly influenced by what happens to us day in and day out as we fill our roles as employees. I remember when I was cutting timber for a living. I was riding all over the state of Ohio passing beers up to the front seat to two drinkers while I was attending AA meetings after work. It wasn't long until I was drinking again. Who we socialize with at work and after work can have far reaching significance in our lives, both positively and negatively.

You are free to choose where you work and the relationships that result. Just remember, who you become is hanging in the balance. What goes on in the workplace and who you socialize with afterward will change you, for better or worse. Before you take a position ask yourself, "Is that change in harmony with my freedom and vision?"

The commands of the Lord are clear, giving insight for living. They are a warning...
A great reward for those who obey them
PSALMS 19:8, 11

THE STRAIGHT LIFE

The straight life of a working man involves forcing your exhausted frame out of bed five days a week for fifty weeks out of the year. It is the humble pleasure of a two-week vacation once a year to a place the wife and kids choose. The straight life is living on a budget and spending your money wisely when you would rather indulge in the newest toy that boosts your ego; it is coming home after a long day's work to chores that can no longer be avoided; it is spending your days off using your time to be a real husband and father. The straight life is taking your family to church on Sunday when for once you'd just like to sleep in; it is paying your bills with the money you've made and hoping for enough left for your other necessities.

When it comes to living the "straight life" our gut level response may be to withdraw. This old mindset may be screaming inside, "I just don't think I am cut out for this life; get me out of here!" Those who appear to be well-suited for the straight life seem to be a different breed of humanity. Our natural rebelliousness provides the arrogance necessary for us to stop short of life's standards – of God's standards. Our natural dislike of the straight life provides us with a desire to stop short and turn back to experience the temporary pleasures of the past. The result of failing to be a man according to God's definition (see beginning of chapter) are always tragic. In the end, reality always finds us on the road we sought to avoid – being held responsible and accountable. Trust me, nothing is going to work in your life until you do.

A LACK OF VISION

Without a vision for success there can never be inspiration. Visions are what energize us and drive us. They lift us above our challenges to see the desired goal that lies beyond them.

When you are released from prison you can't afford not to see any higher than the barriers and challenges you will face. You must forge a vision that will help you see above and beyond what you are going through – a vision that includes hard work and steady employment.

When considering the straight life, remember the revelation of our late great President Theodore Roosevelt: "It is not the critic who counts; not the man who points out how the strong man stumbles, or where the doer of deeds could have done them better. The credit belongs to the man who is actually in the arena, whose face is marred by dust and sweat and blood; who strives valiantly; who errs, who comes short again and again, because there is no effort without error and shortcoming; but who does actually strive to do the deeds; who knows great enthusiasms, the great devotions; who spends himself in a worthy cause; who at the best knows in the end the triumph of high achievement, and who at the worst, if he fails, at least fails while daring greatly, so that his place shall never be with those cold and timid souls who neither know victory nor defeat." This is the view of the straight life through the eyes of a man who had a vision of something he was aiming for. In Mr. Roosevelt's case, it was the endless labor and vision of building a better nation.

The famous writer and author Helen Keller was blind and deaf. Once she was asked if there was anything worse than being blind. She replied, "Yes, being able to see and having no vision." The word of God makes a big deal out of vision. They are what we are to expect from abiding in the revelation of His Word. It also tells us we self-destruct without them.

Where there is no vision, the people perish
PROVERBS 29:18

The evidence is all too clear. A lack of vision is responsible for the two-thirds of ex-felons who return to prison nationally. Incarceration is becoming an epidemic in younger generations, because they lack a breakthrough vision for their lives. It was only when I lost the vision I had gained for myself that the brutal realities of life took dominion, and pleasure took priority over principles in an effort to escape those realities.

This was the major problem I faced. I had no steady flow of revelation to sustain my vision. The better things got, the less I focused on faith and revelation. The lows of disappointment and even the highs of victory began to overwhelm me. I was now dominated by what I was going through and lost focus of the vision I was going to. I was no longer anchored in the revelation that kept me in a state of stability during those highs and lows. I began to seek out the old familiar ways to escape and medicate their impact on my life. In the end, I returned to prison.

I am utterly convinced it isn't the social barriers, personal barriers, or any other experience you could face that will defeat you upon release but rather a lack or loss of vision from revelation. In the three times I have been released from prison, I don't remember a single person in those halfway houses who couldn't become employed and excel in life if they really wanted to. It was keeping it that so many failed at. The problem for most of us is not a mental deficiency, but rather a character deficiency, marked by instability as a result of a lack of vision for the future. Life experience and the Word of God proved beyond any doubt that failure revolved around a lack of vision that comes through revelation.

Your promises have been thoroughly tested; that is why I love them so much.
Your justice is eternal, and your instructions perfectly true
PSALMS 119:140, 142

Let's take a few moments to reflect on our need for employment upon release.
- Which of the fifteen qualities of employment success are your strongest points? Which ones do you need the most work?
- What employment barriers could you most identify with?
- Have you begun to create a vision for your future that includes employment? How strong is your faith in believing things will work out?

With the answers to these questions in mind, let's move onto the last and final chapter on Goals and Vision.

CHAPTER EIGHTEEN

Goals

—⚍—

Your goal is to create a beloved community, and this will require a qualitative change in our souls as well as a quantitative change in our lives.

— MARTIN LUTHER KING, JR. —

Visions

—⚍—

The idea is to seek a vision that gives you purpose in life and then to implement that vision. The vision by itself is one half, one part of the process. It implies the necessity of living that vision, otherwise the vision will sink back into itself.

— LEWIS P. JOHNSON —

Where are you going in life when you leave prison? Have you taken the time to consider the vital importance of this question? If you cannot answer that question you cannot know anything about your destination. People do not arrive at a destination merely by intentions. The direction you are traveling determines your destination. Wonder how you got to where you are when you didn't mean to end up there? Paths determine destination.

They err in vision, they stumble when pronouncing judgment
ISAIAH 23:7

Prison means you followed a path that led you to the lowest position of human existence while still breathing. Regardless of that position, your adversity has the potential to become the greatest university. Adversity is the last school of higher learning. If you can't learn these truths about paths leading to destinations as a result of incarceration, you are not going to learn them when you are released. The vision you hold most in mind and imagination is the master power that molds and makes the paths you follow.

MAP MAKER OR FOLLOWER?

As a man who has been released from prison three times I can assure you of one thing: The poorest man upon release is not the man without a nickel; it is the man without a vision for a better life. The vision you choose will determine the future you create. The map for your future has always been inside you. It has never been on the outside of those prison gates. You are the map maker of your future. Until you understand this you won't invest the time to draw up the map.

As an incarcerated man, it's a matter of great urgency for you to decide who is going to draw up the map for your life. Who will write out the details? Who will determine what the destination is and what roads will you follow to get there? Who will determine if that destination is triumph or tragedy? One thing you can be sure of, if you aim at nothing upon release you are bound to reach it.

The real question is, are you content to let the final details of your life be mapped out without having participated in any significant way in what the outcome was? It's so easy to "go with the flow" and follow the herd down the path of little effort and least resistance. It's so easy to be a follower instead of a map maker, stumbling onto whatever road is in front of you and following it where it takes you.

It's so easy not to be a map maker because it allows you to avoid the pain of problem solving and the hard choices of mature adulthood. This type of aimlessness just lets life happen, ducking and dodging, reaching and grasping at whatever comes along. If this is what you want to be, I can promise you, at least you will have lots of company.

These men turn from the right way to walk down dark paths
PROVERBS 2:13

Far too many people are willing to accept the aimless life. They attempt to make an art out of taking life as it comes. They are not visionaries when it comes to their own future – never fighting to map out their own lives and create their own chances. The motto has become "it is what it is," rather than "it is what you make it." Are you one of them?

THE PATH OF LEAST RESISTANCE IS FAILURE

It can often feel safe and comfortable to let our life unfold without a map, a moral compass, and a destination. You may not like the outcome, but you can always shrug your shoulders and claim you couldn't help it; you really didn't have a chance. You can claim it is out of your hands and let life unfold on its own, forfeiting your opportunity to determine your own destiny. The problem is, when you choose this method you can't be sure it won't end in another incarceration, one that is much longer and much harder.

It is pleasant to see dreams come true, but fools refuse to turn from evil to attain them
PROVERBS 13:19

Those who are living out the direction of their lives that chance defines for them do, in fact, obtain a type of freedom – freedom from any worry whether they are doing the right things in life. Those that want to justify this shallow, fruitless type of freedom stand on the sidelines of life, hustling short cuts and quick fixes. They never experience the sense of mission and purpose that comes with charting out their own map for life. Unless you deny reality (as we often do) you will always know who and what you are was never something chosen but merely accepted. Map makers are daring people who realize the cost of what they decide. They know the pain and work involved and are still committed to living out the map for their lives they participated in defining.

ARE YOU BITTER OR BETTER?

There is a reason this chapter holds the last position in this book. Our trials will make us bitter people or they will make us better people. Taking life as it comes and following whatever path that is in front of us often leaves us all in varying degrees of bitterness. Bitter roots can only produce bitter fruits. Bitter fruits can leave us with bitter expectations on release.

Get rid of all bitterness
EPHESIANS 4:13

It's hard to be a visionary with goals for a better life if we are full of bitter expectations. The hope is that when you have traveled this far on your journey in this book you will have made at least two conclusions. First, "I can have a better life." Second, "I am responsible for it." You define your circumstance, right here and right now; they don't define you. Your circumstances define you when what is in them gets into you. You define your circumstances when you prevent that and get into your circumstances and redefine yourself.

Dare to draw your own maps – be your own map maker of your future, instead of letting others and the world (circumstances) decide for you. In spite of all the stresses and strains, sorrows and disappointments that sometimes come with daring to draw your own map, it is only these men who will experience authentic manhood because they really choose who they will be and what they will do in spite of their circumstances – and not simply pretend to do so.

MAP MAKING REQUIRES FAITH

For better or worse, the lives of map makers really are their own. These men are willing to assume responsibility for their own future by exercising their decision-making power to plan and determine their own destiny. They are unwilling to accept the status quo of their circumstances. Are you one of these? I am today, and I have four prison numbers. No matter how many times you have failed or what your past is, you can be one of them too if you have faith in your God-given potential. Even the true believer in God, a person of true faith in God's plan for their life, has choices to make and a map to write out (Habakkuk 2:2-3). Without a vision of faith in the unseen and a map of where it leads, you will grasp at whatever is in front of you upon release.

You spoke in a vision to your faithful people
PSALM 89:19

It is not enough to hear the good news about what you can be in the pages of the Bible, this book, and from others. You must think about it. You must write it out, and then you must act it out in faith that you can reach your destination. The time is at hand to really go for it. Each day that passes you are closer to being thrust back into society. It is time to make some decisions and step out in faith on them. You won't succeed without faith. Your faith is energized by a vision and goals for a better life.

PLOWING FORWARD REQUIRES LOOKING FORWARD

You have to ask yourself if you want the future to look like the past. Fear is a type of faith that gets its strength from rehearsing the past. In the end, will you ever be satisfied to remain who you are? If the answer is no, it's time to understand that you have the God-given authority to choose differently and the power to make bold changes in your life. You create the vision, and then the vision creates you.

What type of person you eventually become is up to you. You are capable of rising above your past and becoming the man you always knew was in there and waiting to come out. Your past failures do not mean the denial of your dreams, only a delay. Prison doesn't mean dreams are over – a graveyard does. Unless of course, you keep living in the graveyard of the past.

No one who puts his hand to the plow and looks back [to the things behind]
is fit for the kingdom of God
LUKE 9:62

Your past is a prison cell that opens from the inside, and your future is like the security doors in the prison – the one you are standing in front of won't open until the one behind you closes. When your goals and visions are bigger than your memories, you will discover your faith and terminate your past, as I have. Forgetting those things behind you (Philippians 3:13) is not the same as denying those things which are behind. It is disconnecting from who you were and connecting to who you are becoming.

Write the vision and engrave it so plainly upon tablets…the vision is yet for an appointed time and it hastens to the end [fulfillment]: it will not deceive or disappoint. Though it tarry, wait [earnestly] for it, because it will surely come
HABAKKUK 2:2,3

THE FIRST CREATION PRINCIPLE

As co-designers and map makers, we can begin to give expression to what we want to be and what we want to do with our lives by writing out our own personal reentry resolution. However, we must have a revelation before we can have a resolution. It's called the first creation principle. We must be able to see it on the inside (inner vision) before we can make it real on the outside. Visions require that we use all our mental powers, including the powers of imagination and creativity.

I have multiplied visions [for you] and [have appealed to you]
HOSEA 12:10

As men made in the image of our Creator, we can use the powers of self-awareness and self-examination to visualize what needs to be removed from our lives and what we need to add. This requires that we shut out what is around us and journey inward. We can so easily develop a habit of letting all our mental powers get caught up in the daily thick and thin of things in prison. In the midst of all our distractions what matters most for us as incarcerated men (building a better future) gets buried in all the layers of aimless activities, minor concerns, petty problems, as well as emotions and misguided impulses.

Visualization is a natural part of effective life management. What can emerge out of it is a foundation of well thought out purposes and values that become the center of a person's life.

Exercising our mental powers through visualization can be extremely powerful in rescripting the directions and destinations of our lives. Revelation that leads to vision is central to enduring spirituality, clothed in the practice of study, meditation, and prayer.

TAP INTO YOUR VISION

Let's try a brief exercise to see how this power of visualization might work. Try to stand apart from yourself as if you have just stepped outside of your own body. Can you look at yourself as if you are a second observer? Think about what mood you are in? Can you identify it? What are you feeling? Next, try to describe your present mental state. Think for a moment about how your mind is working. Is it quiet and alert? Is it distracted? This second observer exercise allows us to practice our skill of conscious awareness.

Let's try another one. Look back to a time when you were driving or riding in a car. Take a moment to see it. Were you happy or sad? Was it a good experience? Take a moment to allow yourself to feel it again. Where are you going? Now, look forward to the future and picture yourself driving or riding in a car after release from prison. Picture yourself happy and successful. What do you see yourself wearing? Where do you see yourself going? What else do you see or feel that is different about you?

The ability to do what you just did is an awesome and uniquely human power. It is almost like having a mind with a separate consciousness that allows us to analyze ourselves in the present, look backward, and even forward into time. We have these powers because we were made to reflect God's image. We can create something in our mind (the first creation principle) and then make it a physical reality (the second creation principle). These powers allow us to evaluate and learn complex information from others, like this book, and use it to formulate a new vision of ourselves for a better future.

VISION AND SUCCESS

Research on peak performers like athletes and businesspeople has shown that almost all who were on top of their fields were visualizers. They see it, they feel it, and they actually experience it through the first creation principle of visualization before they actually make it a physical reality. These successful people begin with the outcome and destination in mind, and they visualize the paths it will take to get there. They plan big but think logically and realistically.

There is a God in heaven who reveals secrets....
Your dreams and the vision in your head upon your bed are these
DANIEL 2:28

You can begin to visualize every area of your life before you are released. Once you are released you can visualize outcomes daily before every challenge. You can visualize a job interview, your first car, your first home, and every other reentry goal. See it clearly, vividly, relentlessly, over and over. What you create for every challenge is an internal comfort zone.

When you get into the situation it's not unfamiliar, and it doesn't rattle you. What you create for every other goal is the hope and belief that you can reach the goal, as well as the plans and energy to get there.

The vision to mentally create an experience internally before we create it externally is one of our most important reentry assets. This applies to the first creation principle of writing out our reentry resolution and the second creation principle of making it a reality in our lives. You can be sure of one thing. If you use this tool of vision in your life day after day, your life will change for the better. Instead of living out past visions of self-defeat, you will be living out the map of your visions and goals for a better life of security and stability.

A TOOL OR WEAPON?

The power of vision is not a new concept for us. What's new about it is not the concept, but rather the application. We have all practiced these skills in our fears, destructive fantasies, and crimes. We are simply taking charge of our thought life. We are using these resident powers of visualization for self-preservation and progress instead of our self-destruction. It will mean you are giving your visions, your words, your writing, and your actions new direction.

There shall be no more any false, empty, and fruitless vision
EZEKIEL 12:24

POINT YOUR VISION IN THE RIGHT DIRECTION

A good plan to begin activating these powers of vision is by answering the question our incarceration constantly poses to all of us: "What's really important in life?" If we haven't heard our incarceration ask that question, it doesn't mean our circumstances haven't been posing it every single day, but rather that we haven't been listening. We have to slow down and be silent before we can hear it. For some of us, we stay just busy and distracted enough so that we don't have to hear it.

If incarceration is not initially seen as a catastrophe in our lives, we have some real problems about how we value ourselves and our freedom. Such a catastrophe should move us to ask some really important questions. We can only respond with an answer by how we live our lives today. Let's look at a few of those really important questions.

Write out your answers to the following questions:
1. What kind of life do I really want to experience?
2. What's really important to me?
3. What do I value most in life?
4. What is my purpose, or why am I here?
5. What contribution to life can I offer?
6. If there is a design for life, how is that design best lived out in my life?

When people seek to identify what really matters in their lives – what they want to be and what they want to do – it is likely to elicit a couple of powerful experiences. They become (reverent); prayerful, have feelings of deep respect for God and life, mixed with awe and wonder. They become (reflective); thoughtful, looking both back upon life and forward to a better future. Becoming reverent and reflective requires that we think in terms much larger than just today or tomorrow. Let's take a look.

Consider the matter and understand the vision....
And he understood the word and had understanding of the vision
DANIEL 9:23, 10:1

BEGIN WITH YOUR DESTINATION IN MIND

You can think in larger terms than today or tomorrow by beginning with a specific future destination in mind. One powerful application is to define your life from an expected end. You can visualize your own funeral and write out the details of your own eulogy. If you are willing to invest the time to envision your own funeral in advance, it will help you reflect on what you truly prize as important then. It will teach you a great deal about what should be important now.

If you can visualize yourself at the end of your life and then reflect on things up to now, you undoubtedly would make some judgments that would be best made in the present. Far above any of the other conquests that a man will be remembered by is what those you leave behind will have to say about you when you are gone. People won't talk about how well you dressed, how much gold you wore, how big your house was, or what kind of car you drove. You won't be remembered by those things, because in the face of death, these things are insignificant to who you really were as a person. What you imparted on the inside of each of them is what you will be remembered by.

You will only be remembered by your love and your character, and the contributions to the lives of others that those internal qualities made. What about you? Will they remember your selfless sacrifice to something worthwhile and of lasting importance to life? What will they remember about the good in your life that became the good in their lives? Will they miss you?

If these questions are not a concern for you now, I can absolutely promise you that the day will come when they are most important. As you age, you will feel the growing significance of these most important matters. It's a destination no one can escape. We can only hope that when we reach that day it will not be too late to assure the best possible answers.

How do you know what your life will be like tomorrow?
Your life is like the morning fog – it is here a little while, then it is gone
JAMES 4:14

Wouldn't you really like to leave behind people who would say about you, "He had a rough start and made some wrong choices, but he chose to face himself and rose above it. People no longer feared him being around. They respected him. He was an overcomer; a man of true character and integrity." If you want people to remember you that way when you are gone, you will need to start working on your life now to make it happen.

MY FATHER WAS NOT A MAP MAKER

I remember my father's funeral. I was twenty-two when he died. I remember how the funeral parlor was empty. The only sound echoing through the empty parlor was the sound of my older brother Rick crying out like a little boy with a broken heart. Little did I know that he would be killed by a drunk driver the following year. I just sat there at my father's funeral, feeling extremely awkward. I didn't know my father well enough to share in my brother's level of sorrow. I didn't know him from the position of the strong male guidance of a role model and father. That was the legacy he left me.

Nevertheless, I loved him because he was my father. The funeral parlor was empty because my father had no real friends or family members that he was close to. He had only drinking buddies and bar friends. My father was a practicing alcoholic for most of his life. Alcohol killed him at the young age of sixty.

Nothing mattered much in his life except him and his booze. In the last couple of decades of his life he couldn't function well enough to hold down a job. He chose to survive on state assistance and odd jobs and lived in a roach-infested apartment. When he ran out of money or needed something he called and begged family members who were at their limits with him.

I remember his last thirty days in the hospital before his death. I used to go and sit with him after work and stare at him. For the first time in my life, I realized how much I looked like him. One evening at the hospital, his brother and sister, my mother and brother, and a few others were present. I sensed the atmosphere was not of a distinguished human being passing: it felt more like someone being put out of their misery. It was not a pretty picture for his two young sons to experience.

I am confident it was not his intention for his life to turn out that way. He simply was not a map maker for his life. Neither was it my intention to have four prison numbers. I was not a map maker either, until now. The French philosopher Jean Paul Sartre reminds us, "Not to decide, is to decide." In reality, to wait to decide what the last days of your life will be is, in most instances, to let other people and circumstances decide for you.

For example, if you don't have a ride from the prison upon release, and do not decide to take the 12:00 pm bus to your city, at 12:01 pm you will find that the decision has been made for you. So it is with our lives. We can put off trying to decide whether or not to make a map and choose a destination. In the end, we will probably find that what we have been trying to decide has been decided for us. I am so grateful you and I can still decide to be a map maker, pick up a moral compass, and chart out our destination. Without deciding on these things there is no way to tell for sure how tragic our ending will be, or how fruitless the years between now and then might end up. God's instructions are perfectly true, and this includes our need for vision.

Where there is no vision…the people perish
PROVERBS 29:18

THE VISION OF YOUR OWN FUNERAL

Let's decide how our end will be. We will begin with the end in mind. Let's do a potential life-changing exercise and visualize our own funerals. We can begin by clearing our mind of all concerns and distractions. Get into a comfortable position and close your eyes. Take a couple of deep breaths and release them slowly. Now complete the following exercise.

Begin visualizing in your mind you are going to the funeral of a loved one. Picture yourself walking up to the funeral parlor door. As you open the door and walk in, you notice all the flowers and hear the soft organ music playing. Now clearly see all the faces of family and friends as you walk deeper into the parlor. Notice the atmosphere. Are they sorrowful or peaceful about the passing?

As you walk up to the casket and look down inside, you suddenly come face to face with yourself. This is your funeral. All these people have come to say goodbye to you and honor your presence in their lives. Several have put their memories and tribute to you down on paper so they could sum it up in a speech for the rest of those saying their goodbyes. You were deeply cared for and loved. For this reason, people want to pay honor and tributes to your life.

There are letters from your wife and children, and your brother and sister. One speaker was a close friend, another from where you were employed. There was a speaker from your church, the city mission, and other people in the community where you touched their lives. Now open your eyes. Before we go any further, stop here and write down your impressions about how this experience made you feel.

YOU CAN DETERMINE YOUR OWN EULOGY

What will each of these people say about you? What type of person are each of them describing? What contributions to their lives have you made? What are they going to remember most about you? What kind of difference did your character make in their lives?

When I had seen the vision, I sought to understand it
DANIEL 8:15

Now it is time to decide what type of person they will remember you as. It is time for you to write your own eulogy. A eulogy is a speech or writing of praise honoring the deceased at their funeral. It can be in a random list or letter form. Write down the names of the speakers you would want at your funeral. Review each question in the prior paragraph. Answer each question for each name on your list. With your list of names and the questions in front of you, write out your most desired responses. Take a couple of days and do not rush your eulogy. Once it is complete, do not put it away and forget about it. Read and reflect on it.

Now that you have examined your eulogy, it is time to consider what type of values it will take for your life to represent what you have written. Return to the chapter on Consistency. Look under the headings: Qualities of Love and Fruits of Maturity. Using these two lists of values, write down all of them you feel you will need to incorporate to become the person you have described in your eulogy. If it is all of them, write down all of them. Underline the ones you feel you need the most work on.

YOUR PERSONAL REENTRY RESOLUTION

Now that you have identified what values are important to reaching your intended personal character, it is time to take the next step and write a reentry resolution. Your reentry resolution becomes your own personal constitution – a solid expression of your values in action upon release. Your reentry resolution will consist of your reentry resolution statement and your well-defined reentry resolution goals.

Rebuild the road! Clear away the rocks and stones....Return from captivity
PSALM 57:14

Our reentry resolution helps us succeed in reentry because it is based on clearly defined values. It forces us to think intentionally about our priorities in a world that calls our attention in so many different directions. Like our nation's Constitution, it is written from self-evident Biblical principles that are timeless and changeless. These self-evident values empower our reentry resolution with enduring strength, even in the midst of a chaotic world of change and challenge.

We have already decided that once you are released you will be heading somewhere. Writing a reentry resolution is simply making a conscious choice of where your destination will be. It's your reinstated liberty to choose responsibly and in a mature way what your future will look like. Our reentry resolution can provide the same kind of security, stability, and prosperity as our nation's Constitution when it is built on the same values and truths. It becomes the basis for our daily decisions in the midst of constant social uncertainty.

YOUR REENTRY RESOLUTION STATEMENT

The most effective way to map out your destination is to decide what route you will take. The route always holds us on course toward our destination. It's important to consider what route has the best roads and plenty of support along the way. The route is your reentry resolution statement that supports your journey toward your goals and destination. Do not fear mistakes or falling short of your destination. Fear only wrong roads – stepping outside of your own values and violating your freedom-supporting reentry resolution statement.

Your reentry resolution statement is not something you write in one setting. In light of the need for careful analysis and thoughtful reflection, it may take days or even a week to write. The idea is to work on it until it is detailed and has a clear expression of your innermost values and directions. From your values list and the examples provided, begin now to write out your own reentry resolution statement.

MY REENTRY RESOLUTION STATEMENT
[FREEDOM TO]

1. I WILL value the rights and freedoms of others in society.
2. I WILL fulfill my duties and responsibilities in every area of my life.
3. I WILL live my life centered on family and community.
4. I WILL live my life trustworthy in my manhood.
5. I WILL base my decisions and actions on how they affect everyone.
6. I WILL cherish and protect the gifts of freedom and liberty.
7. I WILL give more than I take.
8. I WILL develop habits that free me from old labels and limits.
9. I WILL keep myself free from addictive and destructive habits.
10. I WILL seek to discover and develop my talents for the benefit of everyone.

In the chapter on Consistency, we discovered the two freedoms. FREEDOM TO: choose, have, become, relate, and achieve; FREEDOM FROM: immaturity, impulsive behavior, compulsive/addictive behavior, self-obsession, fear, and falsehoods. It was briefly discussed that what we want freedom to do is most often much more obvious than what we need freedom from. Likewise, consistently navigating between what we need to break away from and what we want to work toward is adapting to survive our freedoms.

Return to the chapter on Consistency and use the two charts, Qualities of Fear and Fruits of Immaturity, for the next part of your reentry resolution statement. Write down all the negative traits you will need to release to become the person you described in your eulogy. Write down all the ones that apply to you. Underline the ones you feel you need the most work. Using this list, and the following example of my list, complete your reentry resolution statement.

MY REENTRY RESOLUTION
[FREEDOM FROM]

1. I WILL NOT focus on what's wrong, only what's available.
2. I WILL NOT recycle the past.
3. I WILL NOT let false pride govern my life.
4. I WILL NOT focus on outcomes, only efforts.
5. I WILL NOT compare myself to others.
6. I WILL NOT exchange the truth for a lie.
7. I WILL NOT run from problem solving.
8. I WILL NOT love things and use people.
9. I WILL NOT mistreat or violate anyone.
10. I WILL NOT give up.

REENTRY RESOLUTION GOALS

Reentry resolution goals are clarified by setting down in clear and specific words the purpose and goals of your life upon release. It is a detailed map of what will make your life a success. If it is taken seriously, it can generate tremendous motivation. Writing your reentry resolution goals can be one of the most important exercises of your life, because it becomes the point where you are finally able to see what will give your life purpose and meaning.

Hope deferred makes the heart sick, but a dream fulfilled is a tree of life
PROVERBS 13:12

If these goals are an extension of our reentry resolution statement, based on correct values, they will be vitally different from our old method of serving only self-centered objectives. It means our goals will be in harmony with correct principles of truth. Setting goals that reflect our deepest values gives us the greatest source of power to achieve them. We must be certain that we are not submitting ourselves to map making that is not in harmony with the values that secure our freedom.

Our goals no longer focus on what produces the most pleasure or feeds an over-inflated ego. Our reentry resolution is intended to be used to transcend self-obsessions and create the life we desire for ourselves. It represents a life based on principles and values that govern the society we seek to thrive in. Writing out the goals of our reentry resolution crystallizes and clarifies this new life direction.

Effective reentry resolution goals focus on results. It helps us to identify where we want to end up, and in the process helps determine where we are. It gives us important information on how to get there and tells us when we have arrived. Our reentry resolution goals unify our vision and efforts while giving purpose to all that we do. It translates into daily activities that make us proactive and in charge of our direction.

ROLES HELP DETERMINE GOALS

It will help our reentry resolution goals to be much more manageable and balanced if we break them down into the six areas of our design, and then the specific roles we play in each of those areas. For example, what roles we play in the areas of family, such as husband and father. We determine what roles we play in the social areas of lives, such as employee, friend, coach, community member, and so on. Every one of these roles are important. When we are able to focus on our roles, we can be much more in touch with writing out our goals. "I was not disobedient unto the heavenly vision" Acts 26:19.

GOALS AND THE HUMAN DESIGN MODEL

One of the major mistakes that often arises when people work to become more effective in life is that they don't think broadly enough or holistically. This can cause us to lose our sense of proportion and dimension. The result is a loss of the natural sense of balance necessary for effective living. For example, people get consumed with their financial goals and lose sight of the most important relationships in their lives. We break our lives down into small chunks, so we can put it all together the right way to represent our goals. Then our goals, like our life, represent wholeness, relationship, balance, and order.

OUR CIRCLE OF POTENTIAL AND PERFORMANCE

Our uniquely designed potential is the only instrument we have in which to deal with life. We are the instruments of our performance. The six areas of our Human Design Model are the center of our circle of potential. To be effective map makers and goal setters we need to recognize the potential of that design. Then we can take the first step of being responsible for our first creation vision in all six of those areas.

The Master Model of Manhood is our perfect example of a man with a vision and a mission for His life. He did what His Father sent him to do, which was initiate and reveal God's Kingdom (John 6:38). Each of us would do well to understand and follow His example. Like Him, we can set forth clear terms for our mission according to the word of God, and then commit ourselves to living it out. However, even the Master Model of Manhood had to spend time alone in prayer, reverence, and reflection to assume His mission. This is what the story of the forty days in the wilderness is all about. He took the time necessary to fully grasp His mission. This is your wilderness journey. Will you discover your mission?

It is important to take time out of our schedule to pray and reflect before we write out our goals. There is no set amount of time to complete your reentry resolution goals. However, we are not likely to thoughtfully produce a map for our future in one or two hours. It will probably be more like several days of effort. If you can't afford several days, I am sure we can all afford a weekend. It's your future – just how important is it and how serious are you? It won't get any easier to do this after release when the full weight of freedom is upon you.

I the Lord make Myself known to him in a vision and speak to him in a dream
NUMBERS 12:6

HOW TO PREPARE YOUR REENTY RESOLUTION

It is important to include others before and after your journey of reverence and reflection in writing. Others will play a crucial role in giving you feedback and assurance that the goals of your reentry resolution fit you. Likewise, others can help you work through some of the means to make it all possible.

Personal responsibility in map making means being proactive in our faith and choosing visions that reflect a new life direction and destination. We don't choose paths that are limited to the provisions we currently have. We choose realistic goals our hearts desire, and then we determine the means to acquire our provisions. You will also need to review your goals and make minor changes as new insights and changing circumstances occur.

Briefly review the six areas of the Human Design Model. Complete your goals in each area in the order they are established. This order represents the developmental order that governs our lives. One area builds upon the next. Long-term goals identify specific destinations. Short-term goals represent points on our map that indicate our progress in that direction. Follow the steps below. Some helpful examples are provided.

FOLLOW THESE STEPS:

1. Read the chapter that corresponds to the area you are setting goals in.

2. Identify what roles you represent in each area.
3. Pick one long-term goal for each area.
4. Pick two to three short-term goals that represent progress.

NOTE: This model of goal setting is designed to move from general to specific. Once a goal is outlined in this general concept format, write out as many details as you can think of. Be detailed and descriptive.

MY REENTRY RESOLUTION GOALS
[MY BECOMING]

1. SPIRITUAL

Roles:
1. Student/disciple
2. Fellowship member
3. Mentor
4. Model/example
5. Servant

Goal: Attain principle centered maturity

Short Term Goals:
1. Find fellowship group
2. Recruit a mentor
3. Daily study, prayer, reflection

2. MENTAL

Roles:
1. Navigation center
2. Interpret reality
3. Reasoning/judgment
4. Decision making
5. Problem solving

Goal: Renew my mind with truth

Short Term Goals:
1. Continue my education
2. Expand my world view
3. Seek wisdom of others

3. EMOTIONAL

Roles:
1. Gauge needs
2. Understand self/others
3. Empathy/sympathy
4. Energy of action
5. Motivation

Goal: No longer be ruled by emotions

Short Term Goals
1. Learn to understand my feelings
2. Learn to manage my emotions
3. Learn to communicate my feelings

4. PHYSICAL

Roles:
1. Temple of Spirit
2. Represent inner image
3. Connect with life
4. Vehicle of mobility
5. Machinery of action

Goal: Increase health/vitality

Short Term Goals
1. Regular exercise
2. Change eating habits
3. Join softball team

You have set the foundation for the goals of your principle-centered self. This is the process of creating goals that define our desired inner image and reflecting them in our outer image. These prior four goals will provide a platform for the map making of the reentry resolution goals of family and social – of relating and achieving. We can only take into our relating and achieving the substance of what we have become, and are yet becoming, in our principle-centered manhood.

NOTE: If you don't have a family to return to upon release, complete the map for your future family.

If you have family, it is important not to make the final decisions on map making for the family without involving them. Get feedback from every family member by having them separately write out their own view of positive changes for the family. Come together with everyone and their ideas. Look for commonly recognized positive changes. Revise your family goal list using the words from each family member. Get the family talking and communicating on the things that really matter most, which are the beliefs, rules, and needs of your family.

Come together in the spirit of mutual respect, expressing different views and working together to create something greater than any one individual could do alone. These goals become the framework for family map making and for governing the family. When problems and crisis arise, these goals are there to remind everyone what matters most. It can also be helpful for providing direction for problem solving and decision making. It can be typed out on the computer and hung on the family room wall. Below are some examples.

FAMILY REENTRY RESOLUTION GOALS
[MY RELATING]

5. FAMILY

Roles:
1. Husband
2. Parent
3. Man model
4. Provider
5. Teacher

Goal: Determine beliefs, rules, needs

Short Term Goals:
1. Develop open/honest communication
2. Have regular family meetings
3. Develop activities for family unity

SOCIAL REENTRY RESOLUTION GOALS
[MY ACHIEVING]

6. SOCIAL

Roles:

Goal: Live in partnership with society

1. Community member
2. Neighbor
3. Employee
4. Friend
5. Support

Short Term Goals:
1. Obey all laws
2. Support community-church/mission
3. Support common goals, needs, interests

NOTE: This model of goal setting can be expanded to include specific goals for a career, skill or any other goal. We start with these six areas to secure a life that will support our personal development and freedom.

Personal responsibility for your future does not begin and end in writing your reentry resolution. It is an ongoing process of keeping your values and vision before you, then aligning your life to be in harmony with these most important things. Spend a few minutes each day visualizing it. Visualize yourself in situations of having reached your goals.

Earnestly revolving the vision in his mind and meditating on it
ACTS 10:19

The more clearly you can imagine every detail you write out, the more you will experience it, and the less you will see yourself as a spectator. See yourself handling these goals with love, power, self-control, and principle-centered maturity. Journey on, fellow overcomer. I am traveling the same low valleys and the same high mountains. I have faith in you and so does God.

THE BEGINNING!

ACKNOWLEDGMENTS

I would like to acknowledge Yahweh-God and His Son Yahshua-Jesus, whose love transforms the heart and mind of those who trust in Him. He is truly a God of new beginnings. I would like to acknowledge several other people who entered my life by His sovereign will. He always supplies us with who we need and what we need, when we need it.

Joseph Hoeflinger, who shared in my dream of helping me and others learn the truth of who to be free on the inside so we could remain free on the outside. His value in my life as a mentor and friend are beyond measure. Without his guidance and sponsorship this book would have never been possible.

Tom Grogan for teaching me to be a better writer. Together, Tom and Joe believed in me and this work until I was able to believe in it also. I would have never made it through this project without their loving support and encouragement.

The Honorable Judge Jack Zouhary for investing his invaluable time, attention, and direction in my life. His care for my success and well-being have been an incredible inspiration. No amount of words could express my gratitude for this. Sincere appreciation also goes to Ben Syroka for his steadfast assistance with both my re-entry and this book's publication.

Mark Hanusz of Hanusz Publishing (and Toledo Law!) for his belief in my work and seeing its need and value in reducing crime and recidivism. His insight and decades of experience have made what you are about to read possible. Thank you Mark. Your selfless investment with no thought of monetary reward is astounding.

My mother, Violet Lenora Thompson, for loving me unconditionally and never giving up on me, for seeing the potential in me that I could not see, and showing me what loving sacrifice is all about.

The countless fellow prisoners who are too numerous to name, for their part in making this dream a reality. Thank you. I dedicate this book to you all. The invaluable human beings inside the razor wire who have a vision for changed lives and remaining free. They are men the world may never know, the men I will never forget. I have suffered with you, pray for you, and seek your deliverance.

If this book helps you in any way, honor God who put the vision in my heart to write it, supplied the wisdom, and opened the doors. I just showed up and said "yes."